In Search of
Germany

In Search of
Germany

Edited by
Michael Mertes
Steven Muller
Heinrich August Winkler

Transaction Publishers

New Brunswick (U.S.A.) and London (U.K.)

Library of Congress Catalog Number: 95-45854
ISBN: 1-56000-880-6
Printed in the United States of America

Library of Congress Cataloging-in-Publication Data

In search of Germany / edited by Michael Mertes, Steven Muller, and Heinrich
    August Winkler.
        p. cm.
    "Augmented version of a special issue of Dædalus, Winter 1994, 'Germany in transition,' Volume 123, Number 1, of the Proceedings of the American Academy of Arts and Sciences"—T.p. verso.
    Includes bibliographical references and index.
    ISBN 1-56000-880-6 (alk. paper)
    1. Germany—History—Unification, 1990. 2. Political culture—Germany. 3. Germany—Historiography. 4. Germany—Politics and government—1990- I. Mertes, Michael. II. Muller, Steven, 1927- . III. Winkler, Heinrich August.
    DD290.29.I5   1996
    943.087'9—dc20   95-45854
                                                                      CIP

Contents

Preface

I F ONE ACCEPTS THE PROPOSITION recently advanced by Eric Hobsbawm that the twentieth century was a short one, beginning in 1914 with the outbreak of World War I and ending in 1991 with the dissolution of the Soviet Union, we are already well into the first decade of the twenty-first century. For those whose eyes are focused principally on the tragic events in the former Yugoslavia, the continuing civil war in Rwanda, and the wholly-unanticipated terrorism of Oklahoma City—the question must arise as to whether these and other comparable happenings in Japan and elsewhere are auguries of the twenty-first century. It is obvious that much that has happened in the world since 1989, indeed since 1991, gives cause for elation; there is also much that gives reason for alarm.

The euphoria that attended the dismantling of the Berlin Wall, the excitement generated by the collapse of communist regimes throughout Central and Eastern Europe, the hopes raised in many quarters of the dawning of a new age—characterized by stable and secure democracy and also unprecedented affluence and well-being—have all been seriously compromised by events of the last years. This is not to say that the utopian expectations of the late

1980s and early 1990s are wholly extinguished, or that the kinds of catastrophes that figured so largely throughout the twentieth century are again thought to be imminent, but only that there is widespread unease, uncertainty, confusion, and doubt. It exists in Germany, as it does in every part of Europe.

A book that bears the title "In Search of Germany" will necessarily reflect contemporary conditions, even when they do not touch Germany directly, but such a work must be read also in the context of the nightmare of a century that the twentieth proved to be, and not only for those who lived within the changing borders of what at one time or other was defined as the German Reich. Half a century after the end of World War II, there is interest not only in the policies pursued by the Nazi regime, the crimes it perpetrated throughout Europe, the suffering it inflicted on hundreds of millions, but also on what preceded that unprecedented tragedy and what followed it.

The Weimar Republic, a short-lived and ill-starred political experiment, is today the subject of new and important inquiry; so, also, are the much longer decades when the Federal Republic and the German Democratic Republic co-existed, in open hostility initially, in somewhat more normal relations, at least on the governmental side, in response to *Ostpolitik*. When the "crisis" of 1989 erupted, in the midst of the fortieth anniversary celebrations of the birth of the G.D.R.—considered by many to be the most successful of all the Communist states, rivaled only perhaps by Hungary—the world watched in amazement the unraveling of what had appeared to be so tightly-knit a regime, and then looked with awe on the political and diplomatic skills demonstrated by the German Chancellor in his dealings with reluctant allies and a suspicious Soviet Union, achieving German unity on terms that few would have imagined possible six months earlier.

Germany, like much of the rest of the world, seemed to have embarked on a glorious new adventure in politics. When the full dimensions of the East German situation became known—when the lies disseminated by very able Communist propagandists were laid bare and the story of the *Stasi* began to break, when the citizens of the former Federal Republic fully realized the costs they would be required to pay to bring East Germany into some economic parity with the old Federal Republic—there was complaint and grumbling, but not enough to diminish seriously the nation's enthusiasm for unification. If *Ossis* came to detest *Wessis*, feeling keenly their humiliating condition—living as paupers in a world of plenty—other kinds of grievances were no less openly expressed on the other side. The two states, having lived apart for half a century, having established political, social, economic, and intellectual institutions that did not incorporate the same values or provide the same protections, could not be expected to have an easy early marriage. Their difficulties, certainly exacerbated by the world-wide recession that caused unemployment to escalate in certain of the *Länder* to levels not known since 1933, created a certain anxiety and turmoil, but nothing approaching what Germany had known at other times in the twentieth century.

Today, with the recession officially declared to be over, Germany, certainly in comparison with her other European Union partners, seems again to be a quintessentially stable state, the Federal Republic of yesterday, this time writ large. Having few doubts about the virtues of the European Union, scarcely sympathetic to the doubts expressed by the United Kingdom, knowing little of the mass unemployment that continues to plague France and Spain, having no experience of the currency and debt problems common to Italy, so greatly exacerbated by the parties of the Right, evoking memories of fascism, the new Germany seems to have weathered the major post-1989 storms. Its deutsche mark remains as strong as ever; its democratic institutions are unchallenged; no power in the East threatens its new borders. What more could Germans possibly hope for?

Yet, those who visit the country know that *alles gut* has not become its principal slogan. Though many of the problems in the new *Länder* are in fact being tackled, though the former Communist states in the East are experiencing significant economic recovery, this being particularly true of the Czech Republic, Poland, and several of the others, the fragility of their recovery is recognized, not least in Germany. While great pride is taken in what Germany has been able to do to help Russia economically, the political instability of that state, not to mention its social and moral dilemmas, creates unease. The situation in Ukraine, and in any number of the other former Soviet republics, is no less distressing. And then, quite obviously, the hopes for the European Union, as they existed in

1992, are not so long buried. While some would like to believe that the promises of Maastricht will be realized in time, perhaps even before the year 2000, Europe is clearly not moving in the bold directions once confidently prophesied. If relations with the United States remain good, at least on the surface, neither Germany nor its NATO allies quite know what to do with that Cold War institution, and all are massively confused about what needs to be done to reform the United Nations. To speak of a German seat on the Security Council seems to evoke the ambivalence that many feel. Are these, then, the reasons for German anxiety?

Only very partially. Germany, though boasting the most successful capitalist economy in Europe, wonders how long it all will last. Can a rapidly-aging society, with low fertility, very high salary scales, and generous social welfare benefits continue to live on the level it has managed to climb to in recent years? Some speak of Germany's labor force needs, of how the country will have to depend on foreign workers at a time when the immigration of non-Germans has become a sensitive political issue. Others worry about what they perceive to be the moral decline in the society, and not in Germany alone, of the intellectual aridity of this fin de siècle, and not only in Europe. Politics necessarily figure, and not simply in terms of what will happen when the longest-serving Chancellor since Konrad Adenauer leaves office. What is the quality of the political class that governs in Germany today? Is the society, despite its European connections, too provincial, too self-satisfied? Where there is so much doubt about what the twenty-first century will bring, it is useful to hear the opinions of Germans in many professions, in very different ways aware of the problems confronting the new Germany. While not agreeing among themselves on which issues deserve priority, no one of them believes that German society is poised on the brink of catastrophe; there is no Cassandra in this book, but neither are there any Polyannas.

Having said that, it must be acknowledged that there is little prophecy in this volume. The authors have deliberately eschewed making predictions about the world as it is likely to appear in the year 2000 or beyond. Still, such concerns have not been absent from their deliberations. I wonder how a number of the authors in this book would react to a statement made in *Dædalus* in the spring of 1995 in an issue entitled, "What Future for the State?" On that occasion, I wrote:

> Men like Václav Havel are right when they speak of the "post-Communist nightmare," when they think back to how very fragile so many of the new democracies created on the morrow of World War I proved to be. There is no reason to believe that the regime changes that have occurred since 1989 in that corner of the world have in fact established governments that will be able to satisfy popular demand. Those who speak of "rogue states"—Libya yesterday, Iraq today, and one can only imagine which of the several candidates for that very dubious distinction it is likely to be tomorrow—are also addressing a very real problem, however hyperbolic their language may be. So, also, those who speak of the growing hazards posed by Islamic fundamentalism—a theme that has been figuring very conspicuously in the last decade and is likely to become even more common in the next—are focusing on very real issues that cannot be ignored. All such conditions and any number of others, including those common to the very poor states of the world, the ones so casually dismissed as "basket cases," cannot fail to interest all who have any concern with the international system, with how instability in any one state, however small and seemingly unimportant, can disturb the so-called "world order," creating dangerous resonances elsewhere.

This is much more than a collection of essays, written by German professors, journalists, and civil servants, with an industrialist, foundation head, and editor thrown in to give it greater leaven. It is a dialogue among Germans, but also a dialogue with European and American counterparts. The contributions from scholars in the United Kingdom, France, and the United States are central features of the book. The planning for it began with a meeting at Coppet, in Switzerland, the home of Madame de Staël. We are much beholden to Count d'Haussonville for making this historic site available to us. It seemed very appropriate that a collection of essays on contemporary Germany should have its beginnings at Coppet, where one of the great classic works of an earlier Germany was composed. The authors met later in Prague, to discuss early drafts of their essays, and there, too, the symbolic importance of the city was not lost sight of. This book, in dwelling on Germany both as an Atlantic and European partner, is seeking to place that experience in a context that takes account of how much the problems and opportunities of today are related to what has gone before, and how much they depend on very candid consideration of the delicate and confused conditions of modern, industrial, democratic society.

A great debt is owed to many who have made this book possible. I would like to acknowledge the support of the Ministry for Foreign Affairs of the Federal Republic of Germany, which so very generously encouraged the creation of a book that would have scholarly merit, that would not seek to avoid controversy, that would depart from the more conventional clichés that abound about Germany.

Thanks are due also to the Fritz Thyssen Stiftung, the Robert Bosch Stiftung GmbH, the Körber-Stiftung, and the German Marshall Fund of the United States. They have helped to support the meetings and editorial work that have made this book possible. Needless to say, the opinions expressed by the authors are their own, and not of the bodies with which they are professionally associated. Every effort has been made to render these essays readable to a wide public. Germany matters, to Europe, the United States, the world in ways that are not always adequately perceived. A great debt is owed to Michael Mertes, Steven Muller, and Heinrich August Winkler for agreeing to be editors of this book, which had its origins in a *Dædalus* issue, now revised and in important ways expanded. Their Coda helps to bring the story up to date, if such a thing is at all possible in a world thought to be so rapidly changing.

Stephen R. Graubard

Michael Mertes

Germany's Social and Political Culture: Change Through Consensus?

WORDS AND THINGS

I S GERMANY A *PAYS LÉGAL*, OR IS IT ALREADY A *PAYS RÉEL*? How can one write meaningfully about the social and political culture of a country that, after decades of division, has only recently recovered its state unity? Is it not more appropriate to talk of social and political *cultures* that are still distinct, and are likely to remain so for quite some time?

There is a great deal of confusion about words. Is it only about words, or is it also about things? Take, for example, the term *neue Länder* (new states), meant to denote the five East German states plus the Eastern part of Berlin. Why "new"? After all, an East German *Land* (state) like Saxony is in fact a few hundred years older as a political entity than, for example, North Rhine-Westphalia, created as late as 1946. Saxony is "new" only because it joined the Federal Republic of Germany (FRG) in 1990. More precisely, it is *called* new because the West Germans perceive it as such. And yet, most East Germans also use the term *neue Länder*; no doubt *neue Länder* sounds less unfriendly than *ehemalige DDR* (the former GDR), more refreshing than *Beitrittsgebiet* (acceding area: an ugly, though legally correct expression invented by an anonymous West German bureaucrat).

Take another example. What is one to call the pre-reunified Federal Republic of Germany? Most call it *die alte* (the old); some call it *die frühere Bundesrepublik* (the former Federal Republic), as

Michael Mertes is Director-General for Social and Political Analyses and Cultural Affairs, Federal Chancellery, Bonn.

1

if it had suddenly disappeared; still others prefer the seemingly neutral term *Westdeutschland* (which can either mean western Germany with a small "w" or West Germany), corresponding to *Ostdeutschland* (eastern or East Germany) for the "new" states. Is this mere quarreling about words?

One may also spend time discussing whether *Wiedervereinigung* (reunification), *Vereinigung* (unification), or *Einigung* (an untranslatable cross between agreement and unification, gingered up by a small dose of togetherness) denotes what happened on October 3, 1990. Adherents of *Einigung* point to the *Einigungsvertrag* of August 31, 1990, the official short name for the "Treaty on the Establishment of German Unity" between the Federal Republic and the German Democratic Republic (GDR). A majority of German journalists and politicians prefer *Vereinigung*. What they mean to convey, wittingly or unwittingly, is that today's Germany is neither Kaiser Wilhelm's *Reich* nor something very much nastier. The hidden presumption is that history began in 1949 when the Federal Republic and the GDR were founded: ex nihilo, on no-man's soil, so to speak. In Germany's European neighborhood, people use the word reunification. For them, Germany ("a former country in central Europe," as the Random House Dictionary of the English Language used to define it) is back again. What kind of Germany? You do not escape the question by resorting to words.[1]

EAST GOES WEST

What, then, is the real thing?   The least sophisticated answer belongs to what can be called the "Fourth Reich" variant: "I think Germans collectively are unsound. I think they have a gene loose, though I don't know what the gene is."[2] The emphasis is on "collectively"; it appeals to the eternal myths about "national character." According to a second answer, united Germany is the merry old Federal Republic (or the "Bonn Republic," as some prefer to call it now) writ large, expanded by five "new" *Länder*. The "Bonn Republic" theorem presumes that nothing has really changed. Is this not a fundamental error?

Germany was reunified by accession of the "new" *Länder* to the Federal Republic. Minor exceptions notwithstanding, this meant that the constitutional, political, legal, and economic system of the country's Western part was instantly adopted by the East. Democratic legitimation for this procedure was provided by the East German *Volkskammer* election on March 18, 1990. An overwhelming majority of 75 percent voted in favor of parties that had strongly advocated the accession path to state unity during the election campaign. The competing models were implicitly rejected: maintaining the division of Germany and building up a truly democratic GDR on the one hand, or creating a single German state under a new constitution, to which East and West would accede, on the other. Both options were more or less inspired by "third road" visions, ideas of some German *Sonderweg* (separate course) between "capitalism" and "socialism," of pacifist neutrality vis-à-vis so-called "Rambo" America and what was then still Soviet Russia.

The Bonn Republic theorem is supported also by the trivial, but not unimportant, fact that three-quarters of the German population lives in the West, that an even much greater portion of the country's national product is created there. In essence, though, the massive preponderance of the West is based on the demonstrated superiority of free democracy and open society as opposed to centralized authoritarian systems. Even before the Berlin Wall fell, the collective wishes and dreams of Germans followed a one-way street from East to West. In many respects, the path of seventeen million East Germans after World War II may be seen as a detour full of privations towards the modernization and Westernization granted the West Germans during the same period, thanks in considerable part to American farsightedness.

Claiming to be the main road of postwar German history was a central element of the Federal Republic's *raison d'état* from the outset. The West Germans built a free democracy and an open society "also on behalf of those Germans who were prevented from participating," as the Basic Law (constitution) of 1949 put it. West German hubris? Only if it is arrogant to say that liberty is superior to oppression; only if the West Germans mean to compliment themselves for individual merit—which many of them are inclined to do nowadays—accusing the East Germans of individual failure.

The East German rulers understood very well that the Federal Republic's "all-German" claim was a permanent threat to their own legitimacy. Granted, the old Federal Republic did not constitute a full-fledged nation.[3] This is why so many felt the irresistible need to waste energy and ink trying to solve the puzzle of what the (West) German true collective *Identität* (identity) might be. However, there was never any serious doubt that the West German state represented the best polity ever in German history: "civil, civilian, civilized," as Timothy Garton Ash put it. The East German state never succeeded in providing a rationale for national identity either. The sole raison d'être left to the GDR was to represent the "socialist alternative to the FRG,"[4] as Otto Reinhold, one of the leading East German ideologists, unequivocally put it. This was in August 1989, when a majority of West Germans still believed that the GDR would last for an eternity.

The greatest cultural achievement of the Federal Republic is the ease with which West Germans feel themselves to be a part of the West and its political civilization, a community of European nations that is continuously growing closer together. Today, European integration and Atlantic ties are at the core of Germany's *raison d'état*. The main cultural challenge is to anchor this consciousness in the minds and hearts of East Germans: Western-mindedness is still significantly, though not dramatically, stronger among West Germans than among East Germans.

There is, of course, no single criterion by which degrees of Westernization may be measured.[5] One would certainly not call the United Kingdom a less "Western" country than Germany for being less enthusiastic with regard to European integration than Germany; the Danes ought not to be accused of a weaker cosmopolitan spirit for being more in favor of restricting the rights of immigrants in the European Union (EU) than the Germans.[6] A number of intersecting indicators would have to be used. They would, for instance, include adherence to or rejection of "Western" values; approval or disapproval of democracy and its way of life; strength or weakness of cosmopolitan (postnational and proforeigner) attitudes; and, not least, positive or negative views of European integration and North Atlantic Treaty Organization (NATO) membership—or, more specifically, of France and the United States. It appears that no real dividing line can be drawn between "center Right" and "center Left" in terms of Western-mindedness: Among the members and adherents of the mainstream political parties, there is a broad pro-Western consensus, to which equally clear anti-Western resentments on the fringes correspond. Notwithstanding this, the social and political elites appear to be more pro-European than the general population; Christian Democrats[7] tend to be more pro-NATO and pro-American than Social Democrats; and postnational as well as proforeigner sentiments are stronger among younger than among older people.

One month after reunification, 77 percent in the West and 48 percent in the East declared themselves "in general satisfied with our [*sic*] political system" ("unsatisfied": West 13 percent, East 26 percent; "undecided": West 10 percent, East 26 percent). Of the younger generation, 47 percent in the West and 68 percent in the East endorsed the statement: "I am proud to be a German" ("not proud": West 48 percent, East 31 percent); 97 percent in the West and 83 percent in the East say they have made, or could think of making, friends with their non-German peers. As for attitudes towards the United States, nearly 75 percent of Germans view themselves as pro-American; 55 percent support maintaining a residual American military presence on German soil; 51 percent in the West and 37 percent in the East "like the Americans" ("undecided" or "no opinion": West 27 percent, East 40 percent).

What do the relatively high "undecided" and "no opinion" figures in East Germany indicate? First, they point to an obvious lack of information. Politically speaking, they mean that the odds are in favor of the West, but only if certain opportunities are seized. Political education in the "new" *Länder* must be intensified; international contacts of East Germans, particularly younger ones, need to be increased.[8] However, there are encouraging signs that some of the old prejudices East Germans harbored toward the United States are starting to break down: for example, their support of a residual American military presence in Germany has doubled from 12 percent in 1991 to 24 percent in 1992 (in the West it increased from 43 percent in 1991 to 63 percent in 1992).

STABILITÄT ÜBER ALLES

All this would be quite reassuring but for the fact that in the younger generation no less than 63 percent in the West and 72 percent in the East oppose a European Economic and Monetary Union (EMU). The EMU project, stipulated by the Treaty of Maastricht, is meant to be a centerpiece of further European integration. The pollsters asked people whether they liked the idea of replacing the deutsche mark with a single European currency called the ECU ("Esperanto money," as chauvinist critics have dubbed it). Most did not. This has to do with a basic trait of German political culture: the marked desire for stability—or, to put it more exactly, the loathing of instability. Many national goals are defined not in positive terms, but as "Never again!," referring to errors, mistakes, and sins that paved the way for the National Socialist tyranny and, indirectly, the communist dictatorship of the GDR. If there were something like a civil religion in Germany, its liturgical expression would take the form of a cry for exorcism rather than a credo. "In today's world," an American expert on German history remarked in early 1993, "the Germans must surely be the most ardent believers in Murphy's Law, that if anything *can* break down it *will.*"

The abhorrence of instability expresses itself in the strong affection—almost devotion—for the deutsche mark, which has developed into a kind of national symbol. The hyperinflation of 1923, with its devastating consequences for Germany's social and political stability, is among the traumatic experiences that have remained deeply fixed in the collective German conscience and have shaped much of the German "safety first" mentality. Directly after the end of World War II, Germany suffered a second hyperinflation, which was brought to an end in 1948 in the three Western zones through a drastic monetary reform. Out of "Trizonia," as it was then called, emerged a politically stable community: the old Federal Republic. The categorical imperative *Keine Experimente!* (No experiments!) became the most successful (West) German campaign slogan, a cantus firmus in accord not only with the pragmatic spirit of the 1950s. The opposing position—"No fear of experiments!"—(primarily expressed in the decade between 1965 and 1975 and, even more specifically, the years between the "student revolts" of 1968 and the Oil Crisis of 1973)[9] did not long maintain the upper hand.

STRIVING FOR HARMONY

The German preference for maximum stability, corroborated by the success story of the old Federal Republic, explains to a great extent their striving for the broadest social and political consensus. The traditional German "yearning for synthesis," as Ralf Dahrendorf put it, also plays a role, though softened by the spirit of pluralistic competition: the search for compromise has become a strategy not to avoid conflict but to settle it in a civilized manner. In only a very superficial assessment is the spirit of Kaiser Wilhelm (the tendency to sweep domestic conflicts under the national rug) still alive. What is alive, though, is some memory of the devastating effects that sanguinary religious conflicts and other rivalries on German soil since the Reformation have had on the nation's ability to unite. The same holds true for recollections of historic times when Europe's center was torn between Great Power interests in the East and the West, the North and the South.

What would an investigation of German political rhetoric reveal? Most probably, a predilection for key concepts and catchwords that conjure up continuity and harmony in domestic as well as foreign affairs: *Friede* (peace), along with its derivatives *sozialer Friede* (social peace), *innerer Friede* (domestic peace), and *Friedenspflicht* (literally, peace obligation, the banning of "wild" strikes); *Versöhnung* (reconciliation) and *Verständigung* (understanding, agreement); *Normalisierung* (normalization) and *Normalität* (normality); *Dialog* (dialogue) and *Ausgleich* (balance, compromise); *Partnerschaft* (partnership) along with its derivatives *Sozialpartnerschaft* (social partnership) and *Sicherheitspartnerschaft* (security partnership); *Augenmass* (sense of proportion), *Vernunft* (common sense), and *Mitte* (literally, center, meaning something like mainstream); *Kontinuität* (continuity), *Berechenbarkeit* (predictability), *Verlässlichkeit* (reliability), and *Behutsamkeit* (a mixture of caution and gentleness, the opposite of abruptness); peculiar, difficult to translate neologisms like *konzertierte Aktion*[10] (literally, concerted action), *Solidarpakt*[11] (solidarity pact), and *Streitkultur* (culture of dispute; in this combination, the irenic *Kultur* neutralizes the abhorrent *Streit*). In such a dictionary of German political rhetoric, we cannot leave out the word *Geborgenheit* (an untranslatable cross between shelter and warmth), idealizing the actual living conditions in the former GDR. Even if fairly well heated, a prison is never a cozy place.

The jargon of harmony expresses both the patterns of behavior and the priorities that led to the success of the old Federal Republic, both in domestic policy and in dealings with its neighbors and partners as well as the international community. It also implies a

German conception of the world that does not allow for Saddams and Skinheads, Mogadishus and Sarajevos, "ethnic cleansing" and fundamentalist terror. It is difficult for many Germans today to believe that there are problems and conflicts that cannot be overcome simply through social work and support groups, appeals to common sense and positive encouragement.

At the beginning of 1991, the German peace movement made a deeply disturbing discovery: unconditional pacifism is counterproductive; it only emboldens aggressive dictators. The decisive lesson of the 1930s is not simply "Never again war!" but "Never again appeasement in the manner of Munich!" One cannot wipe aggression off the face of the earth by simply giving in to it. This also holds for domestic policy: The series of xenophobic arson attacks since the events of Hoyerswerda in the autumn of 1991 taught many German supporters of an unquestioning tolerance that, in the interest of a successful battle against terrorist violence and political extremism, you cannot do without a reasonable dose of "law and order," sustained by a more efficient law enforcement system.

Reunification has not weakened the general desire for consensus in Germany; indeed, it has strengthened it. Conflict is less popular among East Germans than among West Germans, who are, after four decades, accustomed to the cold winds of economic and political competition. Fifty-eight percent in the East fully approve of the statement "Instead of permanently fighting against each other, politicians should commonly act in the same direction" (*an einem Strang ziehen*); in the West, only 39 percent would endorse that view. As for the statement "It is the job of politics to give the citizens a feeling of *Geborgenheit*," the differences are even more striking: 58 percent in the East fully agree, as opposed to 31 percent in the West. During the East German steelworkers' strike in the spring of 1993, a television journalist asked an anonymous man on the street whether he deplored the strike, choreographed and directed principally by West German trade-union leaders. The worker's disarming answer—quoted from memory—was: "No. After all, they are better superiors (*Vorgesetzte*) than the former (the Communist) ones used to be." Did he mean to say that he believes in the professional qualities of West German trade-union leaders when it comes to being tough in dealing with obstinate entrepreneurs? Those who like stereotyping may find his reply very German:

disobedience out of obedience. It is true that many West Germans feel that the GDR preserved an old-fashioned, petit bourgeois kind of Germanness, now completely alien to them. However, if they were compelled to face even a small part of the massive changes they expect their Eastern compatriots to accept without muttering, they would react with more impatience, and some would revolt.

It is well known that people tend to cherish most what they miss. The mechanisms of stability and consensus, of continuity and harmony (whose East German caricature used to be state-run *Geborgenheit*) do not work on the "all-German" level yet. Inevitably, there is a feeling of unease that expresses itself in a gap between a high degree of contentment with one's private situation, especially among young people,[12] and a sense of insecurity or uncertainty as to overall developments. At the beginning of 1993, 47 percent in the West and 44 percent in the East said they were optimistic as far as their personal prospects were concerned ("partly optimistic": West 40 percent, East 48 percent; "pessimistic": West 4 percent, East 8 percent); in contrast, only 9 percent in the West and 12 percent in the East were optimistic with regard to the "political perspectives" in general ("partly optimistic": West 60 percent, East 61 percent; "pessimistic": West 20 percent, East 26 percent).[13] Twenty-eight percent in the West and 32 percent in the East no longer felt happy about reunification; 55 percent in the West and 41 percent in the East said they had been and remain favorable to reunification.[14]

That the old Federal Republic was a stronghold of general harmony is as much a nostalgic myth as the fairy tale of GDR *Geborgenheit*. However, those who held responsible positions in society and politics developed the skill of healing wounds torn open by passionate controversies of the great national questions. Three examples should suffice: *1)* the introduction of a *Soziale Marktwirtschaft* (social market economy) associated with Ludwig Erhard; *2)* the *Westbindung* (the integration of the Federal Republic into the European-Atlantic Community) carried out by Konrad Adenauer; and *3)* the *Ostpolitik* of Willy Brandt. In the first two instances, the Social Democrats (SPD) and in the latter the Christian Democrats (CDU/CSU), after long internal debates, renounced all "revisionist" policies. The only major exception, interestingly, was the fierce controversy that shook the Federal Republic in the early 1980s when American intermediate nuclear missiles (INF) were to be deployed on West German soil, following NATO's double-track decision of 1979. It was mainly over this issue that Chancellor Helmut Schmidt lost the majority within his own party, the Social Democratic Party (SPD). The pacifist issue has never really been put to rest; it simply seemed to have become obsolete by what happened in 1989–1990. But the legacy of the unsettled dispute remains. Should Germany be prepared, for instance, to support militarily UN peacekeeping and peacemaking operations? The Federal Republic would probably have had to answer that question whether or not reunification had occurred.

SOCIAL CONTRACTS (WEST)

Geborgenheit is the opposite of *Angst,* one of those German words that, like *Kindergarten,* have found their way into the English language. As such, it is the code word for *Teuto-Pessimismus* (Teutonic pessimism), as Karl Dietrich Bracher affectionately dubbed his compatriots' notorious appetite for biting their fingernails. Yet *Angst* can have other than paralyzing effects; it may also release inventive forces, liberate productive energies, become a motor of change. Stability does not necessarily mean immobility; it may also set the framework for an extraordinary dynamic. This happened repeatedly in the old Federal Republic, and it built the foundation for a new social contract, constructed in the first instance as a survival pact. "Survival" meant overcoming poverty and chaotic socioeconomic conditions and, for the West Germans, securing protection from the expansionist goals of the Stalin-led Soviet Union. The rebuilding of the ruined country could succeed only through a great communal effort of all social groups; this recognition and resolve had a lasting impact.

In the former "Trizonia," the *Soziale Marktwirtschaft* created the parameters within which, out of the survival pact of the first hours, grew the *Sozialpartnerschaft* between employers and employees. That partnership effectively created a balance of interests between the two sides. The *Mitbestimmung* (codetermination) of the workers in factories played a major role in this. As a "unique social innovation brought to life with the help of the allies to weaken German heavy industry through union control," it became in time a great benefit for West German industry: The cogoverning of employees and their trade-union representatives on boards and committees has made factory standstills and painful reforms easier to accept; it has been a force for learning and the sharing of responsibility.[15] The *Friedenspflicht*, stipulated by legislation as well as wage negotiations through industry-wide arrangements of free collective bargaining (employers' associations and trade unions), reduced conflict inside individual companies. The trade unions were no longer organized, as in the Weimar Republic, according to ideological or political party preferences; structured by profession, huge amalgamations, at least nominally cross-party, became possible.

The term *Soziale Marktwirtschaft* is itself one of those "irenic formulas," as Alfred Müller-Armack put it, with which the vocabulary of German political rhetoric is so richly endowed. It describes a social and economic order in which competition and social balance are reconciled with each other—indeed, may be seen as two sides of the same coin. A comparable approach underlies the so-called *Produktivitätspakt* (productivity pact) between employers and employees—the basic understanding that wage increases and reduced working hours are tied to an increase in productivity so that cost stability and competitiveness are preserved. Such arrangements created the great West German pie of which there was a piece for everyone. This process, which was occasionally interrupted, on the whole seemed to be something that could be taken for granted. People altered their consumer habits, and after the *Fresswelle* (wave of gluttony) in the 1950s, travel, sex, and other such waves swept across the Federal Republic. Even many of the supposedly postmaterial values of the 1980s required a fairly full wallet: the proverbial estate in Tuscany, where West Germans, tired of civilization, learned to spend their weekends enjoying bucolic tranquillity over good red wine, was never free.

More and more West Germans have become aware that the high degree of social harmony for which their part of Germany has been famous, and which has made it an attractive place for low-risk investments, is not free either. No less than one-third of the German GNP is being reallocated for welfare purposes by the public and private sectors. Of course, the taxpayers and the socially insured pay a large portion of the social harmony check, but German taxpayers seem to be more indulgent than their counterparts in the United States. Few, if any, would be willing to stage a tax revolt that might risk big changes in their system of free medical care, free college education, and generous pension and unemployment safety nets.

Indeed, even the perfect management of industrial conflict led to a "new social question":[16] Those who could no longer satisfy the increasing demands of the productivity pact, calling for efficiency and professional qualifications, fell out of work into the *soziales Netz* (roughly, social cushion). Unlike the United States, for example, there were no less demanding jobs available for less pay; this is one of the main reasons why sustained unemployment has never decreased after recessions in the same proportion as it has increased during recessions.

In tandem, a second problem intensified: how to make nonorganizable interests, those who stood outside the working world—such as the unemployed or the elderly—count in a corporate society.[17] Despite declarations to the contrary, the trade unions' concern was and is primarily their own constituencies, the employed. Although they see themselves as "progressive," they, like all large organizations, tend to defend the status quo. In these circumstances, a tacit understanding between employees and employers (including, of course, the public sector) has developed. The private sector tends to blame the federal legislature for the high nonwage costs of labor that weaken the German economy's competitiveness. For example, in 1992 employers had to pay an additional sum of DM 0.84 per DM 1 of wages for various social benefits (including paid days off). Of this sum, DM 0.47 could be attributed to industry-wide free collective bargaining or to special arrangements inside individual companies; only DM 0.37 was induced by legal obligation.

Another major risk of the West German consensus model has been encrustation: a sneaking loss of flexibility and dynamics. Conventional wisdom suggests that Germany's recent domestic problems have principally been due to reunification. But this is less than half the truth. Although the public deficits and debts, for example, have strongly increased since reunification, and although Germany is not a net exporter of capital any longer, her overall financial situation is still not as bad as that of most of the major industrial countries, which do not have to meet the historic challenge of overcoming a communist legacy. Chancellor Kohl[18] and others try to persuade their reluctant West German compatriots that many, probably most, of Germany's present difficulties are rooted in structural dislocations that accumulated in the old Federal Republic, mainly consisting in a relative deterioration vis-à-vis competing economies that have become better than they were before. These problems were not caused by, but became more visible as a consequence of reunification—and of the rise of new competitors in Germany's immediate East Central European neighborhood. To name but a few such problems: Germany has the shortest plant (machinery) running time in the European Community and by far the shortest weekly working hours. Her perfectionist bureaucracy is notorious for its exceedingly lengthy approval procedures. Her higher education system generates the oldest university students and her retirement system the youngest old-age pensioners; many Germans spend the first thirty years of their lives preparing themselves for jobs and the last twenty years recovering from them.

This is happening at a time when German society (West and East) is aging rapidly. Such a development, not least due to declining birthrates, is common in other industrial societies as well. But the German case is among the most dramatic. At the end of the nineteenth century, the ratio of men and women older than seventy-five and younger than twenty years of age was 1 to 79. By the end of the twentieth century, the ratio will be 1 to 14; almost 25 percent of the population will be over sixty years old. Whereas today one pension is financed by three employees (who had to contribute 18.7 percent of their gross income to the pension funds in 1990), the ratio may be 1 to 1 in the year 2020 (which would mean some 35 percent of an employee's gross income).

It has been argued that this development could be countered by a controlled immigration policy. The counterargument says this would at best represent a problem shift: immigrants grow older, too. Be that as it may, it is true that there has been no, certainly no well-devised, German immigration policy to date. Used to defining itself as an emigration—rather than an immigration—society, Germany has to learn that newcomers will be a rule rather than an exception in the future. So far, German immigration policy has been almost purely reactive, with the exception of "ethnic Germans" from the former Soviet Union and from East European countries such as Romania. But more and more Germans are beginning to understand that the seemingly temporary import of labor means importing people—men, women, and children, who begin to take root after a while and who want to become full citizens. Only since the end of 1992 has the federal legislature begun to search seriously for a reasonable path between uncontrolled mass absorption of newcomers[19] and a too restrictive naturalization of foreigners. A more liberal approach to the naturalization at least of second and third generation "foreigners" is badly needed.

There are ample reasons for change, and not only in the "new" *Länder*.

THE CROWDED CENTER

In any comparison of Christian and Social Democrats, the absence of an articulated Left/Right dichotomy makes Germany's political culture different from that of many other countries. The orientation of West German—and now, apparently, of "all-German"—politics and its institutions toward the political mainstream corresponds to the striving for social consensus and harmony. In the 1950s, a three-party system (Christian, Social, and Free Democrats) developed on the federal level. Only in the beginning of the 1980s did the Greens join this triumvirate as the fourth party. Whether or not the successor party of the former East German communists will disappear from the *Bundestag* (Federal Parliament) after the national elections in 1998 is difficult to predict; what can be said with a high degree of certainty, though, is that it will keep drawing its strength for quite some time from its East German strongholds—especially those in East Berlin, where the number of former beneficiaries of the ancien régime is higher than anywhere else in what used to be the GDR.

The splintering of the party landscape, characteristic of the Weimar Republic and associated with a dramatic collapse of the political center, was prevented in the postwar years, not least by the election statute that denied a party access to the *Bundestag* if it failed to garner more than 5 percent of the overall vote. More importantly, perhaps, the large parties—the Christian and Social Democrats— were able to absorb and thereby neutralize the political extremes. Indeed, in their own interest, which they very well understood, the

Social Democrats were often obliged to woo voters who were susceptible to arguments from the extreme Right.[20]

A strong institutional tendency toward political consensus stems also from the necessity of *kooperativer Föderalismus* (cooperative federalism). This is true above all when the majority in the *Bundestag* is different from that in the *Bundesrat*, where the *Länder*, represented by their governments, play a part in federal legislation. Even where parallel majorities exist in the two houses, the *Länder* are confident, assertive, and influential actors, often giving their vote only in exchange for hard currency, sometimes in the most literal sense. Their own interests may cross party lines, leading to the most diverse and shifting ad hoc coalitions: "East German *Länder* versus West German *Länder*" has become an additional possible configuration in a complex game made even more complex by reunification.

Christian and Social Democrats can be successful in elections only if they present themselves as *Volksparteien* (people's parties), which means that they must not limit themselves only to segments of the electorate. Until now, the Christian and Social Democrats were able to control the government only when they were supported by the Free Democrats in a coalition. Only once in the history of the Federal Republic, from 1957 to 1961, did a single political group, the Christian Democrats, gain an absolute majority of votes on the federal level, not least because of its ingenious campaign slogan, *Keine Experimente!*

Competition for power has been a constant battle for the center. The profile and attraction of the established parties was almost never determined by their ideological positions on the Left/Right continuum. Rather, for the most part, it depended on the extent to which voters trusted them to resolve concrete (principally economic) problems pragmatically. Whenever the party profiles blurred—as, for example, during the Kiesinger/Brandt coalition of 1966–1969—or whenever the traditional political parties' ability to cope with pressing issues was called into question, gains were made by populist parties on the extreme Right or by extraparliamentarian movements on the far Left. In more recent times, abstention from voting has developed into a means of deliberate protest, too. Such protest reached unprecedented proportions in 1993 in the West (approximately 30 percent) and in the East (approximately 40 percent)[21] where, for obvious reasons, traditional party allegiances are much weaker.

The earlier zero-sum game—the proposition that gains of the Christian Democrats are automatically losses for the Social Democrats and vice versa—no longer applies. "No experiments!," on the other hand, still remains the motto that Germans (West and East) vote for, that they consider especially important. Landslide changes in federal elections occurred only once, in 1953; it is not likely to be repeated. Over the long term, large crises have not so far "diminished faith in the political system; rather they have strengthened it."[22] The parade of lights at the end of 1992 and the beginning of 1993, by which millions in Germany demonstrated their solidarity against the terror of extreme right-wing gangs, is a sure sign that the centripetal powers are still dominant in Germany, having been momentarily paralyzed following the Rostock arson attack. Some will argue that "*Aux bougies, citoyens!*" does not suffice; that its only message is "Look at us! We are good Germans, out for a head count."[23] Still, it is possible to interpret the *Lichterketten* as an attempt to reconquer the cultural hegemony for cosmopolitan values.[24]

MORALPOLITIK

The culturally conditioned striving for consensus and harmony as well as the institutional tendency toward political common ground compensates in part for the lack of a relatively homogeneous elite, formed in the *grandes écoles* or at ivy league universities, which continually reproduces itself in an aristocratic-meritocratic system. Such a band hands down, from generation to generation, a certain vision of a country's role and duties, its status in the community of nations. In "Germany after the Second World War," Wolfgang Zapf observed in 1965 that,

> the individual sectors—politics, administration, economy, trade unions, church, media—were relatively homogenous. There is, however, a noticeable distance between them. The exchange within the sectors is sometimes high, but decreases considerably "toward the outside." There is no free exchange within the elite as a whole. . . .This fact may make a few characteristics of the post-war society more understandable, such as the lack of self-confidence and coherence at the top, the

lack of a "high society" to set the tone, and the relative division between power, income and prestige.[25]

Little has changed in the last three decades. Yet, the term *classe politique* has been used increasingly to describe the power elite, particularly in West Germany. Such terms, perhaps more applicable to the sociopolitical context of other countries, must be used with caution. While it is true that the permeability between individual social sectors has increased in Germany, it is also true that political careers are principally planned and promoted within the parameters of the political parties. If only relatively small numbers of *Seiteneinsteiger*, gifted dilettantes, enter politics "from the side," it is because in a modern, increasingly complex society, politics is not immune to the general trend toward specialization and professionalization. The individualization of life-styles leads to a retreat into the private realm; the willingness to take public office diminishes; the political parties themselves develop into unattractive "dinosaurs of democracy."[26]

In Germany, as in most other Western democracies, the electronic media contribute to a depoliticization of the public, degrading politics, making it a sector of increasingly trivial entertainment. This encourages a trend toward carefully groomed political showmasters—a tendency that may be countered, at least for a time, by the new style introduced by East German politicians. Many, though not including the old Communists, bring a refreshing element of authenticity to their work, deeply rooted in their bitter personal experience under the GDR regime. No jargon. No worn-out formulas. No "keep smiling." While some may see it as unprofessional, it contributes to a regeneration of the overall political atmosphere.

It is sometimes argued that the absence of a metropolitan center where members of cabinet, economic bosses, leaders of the church, field marshals, media czars, university professors, and top writers can share the same space and communicate easily is central to the problem of recruiting new faces into politics, of overcoming what is perceived as parochialism in foreign affairs, in short, Germany's "culture of reticence." Some attach high hopes to the planned transition of parliament and government to Berlin, where, in the shadow of the Brandenburg Gate, a self-confident and coherent

German *classe politique* is expected to emerge. Such hopes may prove to be an illusion, failing to take into account that traditions are not created by volition, but need time to grow. Metropolitan architecture, however grandiose, cannot replace maturation. Germany, having reacquired her full sovereignty only in 1990, is not yet endowed with what might be called mental sovereignty. This would require her leaders to develop an enlightened definition of Germany's national interests, which, in all vital matters, would run parallel to those of her neighbors. It would exclude defensiveness as well as assertiveness, cheap moralizing no less than cynical *Realpolitik.*

The lack of a political class proper turns out to be a disadvantage when so much time is required for metapolitical debates about questions of style and manners. It is not one of the eminent strengths of Germans (if such a collective judgment may be permitted) to find their way between exaggerated intimacy and exaggerated enmity in dealing with others. It is no paradox that discussions about *politische Kultur* (that is, about the rules of fair play in politics) are usually carried out aggressively in tones of indignation. The opponent is invariably the one who is politically uncultivated. The battle for "moral hegemony" should be seen as an element of the battle for power. However, no one ever articulates this; power is labeled indecent, demonic. This all changes, of course, when one gains power oneself; it is rechristened "responsibility."

The most recent addition to the foreign policy vocabulary is the slightly Orwellian neologism *Verantwortungspolitik* (literally, responsibility politics), supposed to be the opposite of *Machtpolitik* (power politics).[27] *Verantwortungspolitik* may be defined as the politics of verbalism and symbolism, the primacy of good intentions over good deeds (apart from giving money, increasingly scarce, and sheltering refugees,[28] always praiseworthy). When the German government, supported by an all-party consensus in the *Bundestag,* successfully promoted the international recognition of Slovenia and Croatia at the end of 1991—whether this was right or wrong will not be discussed here—Germany was exerting power, clearly by diplomatic means. In Germany, this was not considered an act of power. For Germans, only their intentions counted, and these were good, meaning moral. The idea that Germany was taking advantage of her strengthened position as a reunited country was felt to be a hurtful accusation, as hurtful as the conspiracy theory that there was a plan afoot to expand into the Balkans and down the Danube. The Social Democrats' refusal to consent to more or less symbolic German participation in the UN operations for the protection of the civilian population in the post-Yugoslav war zones was thought also to be based on purely moral intentions. A self-contradiction? No: "The word '*Realpolitik*'," a satirist commented, "has been lost in the German language, and will no longer be needed; it lives on in other languages as a foreign expression. In place of it we urgently need the word '*Moralpolitik*' in order to label that which we, out of responsibility, refrain from doing."[29]

CHANGE THROUGH STABILITY

The West German social and political path taken since the end of World War II represents a thoroughgoing modernization process— very much like the process that most other West European industrial states pursued during this same period. This is not to say, however, that some circumstances were not unique to Germany. National Socialism, and the war it unleashed, brought about momentous changes in society. In order to carry out its total claim to power, it had to "destroy the handed-down—in effect antiliberal—loyalties to region and religion, family and corporation."[30] In West Germany, the traditional milieus—especially the Catholic-rural and trade-union-industrial—were able to reorganize themselves after World War II, but the seeds of fundamental change had already been sown. The alleged "restoration" contributed to a structural stability that made social modernization possible. The disintegration of traditional milieus that accompanied this modernization process has been appropriately described as a "failure due to success."[31]

The twelve million refugees and expellees who came principally between 1945 and 1947 from the former Eastern (now Polish or Russian) territories of Germany and from Czechoslovakia, who, together with their offspring, constitute 20 to 25 percent of the present German population, deserve special mention. Instead of developing into an irredentist time bomb — or a kind of fifth estate—they became an additional agent of change.[32] Their integration drastically diminished the tribal and confessional homogeneity of the regions that took them in; their uprooting allowed them greater mobility and flexibility.

In the 1950s, the agrarian sector's contribution to West German economic life decreased three times more rapidly than in the previous one hundred years. The development of a service industry began late; the Federal Republic caught up with the other Western industrial states only in the 1960s. New middle classes arose, especially in the tertiary sector. Along with the increasing dissolution of traditional milieus, the core constituencies on which the Christian and Social Democrats could rely dwindled;[33] the share of floating voters rose.

In different ways, the communist regime of the Soviet Occupied Zone and the later GDR carried out its own destruction of traditional social structures, already initiated by the National Socialists. The "first workers' and farmers' state on German soil"—as it chose to call itself—took away class consciousness from the proletariat, land from the farmers, and independence from the free professions. The lack of a broad middle class today profoundly differentiates the social structure of East Germany from that of the West. Before the Berlin Wall was built in 1961, some three million Germans, who have to be added to the twelve million postwar refugees and expellees, had fled or migrated from East to West. A disproportionate number were highly qualified: self-employed, entrepreneurs, engineers, doctors, and lawyers. Accordingly, the Wall was "justified" by the East German rulers as an act of defense against West German "social aggression." But even after the Wall was built, there was a continuous brain drain from East to West. The communist rulers themselves expelled, "expatriated," or, yes, sold in return for West German ransom some of the most talented East German intellectuals, writers, and artists during the 1970s and 1980s. If an East German Václav Havel had existed, he would probably have been living in the Federal Republic. There was no such personality. Of the five Ministers President in the "new" *Länder*, there were for a time three—all professional politicians—who had been imported from the West. Incidentally, intra-German "migration" has not come to an end after reunification. In 1992, some two hundred thousand Germans from the East went West, whereas only some 110,000 *Wessis* went East.

Until the middle of the 1960s, a fundamental consensus developed in the Federal Republic relating to the crucial domestic and foreign policy decisions of the late 1940s and 1950s. West Germans no longer saw their state as a provisional entity, a mere torso. The unresolved "German question" was increasingly seen to be a hindrance to the much desired *Normalität*. Along with growing prosperity, new views were expressed that can be roughly depicted by catchwords like "individualization," "hedonism," and "emancipation." The "Protestant" ethic—appreciation for hard work, discipline, and austerity—went into decline.

From the mid-1960s to the mid-1970s, dramatic shifts occurred in the West German system of values. In this relatively short period, the educational goals of "independence and free will" became increasingly popular; the educational goals of "obedience and subordination," as in other industrial societies, lost their attractiveness.[34] The "student revolts" of 1968 were at least as much a consequence as a cause of what some have called a "cultural revolution." During this same period, antiliberal ideas of the New Left gained influence. This, above all, brought into question the basic consensus about parliamentary democracy, the social market economy, the Atlantic Alliance. In the GDR, a noticeable change in values took place a full decade later, between 1975 and 1985. At least among the youth, "individualistic, informal, hedonistic values"[35] gained new favor.

FRAGMENTATIONS

In West Germany, opposing forces were constantly called into action by the modernization process and its social, psychological, and ecological costs. The *Modernisierungsverlierer* (literally, the losers from modernization), especially those in the lower middle classes, became susceptible to antiestablishment (that is, to a large extent, *poujadiste*) parties on the extreme Right. The New Left of the late 1960s and early 1970s and the *Ökopax* (environmentalist and pacifist) movement of the 1980s, which partly grew out of the New Left, developed an anticivilization fundamentalism not altogether different from the one that had been a centerpiece of right-wing ideologies in times more remote. A kind of elitist New Right—certainly not an intellectual mass movement such as the New Left—has made itself heard since 1993.[36] So far, it has not managed to attract the nation's most brilliant young minds; veterans of the New

Left, however, may discover some of their own sons and former students among those angry young men.

It is no surprise that the "romantic relapse" of 1968, as Richard Löwenthal has called it, was not in the least accompanied by a rehabilitation of certain elements of "Germanic ideology," to use a term coined by Fritz Stern, with its contrast of *Kultur* (deep, idealistic) and *Zivilisation* (shallow, commercial). In its most vulgar form, this ideology expressed itself—as had already been the case when it was a stronghold of right-wing extremism—as anti-Americanism.[37] The basic tenets of democracy, including, for example, majority rule and state monopoly of coercion, were brought into question. The Greens, however unintentionally, contributed to the strengthening of those who could only see the dark side of modernization.

Germany—until now in the West, but today in the East as well— shares a fundamental experience with other Western democracies: On the one hand, modernity implies an increase in options for the individual; on the other, it means a loosening of ligatures, including a withering away of the committed *citoyen*. Even in Germany, reputed to be the world champion in *Vereinsmeierei* ("clubism" is only a rough approximation), more and more people are opting for the facilities of a commercial fitness center in order to stay fit, preferring it to a permanent tie to a *Sportverein* (athletic or sports club). Religious alliances, of far greater significance, are also weakening. In this, the differences between the country's Western and Eastern parts are enormous: Among young people, 43 percent in the West and 4 percent in the East claim to be Catholic; 43 percent in the West and 17 percent in the East claim to be Protestant; and 11 percent in the West and 79 percent in the East say they do not belong to any religious community.

Serious problems arise when dissolution, imaginary or not, of familiar patterns becomes a new source of *Angst*. This *Angst* appears to be a fertile ground for new forms of violence, of which xenophobic attacks by youth gangs have represented only one, though a particularly grave and visible form of aggression. Antiforeigner violence has not been, as some armchair sociologists have conjectured, a specter haunting merely the big cities. It is common in small towns and rural areas that used to be (or perceived themselves to be) free of such problems, having only recently experienced a mass influx of immigrants. Of the acts of xenophobic violence committed in 1992, 39.2 percent have been perpetrated in small towns (ten thousand to fifty thousand inhabitants), 20.5 percent in the rural areas, 22.3 percent in the metropoles, and 18 percent in medium-sized cities.[38]

In Germany today, the problems of social fragmentation are pronounced. The healing process between East and West is proving to be very slow. New wounds are constantly being torn open that retard the process of overcoming mutual estrangement between *Wessis* and *Ossis*. The latter complain, legitimately, about *Wessi* arrogance, the former complain about *Ossi* self-pity (which may also exist in the beholders' eyes). The project of *innere Einheit* (literally, internal unity, something like social merger as opposed to *staatliche Einheit*, state unity, already accomplished) embraces much more than a purely economic challenge; it points to "mental" differences that may last for a generation or longer.

Second, the Eastern part of German society has been basically atomized for more than four decades by a communist dictatorship that considered every association it could not control to be a threat to its own total claim to power. The much lauded "niches" in the former GDR—including the *Geborgenheit* they offered—were in reality places of temporary refuge only from this total state claim. They cannot serve as building elements of a civil society. Even in the supposed enclaves free from state control, particularly those that the Protestant Church was able to provide for those opposed to the regime, there was no real protection from the agents of the *Stasi*, the State Security Service. Today, the unavoidable structural transformations in the "new" *Länder* are threatening to destroy that minimum social bond that integration into an ordered working world seemed to offer.

Finally, important parts of the elite in Germany, both in the East and in the West, who might have been expected to play a leadership role in the orientation process are at present principally concerned with a self-critical analysis of their most recent past—that is, their own silence in response to the harm done to individuals beyond the former Iron Curtain. It is not only that so many Western political and social scientists closed their eyes to the actual conditions in the GDR.[39] "Stability" was a code word for the dirty little secret that many West Germans shared with other West Europeans: a silent accord with the status quo, characterized by the seemingly innocent short formula "Yalta." There is already, and not only in Germany, an idealization of the "good old days," when the East-West conflict provided for a clear-cut international pattern, enabling all who had the good fortune to live west of the Iron Curtain to enjoy a pleasant existence. This appeasement—*trahison des clercs* (and not only of *clercs*)—makes East German history an integral part of all German history, as indeed East European history must be seen as an integral part of Europe's history. The GDR rulers tried to create an East German "national" identity by shifting the moral burden for the National Socialist past on the old Federal Republic, by claiming an East German monopoly of "antifascism." Nowadays, many West Germans appear to believe that the communist past is a matter only their Eastern compatriots are obliged to cope with. Their argument, basically insincere though well disguised as liberal generosity and a sort of political correctness, is, "We should not be so patronizing as to wish to interfere with their problems. Let those affected, victims and perpetrators, find a way out for themselves."

PATRIOTISM

How can a new consensus be established from this difficult starting point? What is the glue that will keep — or could keep — the German nation together? Are there articles of faith that might constitute an "all-German" political credo, different from the mere exorcisms inspired by *Angst,* or the simple worship of the deutsche mark? The answer depends on whether the Germans will be able to develop a calm patriotism based not only on their indivisible history (not excluding its darkest chapters), their common cultural traditions, but also, and most importantly, on shared democratic values, civic responsibility for their own *respublica,* an active sense of solidarity and togetherness.

This is the true "challenge of normality," a condition neither Germany nor Europe has known for the greater part of the twentieth century. Hans Magnus Enzensberger's definition of what normality might mean in Germany today is particularly helpful:

> Since we are no longer the world champions of Evil, we feel ourselves obligated to be the world champions of Good. We have to lead the

way by setting a good example; we have to be (morally) better than the others. I find all this a bit warped. I would be happy enough if we could just be normal people in this regard, no worse and no better than the others. Normal civil conditions would suffice completely for me. Even the rest of the world would be content with that.[40]

German patriotism is weakened from two sides. There is a premodern and a postmodern element in how Germans perceive their collective identity. The premodern element may be called "regionalism" or "regional tribalism," a spice in what has been called "multi-German society." To give a single example, the Weimar *Reichsverfassung* of 1919 defined the German nation (*Volk*) as a union of the German "tribes" (*einig in seinen Stämmen*); accordingly, German citizenship had been mediated through Saxon, Bavarian, Prussian, and other *Länder* citizenships, exceptions notwithstanding, until the National Socialists introduced a direct German nationality by the infamous *Reichsbürgergesetz*, which excluded the German Jews from *Reich* citizenship.[41] The postmodern element may be found in widespread postnational attitudes, described as attempts to be rid of the emotional burden of a difficult national history. They carry a positive element, genuine cosmopolitanism.

"Patriotism" is a word greeted with enormous reservation by postnational-minded West Germans. Behind it lies the *Angst* that patriotism may be misunderstood as ethnocentric chauvinism or jingoism. In fact, reunited Germany's real though unacknowledged problem may be the weakness of its republican consciousness, for which an enlightened patriotism might be a remedy. There is a telling story to illustrate this point: In order to compensate for the additional nonwage costs of the planned *Pflegeversicherung* (residential care insurance scheme), it had been suggested that one public holiday be dropped, thereby increasing the working year by one day. The churches strongly opposed the abolition of Whit-Monday; the trade unions refused to allow May Day to be dropped as a public holiday. Some proposed that October 3, the "Day of German Unity," the *only* republican holiday celebrated in Germany, might be sacrificed. Is it possible to imagine French *citoyens* wishing to pay for a new social insurance scheme, however reasonable and necessary, by giving up their Quatorze Juillet? Would any American think of sacrificing Thanksgiving or Independence Day for such a purpose?

Postnational-minded Germans may object that there can be no patriotism without a *patria*. And what is the German *patria*? It appears to be characteristic of the Germans that the question "What is German?" never dies out. Roughly a century after Friedrich Nietzsche said this, Timothy Garton Ash, in a brilliant analysis of the German reunification process in 1990, observed that for "the last forty years (some would say for the last two hundred) the question of German national identity has provoked some of the longest, deepest, most contorted answers ever given to any question by any branch of humankind."[42] Have we at last discovered the German "loose gene?" Is Germany a *malade imaginaire*?

Yes and no. The identity issue certainly points to a real German problem in modern history, the incongruity of state and nation. To German ears, *Staat* and *Nation* remain two distinct concepts. It is also true that the "German question" can be put to rest finally if today's Germany is contrasted with what she was during recent decades. Her most recent past may be expressed in the formula "one nation, two states"; her present-day situation may be described as "one state, two societies." In 1990, the (once East) German writer Reiner Kunze said of Germany that "after October 3, 1990, it will prepare itself for this day."[43] That paradox may be refined by saying that the Germans still have to *become* a nation through a *plébiscite de tous les jours*, through a process of learning by doing, which has barely begun. Fritz Stern has introduced the term "second chance" to describe Germany's situation after her second state unification. Even if one does not subscribe to the proposition that Bismarck's Reich and today's Federal Republic confront a similar dilemma, such a comparison may be useful as a heuristic tool.

One of the principal differences is that today's Germany is no longer burdened by the mortgage of irredentism. There is a fundamental consensus, inside the country and among its neighbors, that the borders of the German state coincide with the borders of the German nation. The price, overwhelmingly caused by German guilt, involved the uprooting and expelling of twelve million from East Central and Eastern Europe. What remains are comparatively small "ethnic German" minorities in the East. For the time being, the Federal Republic feels a special humanitarian obligation towards these people. The claim to German citizenship of those who lost it because the areas in which they live now belong to Poland and Russia is treated as a constitutional right. The same holds true for those "ethnic Germans," principally from Siberia and Central Asia (where they had been deported under Stalin) as well as Romania, who, as a consequence of National Socialism, suffer from the accusation of having been disloyal to their "host" nations. It is important to note that most right-wing extremists in Germany today and many of their sympathizers consider "ethnic Germans" to be foreigners, no less so than asylum seekers from Sri Lanka or refugees from Bosnia.

Compare all this to Bismarck's *Reich*: In those days, irredentism was a common sentiment referring principally to Austria, whose German-speaking population was thought to be an integral part of the German nation. The strong Polish and Danish and the large Catholic and Jewish minorities were suspected of disloyalty to the *Reich*. Alsace and Lorraine remained a bone of contention between France and Germany. The German power elites after Bismarck were driven by an unsatiated yearning for a "place in the sun." Not least because of the unprecedented success story of European integration after World War II, the contrast between that period and the conditions that now obtain could not be greater.

There is, however, one major legacy of the past that the Germans must still overcome: The statement "I am German" has not yet the same meaning as the statement "I am a citizen of the Federal Republic of Germany." "All-German" citizenship, which (from the old Federal Republic's point of view) included the GDR inhabitants, had been an important brace holding together a divided nation for four decades. According to conventional wisdom, the issue is rooted in German jus sanguinis legislation as opposed to jus soli. This is not the real question. Jus sanguinis is a rule in most places in the world; children of American parents, for instance, are citizens of the United States even if born abroad. Jus soli and, of course, naturalization are additional ways of conferring citizenship. Apart from jus sanguinis, naturalization has always been a way to acquire German citizenship; the approximately five hundred thousand Poles who immigrated before World War I as permanent settlers in the Ruhr valley are but one example. What cannot be disputed, however, is that the German naturalization laws will have to become more generous. Under the Kohl government, a first legislative step in that direction was taken: As of January 1, 1991, new provisions—capable of and needing further amendment[44]—give a claim to naturalization without considering "ethnic" criteria, such as descent or total assimilation.

Formal naturalization is a necessary but not sufficient condition for full integration of "foreigners." Here, German society is again in the middle of a learning process that will require some patience and republican leadership. *Volk* (people) has a threefold meaning in German: *demos, laos,* and *ethnos.* In the end, *demos* should be the only acceptable connotation. Germans will have to learn to accept each other and themselves: as compatriots, as copatriots.

STABILITY THROUGH CHANGE

The West German success story after World War II has been based on what appears to be a paradox: it was precisely the old Federal Republic's extraordinary, if boring, stability that made breathtaking changes in West German society possible. The slogan "No experiments!" turned out to be a recipe for a thoroughgoing and dramatic modernization experiment. Since reunification, this no longer applies: remaining wedded to the West German status quo will not do with regard to the greatest experiment that the country has faced in its postwar history. This is a message that mainly the West Germans must understand; for their Eastern compatriots, momentous change has become an everyday experience.

Only if there are extraordinary changes in West Germany will it be possible to preserve the old Federal Republic's stability working in and for a reunited Germany. The old Federal Republic has been the best polity in German history. Whoever cherishes its humaneness would be giving counterproductive advice in suggesting that the West Germans should simply act upon the *weiter so!* (go on!) principle.

The Prussian-Protestant *Staatsidee* (roughly, *raison d'état,* or concept of statehood), which governed the first German nation-state, is as dead as Prussia herself. It is wishful thinking—or fear rooted in ignorance—to believe that it can be resurrected in Berlin.[45] Its true spirit was, in any case, more adequately reflected in Immanuel Kant's ethics or in the courageous attempt on Hitler's life on July 20, 1944 than in Kaiser Wilhelm's bullying Teutonism or the stereotyping *"Jawohl, Herr Hauptmann!"* caricatures. But why should there be any question for a new *Staatsidee* for a reunited Germany? It is already there: represented by what the old Federal Republic built, "also on behalf of those Germans who were prevented from participating." The challenge consists in exporting the "Bonn Republic" to Berlin, Germany's old and new capital.

What, then, can the East German contribution to a reunited Germany be? After more than forty years of communist dictatorship, is there nothing left but a sense of vain suffering, of uselessness? No. Timothy Garton Ash gave the most convincing and edifying response to that question. Thinking of Europeans generally, what he said may be applied to Germans particularly:

> At the very least the Europeans from over there. . .have offered us, with a clarity and firmness born of bitter experience, a restatement of the value of what we already have, of old truths and tested models, of the three essentials of liberal democracy and the European Community as the one and only, real existing common European home.[46]

And they have shown us once again that an open society deserves to be defended against its enemies, of which apathy and indifference are not the least dangerous.

This is no cheap consolation. The *plébiscite de tous les jours* by which the Germans have to become a full-fledged nation is a thorny path. The point of no return lies behind. United Germany will happen when and if Germans do not lose the sense of wonder and gratitude for what happened in the days when the Wall fell, when unity was born of liberty, not of blood and iron. Recalling the time when the seemingly impossible happened, not forgetting the suffering of the seventeen million and countless other millions in Eastern Europe, will remind them that the effort of change is worthwhile.

ENDNOTES

[1]Empirical data (such as poll results) which are not attributed to specific sources have been taken from the following publications: *IPOS* Institute (Institut für praxisorientierte Sozialforschung), *Jugendliche und Erwachsene in Deutschland* (Mannheim: *IPOS* Institute, April 1993); European Commission, ed., *Eurobarometer 37* (Brussels: June 1992); Elisabeth Noelle-Neumann and Renate Köcher, eds. *Allensbacher Jahrbuch der Demoskopie 1984 –1992* (Munich, New York, London, Paris: K. G. Saur Verlag, 1993); Ronald D. Asmus, "Germany's

Geopolitical Maturation," in *RAND Issue Paper,* February 1993; Ulrich Becker, Horst Becker, and Walter Ruhland, *Zwischen Angst und Aufbruch. Das Lebensgefühl der Deutschen in Ost und West nach der Wiedervereinigung* (Düsseldorf, Vienna, New York, Moscow: ECON Verlag, 1992); *INFAS* Institute, *Deutschland-Politogramm der Woche;* Institut für Demoskopie Allensbach, *Deutschland im Frühjahr 1995. Die Muster wechselseitiger Beeinflussung von Ost- und Westdeutschen* (Allensbach: 1995); communications of the Institut der Deutschen Wirtschaft, Cologne; the Federal Office of Statistics, Wiesbaden; the Federal Ministry of the Interior, Bonn; and the United Nations High Commissioner for Refugees (UNCHR), branch office for Germany.

[2]Martha Gellhorn, "*Ohne Mich*: Why I shall never return to Germany," *KRAUTS!, Granta 42* (Winter 1992): 206.

[3]See, for example, Heinrich August Winkler, "Nationalismus, Nationalstaat und nationale Frage in Deutschland seit 1945," *Aus Politik und Zeitgeschichte,* 27 September 1991, 18 –21.

[4]Otto Reinhold in RADIO DDR II, 19 August 1989, 7:00 P.M. (quoted from *DDR-Spiegel* of the Federal Press and Information Office, Bonn, 22 August 1989, 7).

[5]Pollsters seldom expressly refer in their questions to concepts such as "the West" or "Western." An exception can be found in *IPOS* Institute, *Jugendliche und Erwachsene in Deutschland,* 91: Was it wrong for the East Germans to opt in favor of "a W*estern* type of political order" (*eine politische Ordnung nach westlichem Muster*)? Seventy-one percent of the young East Germans said it was "right" (wrong: 28 percent). The most interesting, though predictable, result, however, is that approval of "a Western type of political order" is stronger among highly educated (73 percent) than among less educated (62 percent) young people.

[6]Among the EC population as a whole, 34 percent favored restricting rights of immigrants in the EC ("extend": 17 percent). The strongest advocates of such a policy are the Belgians (48 percent; "extend": 10 percent), followed by the Danes (43 percent; "extend": 5 percent), the British (41 percent; "extend": 7 percent), the Germans (41 percent; "extend": 12 percent), the French (40 percent; "extend": 12 percent), and the Greek (35 percent; "extend": 14 percent).

[7]By "Christian Democrats," I mean here and henceforth the *Christlich Demokratische Union Deutschlands* (CDU) and the *Christlich Soziale Union* (CSU). The CSU is an independent party limited to the Free State of Bavaria, while the CDU, on the other hand, is active in all *Länder* outside Bavaria. The CDU and CSU make up a single group in the *Bundestag,* the German Federal Parliament.

[8]In 1992, 48 percent of the young people in East Germany—as opposed to 60 percent of their peers in the West—traveled abroad, half of them only to East European countries.

[9]Compare Karl Dietrich Bracher et al., *Republik im Wandel: 1969–1982* (Stuttgart: Deutsche Verlags-Anstalt, 1986), 285, 288.

[10]Karl Schiller coined this term during his tenure as Minister of Economics of the government of the Grand Coalition of Christian and Social Democrats (Kiesinger/Brandt), 1966 –1969. Within the framework of *konzertierte Aktion,* he gathered together representatives from trade unions, employers, and govern-

ment at a "roundtable of collective reason." Among other terms, the neologism "social symmetry" came from Schiller as well.

[11]This project, led by Chancellor Helmut Kohl, aimed toward a consensus between the federal government, *Länder,* employers, and employees about the adjustments in economic, financial, and social politics necessitated by reunification.

[12]"(Very) satisfied" with own life: West 95 percent, East 83 percent; "(very) unsatisfied": West 4 percent, East 16 percent.

[13]Compare also *EMNID* Institute poll (n-tv, 4 July 1993): "rather optimistic" as to personal prospects 59 percent (West 59 percent, East 57 percent); "rather pessimistic" 35 percent (West 35 percent, East 39 percent). Economic situation in the West "very good" or "good": 33 percent (West 27 percent, East 54 percent); "bad" or "very bad": 59 percent (West 64 percent, East 37 percent). Economic situation in the East "very good" or "good": 18 percent (West 18 percent, East 18 percent); "bad" or "very bad": 76 percent (West 75 percent, East 79 percent).

[14]See *INFAS* Institute, *Deutschland-Politogramm der Woche* 22 (1993).

[15]Karl Otto Hondrich, "Der deutsche Weg. Von der Heilsuche zum nationalen Interessenausgleich," *Frankfurter Allgemeine Zeitung (FAZ),* 23 June 1990.

[16]Heiner Geissler, *Die Neue Soziale Frage. Analysen und Dokmente* (Freiburg im Breisgau: Verlag Herder, 1976).

[17]See Ibid., 17–20 and Ludwig Erhard and Alfred Müller-Armack, eds., *Soziale Marktwirtschaft: Ordnung der Zukunft* (Frankfurt a. M., Berlin, Vienna: Verlag Ullstein, 1972), 44–46.

[18]Compare, for instance, *Bulletin* 26 (26 March 1993): 221 (ed. The Federal Press and Information Office); *Bulletin* 61 (9 July 1993): 648–51; and *Bulletin* 71 (8 September 1993): 745–46.

[19]Approximately 760,000 people entered Germany in 1991. In 1992, there were even 1 million: 230,000 "ethnic Germans," mostly from the former Soviet Union; 440,000 asylum seekers (of whom, according to independent court decisions, only 5 percent had been persecuted in their home countries for political, racial, or religious reasons); 260,000 refugees, mostly from the former Yugoslavia; and 100,000 illegal immigrants. Taking into account the overlap of some of these categories (of the refugees, roughly one half have also been counted as asylum seekers from the former Yugoslavia) and those immigrants who left Germany again, the sum corresponds approximately to 1.2 percent of the current German population. See *Bulletin* 85 (13 October 1993): 969–70.

[20]In the 1950s, "nationalistic tones were directed [at them] which would touch us today, looking back, in an odd way. The former anti-republican and anti-democratic forces that fell for National Socialism after 1930 should be incorporated into the system. They should be won over as members and functionaries of the new mass party of the SPD." See Peter Lösche and Franz Walter, *Die SPD: Klassenpartei-Volkspartei-Quotenpartei* (Darmstadt: Wissenschaftliche Buchgesellschaft, 1992), 135. In Ibid., 376, the authors name Frankfurt am Main as an example of the transfer of social democratic voters to radical right-wing parties taking place in big cities. In this metropole and other communities of the *Land* of Hesse, in the local elections of 7 March 1993, the SPD lost *per saldo*

more votes to the so-called *Republikaner* (39,000) than the CDU (33,000); the Right/Left dichotomy is also contradicted by the fact that in this election the CDU lost *per saldo* more votes to the Greens (23,000) than the SPD (9,000). A very similar trend could be observed in the *Land* elections of 19 September 1993 in the Free and Hanseatic City of Hamburg where the SPD lost an unproportionately high amount of voters in traditional workers' districts and in socially marginalized areas to radical right-wing parties.

[21] According to an *EMNID* Institute poll (n-tv, 14 March 1993), this circle of persons constituted, in March 1993, 40 percent of those entitled to vote (13 percent "N/A"; 27 percent "No Party") in all of Germany. In the 7 March 1993 local elections in Hesse, the "Party of Nonvoters" reached 1.23 million; the SPD, on the other hand, only reached 1.07 million and the CDU 0.94 million.

[22] Hondrich, "Der deutsche Weg."

[23] See Jane Kramer, "Neo-Nazis: A Chaos in the Head," *The New Yorker,* 14 June 1993, 59.

[24] Compare Helmut Willems, Stefanie Würtz, and Roland Eckert, "Fremdenfeindliche Gewalt: Eine Analyse von Täterstrukturen und Eskalationsprozessen" (research report, ed. *Bundesministerium für Frauen und Jugend* and *Deutsche Forschungsgemeinschaft*), Bonn, June 1993, 146.

[25] Wolfgang Zapf, *Wandlungen der deutschen Elite 1919–1961* (Munich: R. Piper & Co. Verlag, 1965), 199–200.

[26] See Jürgen Rüttgers, *Dinosaurier der Demokratie. Wege aus der Parteienkrise und der Politikverdrossenheit* (Hamburg: Hoffmann und Campe, 1993), especially 239–55.

[27] This contrast was introduced (or at least popularized) by the former Foreign Minister Hans Dietrich Genscher as a rhetorical device.

[28] Germany has so far (as of April 1993) accepted three hundred thousand refugees from the former Yugoslavia (Italy: 16,000; Spain: 4,700; United Kingdom: 4,400; France: 4,200). Germany's proportion of the EC's intake of asylum seekers was 58 percent in 1990 and 1991, and soared to 79 percent in 1992. In relation to Western Europe as a whole, it was 47 percent in 1990 and 1991, and no less than 65 percent in 1992. The number of refugees worldwide is currently estimated to be about eighteen million, of whom 8 percent have been admitted by Germany.

[29] Johannes Gross, "Notizbuch Johannes Gross. Neueste Folge," *FAZ-Magazin,* 26 February 1993, 10. For a critical analysis of the purely moralizing German approach to the Yugoslav crisis in 1991, see Wolfgang Wagner, "Acht Lehren aus dem Fall Jugoslawien," *Europa-Archiv* 2 (1992): 31–41.

[30] Ralf Dahrendorf, *Gesellschaft und Demokratie in Deutschland* (Munich: R. Piper & Co. Verlag, 1965), 432, 434.

[31] Klaus Gotto, "Erosion christlicher Wertvorstellungen? Kritisch Anfragen an Kirche und Unionsparteien," in Anton Rauscher, ed., *Christ und Politik* (Cologne: Verlag J. P. Bachem, 1989), 14.

[32] See Albrecht Lehmann, *Im Fremden ungewollt zuhaus: Flüchtlinge und Vertriebene in Westdeutschland 1945–1990* (Munich: Verlag C. H. Beck, 1991),

7; and Timothy Garton Ash, *In Europe's Name: Germany and the Divided Continent* (New York: Random House, 1993), 227: "Looking back from the 1970s, Willy Brandt himself observed that the peaceful integration of these millions of refugees and expellees was one of Konrad Adenauer's greatest services to his country."

[33]See Lösche and Walter, *Die SPD: Klassenpartei-Volkspartei-Quotenpartei,* chap. II 1–4 for the SPD; for the CDU, see Gotto, "Erosion christlicher Wertvorstellungen?."

[34]Helmut Klages and Thomas Gensicke, "Geteilte Werte? Ein deutscher Ost-West-Vergleich," in Werner Weidenfeld, ed., *Deutschland: Eine Nation—doppelte Geschichte* (Cologne: Verlag Wissenschaft und Politik, 1993), 49–50. See also Dahrendorf, *Gesellschaft und Demokratie in Deutschland,* 471.

[35]Value complexes such as "experiences something crazy more often; adventure," "dress fashionably; treat yourself to a little luxury," "completely enjoy love and sex," "purchase a car," "live in a comfortable home," etc. increased in importance. In contrast to the West, however, "idealistic" values related to society declined in the same period. See Klages and Gensicke, "Geteilte Werte?," 54–55.

[36]See as an early example Rainer Zitelmann, Karlheinz Weissmann, and Michael Grossheim, *Westbindung. Chancen und Risiken für Deutschland* (Frankfurt am Main/Berlin: Propyläen Verlag, 1993); for criticisms see, for instance, Heinrich August Winkler, "Westbindung oder was sonst? Bemerkungen zu einem Revisionsversuch," *Politische Vierteljahresschrift* 1 (1994): 113–17; and Ulrich Raulff, "Auch eine geistige Welt. Rechte Replikanten oder Junge Leute in alten Traditionen," *FAZ,* 13 April 1994, 33.

[37]For an excellent analysis of ideological overlaps between the New Left and the New Right, or between the old Right and *Ökopax,* see Richard Herzinger and Hannes Stein, *Endzeit-Propheten oder Die Offensive der Antiwestler. Fundamentalismus, Antiamerikanismus und Neue Rechte* (Reinbek bei Hamburg: Rowohlt Taschenbuch Verlag, 1995).

[38]See Willems, Würtz, and Eckert, "Fremdenfeindliche Gewalt," 41–42, 113–22.

[39]See Klaus Schroeder and Jochen Staadt, "Der diskrete Charme des status quo: DDR-Forschung in der Ära der Entspannungspolitik," *Leviathan,* March 1993, 24–63. See also Timothy Garton Ash, *In Europe's Name,* 312–42.

[40]Hans Magnus Enzensberger, "Die Schwierigkeiten der Deutschen mit sich selbst," interview in *Der Tagesspiegel,* 19 January 1993.

[41]For a more detailed analysis of the history of German citizenship laws and its meaning for the concept of national unity, compare the excellent monography by Hubertus von Morr, *Der Bestand der deutschen Staatsangehörigkeit nach dem Grundvertrag* (Berlin: Duncker & Humblot, 1977).

[42]Timothy Garton Ash, "Germany Unbound," *The New York Review of Books,* 22 November 1990, 15.

[43]Ibid., 12.

[44]The new legal provisions are still little used by those who are entitled because Germany, like several other European countries, demands that those seeking natural-

ization give up their former citizenship rights; compare Der Beauftragte der Bundesregierung für die Belange der Ausländer, *Ausländerinnen und Ausländer in europäischen Staaten* (Bonn: August 1994), 39–45. Further liberalization plans—also with regard to the problem of dual citizenship (which, above all, applies to the 1.8 million Turkish citizens living in Germany)—have been agreed upon after the *Bundestag* elections in the autumn of 1994 by the CDU/CSU and the FDP—that is, by the parties that form the Kohl government.

[45]Compare Wolf Jobst Siedler, "Erkenne die Lage! Rechne mit Deinen Beständen! Ende einer Hauptstadtprüfung: Die Debatte über Berlin muß eine Illusion nach der anderen anfgeben," *FAZ,* 22 April 1995.

[46]Timothy Garton Ash, *We the People* (Cambridge: Granta Books, 1990), 155–56.

Steven Muller

Democracy in Germany

T RAUMA IS A WOUND OR SHOCK PRODUCED by sudden injury, as from violence or accident. For Germany and the German people, the twentieth century has been a succession of traumas: the war of 1914–1918; the Weimar Republic, burdened by the reparations of the Treaty of Versailles; the hyperinflation of the 1920s; the evils of National Socialist dictatorship; the war of 1939–1945; the occupation of Germany by the victorious Allied powers; the loss of territory in the East, involving a flood of Germans fleeing westward; division into two mutually hostile states; and, most recently, unification produced by the sudden collapse of the German Democratic Republic (GDR). Today, Germany and the Germans are still in trauma—the trauma of unification, obviously, but in fact the whole succession of traumas, which followed each other so rapidly that there was not time to recover from the last before the assault of the next. Normal is defined as usual, regular, natural: the one and only decade of the twentieth century during which German national life could be described as normal was the first.

Above all, this series of traumas includes what is now called the Holocaust, which uniquely and permanently colors both German self-perception and the perception of Germans by others. Anti-Semitism, xenophobia, and genocide are anything but unique. What set the Holocaust apart was the unprecedented application of industrial technology and the factory-based manufacturing process to the extermination of several million human beings. This was neither a sudden, brief, and uncontrollable explosion of rage, nor merely the work of a few. Instead, what those who conceived and ordered

Steven Muller is President Emeritus of The Johns Hopkins University.

this extermination called the "Final Solution" was a systematically planned and efficiently executed program to create and operate a new industry solely and explicitly for the purpose of mass murder. Thousands of people were employed in this process: collecting and transporting the victims, storing and putting them to work while in storage, exterminating them, and disposing as productively as possible of any usable remains—for example, fat drained from the cremation process was used to make soap. These thousands worked at such tasks not just for weeks or months, but for several years. Their work in the murder industry was the source of their daily bread.

Even now, with the facts on record, the reality of these events defies understanding and challenges belief. According to the Bible, when God found the sins of Sodom and Gomorrah very grievous, he destroyed the cities of the plain. The Germans, however, have survived. Of all the traumas that have beset them, responsibility for the Holocaust is unique and the worst. It is, understandably, as little spoken of as possible. But it remains an indelible stain.

Could the Holocaust have been perpetrated by any people other than the Germans? The question is obvious, but not the answer. There is nothing in the earlier German past that clearly and inexorably points to such an outcome. The history of the Germans in Europe does to some significant extent differ from that of their neighbors—particularly in regard to the long absence of a German nation-state—but in most fundamental respects the Germans seemed more or less like their neighbors. What appears to have happened is that in 1933, the Germans—frustrated, impoverished, and demoralized—turned to a leader capable of infecting them with his own madness. That madness was institutionalized into a ruthlessly repressive totalitarian system. In the twentieth century, such collective national intoxication with an ideology and a leader, institutionalized by totalitarianism, has not in fact been a uniquely German phenomenon. There are obvious parallels with Mussolini's Italy, Stalin's Soviet Union, Mao Zedong's China, and Pol Pot's Cambodia. In this context, the unique obscenity of the Holocaust could be attributed primarily to the unrivaled evil incarnate in Adolf Hitler and the moral perverts whom he assembled to serve him. The special Germanic ingredient in the Holocaust could, then, be reduced to such proverbial national traits as obedience, efficiency, discipline, and orderliness. Such traits can often prove to be virtues, but in the service of evil they become vices. Doubtless no other people could have perpetrated the Holocaust in precisely the form it took. Yet, given a leader as evil as Hitler and ruthless totalitarianism, not only Germans might collectively participate in organized obscenity on a large scale.

Does the Holocaust doom the German future? Not necessarily, but it will affect that future, inescapably. Ages ago, Euripides wrote that the gods visit the sins of the fathers upon the children. Even if that means no more than a sense of shame and guilt for the Holocaust, that guilt is now part of the German heritage, though there are many ways to compensate for such a sense. There may be, for instance, an excessive pursuit of national virtue, in the hope that championship of good will overcome past championship of evil. There may be excessive national caution, lest any manifestation of boldness might raise the specter of a return to evil ways. There may be denial, not of facts but of relevance to the present. There may be provocation, based on the claim that if the children are condemned to be prejudged for the guilt of their fathers they might as well imitate or even exceed their fathers' sins. There is almost certain to be excessive national preoccupation with the regard of others, looking always for any hint that accusation for the past is part of present dialogue. In these and other ways, the Holocaust will haunt the German future, and it is sharply and deeply part of the present German condition of trauma.

ILLUSIONS OF NORMALCY

There are those who believed that during four decades of peace and growing prosperity between 1949 and 1989, the Federal Republic of Germany (FRG) had achieved normalcy. This belief is mistaken, but it is worth discussing because of the tribute it pays to a grand illusion. During those four decades, the Federal Republic consistently felt the presence of that other German state from which it was separated by force; it accommodated foreign troops on its soil in substantial numbers, not as an army of occupation per se, but as allied foreign protectors against aggression from the East; it tolerated Berlin as a city not only still de jure under foreign occupation and divided, but serving in its Eastern part as capital of the other

German state; and it became the most favored client state of the
United States. None of this was normal. However, during those
same decades, the Federal Republic also became ever more closely
intertwined with its Western European neighbors in general, and
France in particular; it relied for its security on the American
nuclear umbrella and the NATO Alliance; it functioned effectively
as a constitutional democracy; and it became one of the most
prosperous free-market economies in the world. Those Germans
who lived in the Federal Republic, although still traumatized, were
sheltered in an environment that could be likened to a most luxu-
rious sanatorium—one in which they could and did feel better every
day. And there was no expectation that this status quo would not
hold indefinitely.

As late as 1988, there was little inkling within the Western
Alliance that Soviet power would suddenly disintegrate. The division of Europe and the division of Germany were taken for granted
for the foreseeable future. Western Europe had become addicted to
the illusion that it could build its community without regard for
Central and Eastern Europe, firmly and perhaps forever in the grip
of Soviet imperialism. In the Federal Republic, this illusion of the
permanence of the status quo was not only shared with Western
Europe in general but fostered with special fervor. West Germans
enjoyed maximum security with minimum responsibility, plus extraordinary prosperity. The goal of national unification was universally invoked as an unavoidable piety, but with a degree of commitment directly proportional to the perceived likelihood of its impos-
sibility.

The East Germans, for their part, had little illusion that the GDR
was normal. Its durability depended entirely on the ability of the
Soviet Union to maintain its existence—a fact incontrovertibly
proven by the circumstances of its sudden demise. The East Germans did, however, share the illusion that the Federal Republic
represented normalcy. What many appear to have wanted most was
to become instant full participants in that normalcy—an illusory
aspiration, which reality is denying them with a vengeance. Western
Europe and the United States, whose own addiction to the illusion
that the division of Europe would last indefinitely led them also to
share in the West German illusion of the normalcy of the Federal
Republic, now risk perpetuating an illusion when they view unified

Germany as merely a larger version of the familiar, older Federal Republic of Germany.

In fact, the first united German state in nearly fifty years is a new creation. No single action more succinctly symbolizes this novelty than the decision to relocate the German capital to Berlin—no matter how that decision was arrived at nor how it will be implemented. The newness of unified Germany depends on far more than the fact that sixteen million people who had lived apart for forty years were suddenly added to over sixty million who had experienced a drastically different society during this time. What counts far more is, first, the recreation of a single German state and, second, the fact that this state is no longer on the fault line of a Cold War. Germany is, therefore, free — free from dependence on its American patron for security and free to shape its own identity and foreign policy.

It would be difficult to exaggerate the impact on the Germans of the restoration of a unified German national state. While it is not appropriate to make a lengthy detour into German history, it is relevant to recall that long after France and England had firmly established themselves as nations Germany remained an aggregate of principalities—kingdoms, dukedoms, autonomous city-states, and the like. Only in 1871—with blood and iron—was the Imperial German state created under Bismarck's authoritarian direction. And—as already noted—that state both inflicted and experienced trauma during almost the whole of its existence, until its destruction in 1945. During most of the nineteenth century, national unity was a German dream—primarily belonging to reformers because conservatives were wedded to the status quo of the separate principalities—dreamed to bring, at long last, the Germans with their own state into the family of nations. The years between 1945 and 1989 once again denied that dream; and while few Germans would agree that Germany was the principal aggressor in 1914, the post-World War II division of Germany was perceived by many Germans as divine punishment for the evils of National Socialism, the Holocaust, and Hitler's war. In this context, unification into a single German state without bloodshed seems a miracle, ordained to mark the end of penance for past sins. One question before the Germans is whether their newly-united single Germany will fare better than its unhappy predecessor.

THE NATURE OF GERMAN DEMOCRACY

A distinctively German pattern of political democracy has fully taken shape in the Federal Republic, derived primarily from the Basic Law, conceived while what later became the original Federal Republic still consisted of the three Western zones of postwar Allied occupation. This Basic Law serves as a constitution, but contains the provision (ARTICLE 146) that a sovereign united Germany is free to adopt a new constitution. Constitutional revision in the wake of unification was under consideration, but no fundamental revisions of the Basic Law have resulted. The Basic Law owes much to the democratic commitments of the three occupying powers, particularly the United States. While the Basic Law now serves as the constitution of the enlarged Federal Republic, it lacks the hallowed character of the American Constitution, just as Germany herself lacks a historic democratic tradition, such as the British, which grew slowly over centuries. The federal structure, the bicameral legislature, and the Constitutional Court provided for in the Basic Law all show traces of American influence, but they differ significantly from American practice. German federalism is very real. The *Länder* (states) represent the historic tradition of formerly autonomous principalities, although most of today's *Länder* constitute aggregations of much smaller earlier entities. The *Länder* also participate directly in the legislation and administration of the federation through one house of the legislature, the *Bundesrat* (Federal Council), which is comprised of appointed members of the *Land* governments. Unlike members of the US Senate, who are directly elected and do not take instruction from their state governments, *Bundesrat* members directly represent their *Land* governments. However, the *Bundesrat* rarely originates legislation and has substantially less power than the US Senate. The fundamental legislative power in the parliamentary system of the Federal Republic is vested in the *Bundestag* (Federal Parliament), which also elects the Federal Chancellor, who heads the federal administration.

While the German federal system features elements of both separation of powers and checks and balances, and while the *Länder* retain the residual right to legislate insofar as legislative power is not assigned to the Federation by the Basic Law, in practice German federalism displays substantially greater nationwide consistency than is the case in the United States. Not only is there a great deal of concurrent legislation in Germany, meaning that in a great many areas both the Federation and the *Länder* can legislate, and in these cases federal legislative authority has priority, but the bulk of federal legislation is administered by the *Länder* rather than by separate federal agencies. The Federation and the *Länder* share taxes, and the Basic Law (ARTICLE 107) provides for statutory "reasonable equalization between financially strong and financially weak *Länder*." Also, there is no tradition of substantially autonomous local government, so German federalism does not feature a strong third level of government beneath the federation and the states. In short, the German federal system protects and preserves state rights, but it is designed more to facilitate than to inhibit effective government.

The US Constitution, more than any other, reflects the underlying conviction that government is a necessary evil, whose authority must be limited as much as possible. The one absolute value to which the US Constitution is committed is the freedom of the individual (and individual property). To preserve that freedom, the role of government is not only limited, but divided and held constantly accountable by election. The German Basic Law, on the other hand, reflects the belief that the state is indispensable and that its power and efficiency are necessary, even though German experience underscores the urgency of confining state authority strictly to the rule of law and making it regularly accountable by election. German democracy, then, like European continental democracy generally, values and supports the authority and power of government, while subordinating that authority and power both to the rule of law and to the will of the people as expressed in free elections. As German democracy has matured in the Federal Republic, the rule of law has evolved more into its most pronounced feature. Key issues are frequently referred to the courts for adjudication, and in reaction concern has been expressed that the *Bundestag* is becoming a debating society rather than a decisive law-giving parliament. In the press and in academic circles, there is talk of the legalization of the political process. The prevailing characterization of the Federal Republic as a *Rechtsstaat* translates not only as a state under the rule of law, but also conveys the notion of the just state. In this context, Germans appear to look for the just state more in the legal process and in the courts than in the political arena.

There does seem to be a pronounced German inclination toward social justice, defined specifically in terms of social equality. In the ideal German state, degrees of prosperity would not be perceived as a problem, but real penury represents a social injustice that justifies and requires state intervention. A passion for social justice is not usually mentioned in an inventory of German national traits, but such an inventory often includes references to German tendencies to self-righteous assertions of personal rights and virtues under the law and in society, and to even greater readiness to criticize others in this regard. Could one suppose a connection between an acknowledged German thoroughness, sense of order, and self-righteousness, on the one hand, and movements of social reform, on the other—perhaps all the way from Luther to Marx? Was it the label "National *Socialism*" that early on gave the Nazi movement some initial plausibility and appeal? In any case, it does appear that justice for all is one of the highest aspirations of German society, even at the price of some restraints on individual freedom. Where Americans think of "liberty and justice for all," Germans may be more likely to think of "justice and liberty." The democracy of the Federal Republic certainly has given strong evidence of a commitment to social justice and has worked explicitly and hard to combine market capitalism with a strong and extensive safety net for the less affluent. That safety net presumably made it easier to allow for the large and perceptible gap between the life-styles of the well-to-do and the less well-off in the old Federal Republic.

In the GDR, social justice, whether part of the German national character or not, was part of the ruling orthodoxy. (One of the greatest surprises to this observer after the fall of the Berlin Wall was the genuine shock and anger voiced by many East Germans when the relative luxury in which their leaders had lived became public knowledge—one would have thought they would at least have had suspicions.) In light of such past orthodoxy, reinforced perhaps by national traits, how likely is it that East Germans will embrace the harsher social inequalities of capitalism? Since unification, East Germans have been disappointed that their standard of living could not rise to the West German level more quickly, if indeed not at once. They are still waiting, but with greater aware-

ness that, even when the long wait for parity is finally over, affluence will neither be permanently guaranteed nor equally shared. If
they feel dissatisfaction or anger as a result, how, in the long run,
will they—given the new democratic opportunities offered by unification—find political expression for their sentiments? For that
matter, how, over time, will West Germans express their reaction to
the fact that the costs and problems of unification are far larger and
longer-lasting than originally acknowledged?

THE PARTY SYSTEM

The party system that had existed in the old Federal Republic is
increasingly obsolete. Major changes must unavoidably occur, and
quite soon. As long as the Federal Republic was one of two German
states, its entire range of political competition occurred within a
narrow band, frozen very near center. In terms of the traditional
political spectrum, communism, on the far Left, and neo-fascism,
on the far Right, were outlawed. The center of gravity lay with the
Free Democratic Party (FDP)—a minority "liberal" party strongly
committed to the market economy—whose support was necessary
to enable either the Social Democratic Party (SPD) or the Christian
Democratic Union/Christian Social Union (CDU/CSU) to form a
coalition government. The SPD's ability to move significantly to the
Left was restricted by the need to stay as far as possible away from
any resemblance to the Socialist Unity Party (SED), which ruled in
the GDR. The ability of the CDU/CSU to move significantly to the
Right was inhibited partly by the need for support from the FDP, by
memories of the 1930s, and most of all by the moderate centrism of
the majority of German voters. The ecologically radical Green
movement, as it began to function as a party, could only gain in
political influence by moving closer to the political center, even
though such movement served to call its raison d'être into question.

In today's Germany, unified and freed of the other constraints
imposed by the Cold War, the political spectrum has widened, so as
to tolerate greater scope both on the Right and the Left. The big
question, however, is whether the center of political competition in
the gradually maturing unified Federal Republic will continue to be
occupied by two large parties that can alternate in forming governments, albeit in coalition with one or two smaller partners; whether

two large parties will compete by each moving significantly off-center, so as to be more sharply distinguishable; or whether the moderate center of voter sentiment will crumble sufficiently to engender a more fractionated multiparty system, whose existence would inevitably dilute the ability of government to function decisively. The future of parties and party systems in the democracies after the Cold War is, of course, a question throughout Western Europe. In particular, to the extent that the collapse of the Soviet Empire is perceived to undercut the credibility, indeed the viability, of democratic socialism, it remains to be seen on what basis of ideas a party large enough to govern can emerge in opposition to moderate, socially conscious market-economy conservatism. Europe is, after all, not sufficiently Americanized to adopt the more-government Democratic versus less-government Republican traditional political alternation of the United States. At least in the short run, the evolution of changes in European parties and party systems will be much affected by the relative prosperity of European economies. The moderate centrism of voter sentiment in Western Europe during recent decades did not derive exclusively from the Cold War; it was also encouraged by prosperity sufficient to engender majority satisfaction with—and attachment to—the status quo. Protracted absence of prosperity—or at least the visible prospect of prosperity—undercuts the appeal of the status quo, and therefore of conservatism, and thereupon nurtures the appetite for opposition capable of offering opportunity for attractive change. Sooner or later an alternative to liberal conservatism must emerge.

While these general considerations also apply to Germany, the future of the political parties in Germany must include at least two unique considerations. The first is represented by sixteen million new voters who lack previous experience with democratic competition in politics—with the marginal exception of those elderly few whose memories go back to before 1933. The abrupt absorption of the East Germans into the Federal Republic—swift to the point of indigestibility—initially gave them no alternative but to utilize the preexisting party system, which was thrust upon them as part of their new citizenship. As they become more experienced and active participants on the newly unified national scene, however, they must and will inject their voices more distinctively into the political process. In the 1994 elections, *Ossi* resentment of the disappointing results of unification to date produced a significant protest vote. The Party of Democratic Socialism (PDS), the successor to the former East German ruling party, campaigned as the only authentic *Ossi* voice and won four Eastern electoral seats outright. Even so, the majority of East German voters chose between the two major parties. The PDS may indeed play a role for a time as a regional minority party, but the size of its vote will serve more to measure the level of continuing Eastern discontent than to mark a positive contribution to the national German political dialogue. Interestingly enough, also in the 1994 elections, the Greens—organized as Alliance '90/The Greens—gained support in the Western *Länder* but lost support in the East. Having repositioned their earlier radical stance into a more moderate position as the moral conscience of the Federal Republic, Alliance '90/The Greens may now appear too Western to attract Eastern voters who reject the major parties, but may appear more attractive to those West Germans who yearn for the more innocent and purer days before unification burdened Germany with greater power and responsibility. If neither the PDS nor Alliance '90/The Greens appear to be likely candidates for majority party status, and if earlier reflections in this essay on East German longing for social justice are valid, then perhaps the interesting longer-term question might be how such a longing would affect the restructuring—or even replacement—of the SPD.

The second factor consists of the opportunity—and probable necessity—to accommodate a more pronounced and explicit sense of national identity. The success of unification itself depends on some shared sense of national identity among *Wessis* and *Ossis*. Yet, neither West nor East Germans bring much to the table in this regard. West Germans, who have been consciously—indeed, self-consciously—living down the repellent nationalist excesses of the Third Reich, managed to finesse the issue of national identity by sheltering behind the fact that they represented only a portion of the German people and also by proclaiming their allegiance to the then European Community (EC), to which their attachment was indeed pronounced and unfeigned. In time, West Germans were, in addition, able to express an apparently satisfactory degree of national pride in terms of their economic prowess, the unrivaled excellence of their standard of living and, as mininations often can, the triumphs of their athletes. The East Germans, for their part, were required to demonstrate enthusiastic national commitment to a state that was imposed upon them and to virtues most of them doubted. Now that German politics cannot fail to be explicitly responsive to unified German nationhood, German parties and voters face the unavoidable task of confronting and mastering the delicate subject of national identity. The manner in which different parties respond to the question of national identity may initially prove to be divisive, perhaps to the point of becoming a principal political issue between or among the parties. Some more pronounced political assertion of German national identity is required because it is healthy—or, perhaps better said, because its absence would be unhealthy. Assertive German nationalism, however, would raise obvious problems that would be bound to produce controversy. Thus, the way in which Germans resolve the matter of national identity will play a large role in determining the evolving course of the German political parties and of the workings of German democracy.

GERMAN NATIONAL IDENTITY

Speculation concerning the evolution of German national self-identification begins with recognition of what Germans today do and do not carry with them from the past. Obviously absent from their past is a long, mature, and rather clearly defined tradition of life together in a national state. For centuries before 1871, there were Germans who knew that they were Germans and who shared a language and a rich national culture, but not a national state. The so-called Holy Roman Empire of the German Nation remained a myth and a convenient fiction rather than a reality, and in effect served largely to prevent a unified German state from coming into being in the very center of Europe by sustaining a rationale for the preservation of over three hundred separate German principalities. There was a recognizably—even distinctively—German culture, the *Kulturgemeinschaft* or *Kulturstaat*, still so much admired by Madame de Staël in *De l'Allemagne* just barely over two centuries ago. Without a clearly defined national state, Germany was more a state of mind than an actual fact, a matter of blood and descent rather than national citizenship. It is no accident that to this day German citizenship rests on jus sanguinis, the nationality of the parents, rather than jus soli, the place of birth. There may long have been "German soil," but it was not legally part of the territory of a German national state.

What is missing in the German past is the shared political experience of life together in a common national state. It is tempting to make too much of this, but a German past splintered for so many generations into so many separate, small political establishments left perceptible traces. To this day, for instance, a visitor is apt to notice that Germans tend to make rather sharp comments about differing tribal origins: Bavarians about Prussians, Rhineländers about Saxons. This kind of comment is common in other European countries as well, but among Germans there is often an edge to it so cutting that one may wonder if its sharpness betrays the absence of the greater tolerance bred by centuries of common political citizenship. For a people based in the middle of Europe, the Germans also sometimes seem unexpectedly and profoundly provincial in some of their attitudes. One may wonder whether this provincialism, too, is the legacy of parochial political life, in the absence of the unifying nation-state. There was no German empire at the time that the Spanish, Dutch, Portuguese, French, British, and Swedish empires flowed and ebbed across Europe and over the seas. Germany acquired colonies only between the first unification in 1871 and the end of World War I. If colonialism breeds cosmopolitanism, this has not been part of the German experience. The absence of a German state also delayed the emergence of a national German political class, accustomed to govern on a national and international basis. Without a state, there were no German statesmen to rival the French, British, Spanish, and Austrian national leaders of more than two centuries ago. The Hapsburg Empire was a major national actor on the European scene for centuries while there was no German state.

Only five generations ago German nationalism was a romantic aspiration rather than a fearsome threat. The very recency of its more current reputation should be recognized. Prussia achieved German unification by force of arms and persistent aggression. Political and military German nationalism was obviously perceived as a threat by Germany's neighbors. Fear of German power was a major factor in 1914, and the crippling of German power was a major objective at Versailles. Then came Hitler, then 1945. A

48   *Steven Muller*

familiar, unhappy story, but an unavoidable reminder that the
experience of Germany's political and intellectual leadership with
actual nationhood was both brief and erratic. Initially, with only a
few distinguished exceptions, leading German intellectuals and political and economic leaders supported German nationhood as a
progressive and reforming step away from petty despotisms and
toward a modern, free-trade market economy. Subsequently, they
became more appalled by the terrifying excesses of nationalism—
except for those who themselves became party to those excesses.
Finally, after 1945, the intellectuals in West Germany began to
think that they were able during the Cold War to dismiss nationalism as an anachronism. Those in the East either pretended that the
GDR was a nation or said nothing. Now, presented unexpectedly
with a unified national state again after all, they are confused but
often find their confusion difficult to admit. The fact that many of
these German intellectual and political leaders have sublimated
their confusion by invoking the vision of supranational Europe
offers an eerie parallel to their predecessors, who, after Napoleon,
tried to invoke a supranational pan-Germanism.

One may speculate further as to how and whether this historic
and literal German parochialism relates to German xenophobia.
Negative reaction to strangers is, of course, not a uniquely German
problem. Nevertheless, German xenophobia—directed not only
against non-Caucasians but particularly against Jews, Gypsies, Eastern
Europeans in general, and to some degree against all non-Germans—appears to be exceptionally strong, deeply felt, and edged
with contempt. This xenophobia was not a product of National
Socialism—it was already present for the Nazis to exploit—neither
was it merely a contemporary expression of resentment against the
punitive peace imposed by the Treaty of Versailles. Nor, despite
some illusory hopes to the contrary, was xenophobia purged from
German society as part of the destruction of the Third Reich.

An effort to find roots for German xenophobia might begin with
the thought that "Germanness" was for so long a matter of ethnicity
(common blood) and language (common speech) rather than statehood (common citizenship); that so-called bloodlinks and shared
cultural attitudes tied Germans to each other more sharply than
could shared citizenship—that has been and is the case for other
peoples long accustomed to common statehood. Next, one might

consider that over time feelings of envy developed among Germans of those other neighboring peoples who had achieved national statehood—and whose armies perennially marauded over Germany's soil and population. Such envy would have been very likely to produce feelings of inferiority, which threaten self-esteem. Because Germans continued to lack political statehood, to which they might have looked for the restoration of self-esteem, they fell back on the virtues of the blood ties and the shared language and culture that for them was the essence of their sense of national community. Overemphasis on the virtues of their blood and culture could thus be interpreted as a classic manifestation of aggressive-defensive response to deep-seated feelings of inferiority on a national basis. The widely noted German tendency to lecture self-righteously to others as to proper thinking and behavior could also be related to a national sense of cultural and ethnic superiority that developed in compensation for the enduring absence of a German nation-state. Sometimes one does get a sense both of a heavy-heartedness (*Schwermutigkeit*) in the German character, which may be shared with other peoples who live in cool and often dreary northern climates, and of a self-conscious sense of German clumsiness (*Unbeholfenheit*), derived from the fact that German culture does not feature the lightness of wit and spirit that Germans find diverting among other peoples, whose lighter touch they envy even while deploring their lack of seriousness.

With respect to the intensity of German anti-Semitism, even that could perhaps relate to the long existence of hundreds of small German principalities. The presence of Jews in Central and Western Europe in recent times is, without question, related to the evolution of mercantilism and the rise of cities. The development of market economies required bankers, moneylenders, merchants, and traders. In order to profit from growing mercantilism, those in power licensed and indeed sponsored Jews to play those roles that were regarded as un-Christian and unworthy of the nobility and, of course, beyond the abilities of peasants and servants. While Jews continued to be objects of contempt—identified as a strange and repellent tribe collectively responsible for the death of Christ—they nevertheless were treated with relatively greater tolerance in proportion to the perception that they were useful, even indispensable. In existing nation-states, the highest social power was in the hands of the national rulers and was most heavily concentrated in the capital cities. As a result, the Jews who served the rulers were primarily visible in the capital cities. Among the Germans, each small principality had its rulers and their seats of power; each in due course acquired its Jews to deal in money and trade; and, therefore, the Jews in each principality were a visible and despised presence to almost all those who came to the growing cities to trade and, ultimately, to borrow. To know Jews in each of the German principalities became almost unavoidable, in the context not only of who they were but of what they did. And what they did was not only un-Christian but increasingly powerful: both rulers and ruled became dependent on the Jewish network of money and trade that extended throughout the German principalities. As the market economy grew, so did the influence of Jewish bankers and traders, thus facilitating the myth of an evil, corrupting Jewish conspiracy to make an indecent profit from the honest labor of Christian folk.

However much on or widely off the mark these thoughts may be as to its causes, the fact of German xenophobia cannot be denied. It erupted into the organized genocide of the Hitler period—directed primarily but not exclusively at Jews. And, despite the awful consequences of that eruption, it is manifest again in the newly unified Germany. In Germany today, however, the expression of xenophobia by violence is against the law. Great multitudes of Germans— the very kind of people who kept quiet under the Nazis—have taken to the streets in protest against xenophobic violence and desecration. The hope must be that the new Germany will, in the long run, outlive the negative legacies of the past and that, in the short run, the rule of law and the democratic process will restrain the manifestations of xenophobia within the bounds of civic decency. The larger question is whether xenophobia can be excluded from German national self-identification. That can only happen if German self-identity is defined less by aggressive-defensive attitudes toward the outside world and more by greater emphasis on the positive virtues of German nationhood. There is also hope in the realization that xenophobia is not an inbred characteristic but an acquired condition, susceptible to being unlearned.

The most difficult but also quintessential task before the Germans and their intellectual and political leaders today is simply to manage unified Germany with self-confidence. The basis on which self-confidence can be nurtured and grown is present. For almost five decades, Germans have been neither aggressors nor victims. In sharp contrast to the past, their national unification was attained without force of arms or spilling of blood. In the Federal Republic, a political system has been adopted that provides both democratic process and the rule of law. While this system has initially been imposed in the five new *Länder* without preparation, there is, in principle, no reason why the East German population will not adapt to its use. For five decades, then, the Germans have done nothing wrong (a statement that only makes sense in the context of the many wrongs perceived as resulting from German action in the eight decades from the 1860s to the 1940s). While separated, the two German states proved to be satisfactory neighbors to their respective allies, and their neighbors put no obstacles in the way of their unification. United Germany claims no land from its neighbors and seeks to work in partnership with them. And the national statehood that Germans for so long had lacked, that Germans had earlier gained by aggression and twice lost in bitterness and hatred, was suddenly bestowed upon them virtually without their doing.

National self-confidence has been a problem in the German past: undercut by self-pity during the long era when the Germans lacked a national state; troubled throughout by a deep sense of insecurity reflected in intense preoccupation with external opinion; and distorted into self-assertiveness and self-aggrandizement once unified statehood had been gained at the expense of Germany's neighbors. Must national self-confidence remain a problem in the German future? If so, this would be due less to current reality than to the legacy of past traumas. That legacy persists in at least two respects: In the first instance, there is the question whether a nation burdened with guilt for the Holocaust can ever hope fully to recover national self-confidence. The regime that perpetrated this atrocity was totally destroyed, its actions universally denounced, its surviving leaders tried and convicted of crimes against humanity, and its former citizens now nearly all aged into death. Today's Germans need not perceive themselves nor be perceived as directly or collectively guilty for past crimes. But what of collective shame and self-conscious awareness that German national self-assertion is bound always to kindle recollection of the darkest hours of German history? Both, in fact, are likely to persist, but not necessarily so as to inhibit national self-confidence, which stops short of self-aggrandizement and self-glorification.

A second challenge to the self-confidence of German national self-expression lies in the persisting tensions between citizens of the old Federal Republic and citizens of the five new *Länder*. Four decades of separation have left their scars, and mutual ill will between East and West Germans is perceptibly greater than was the case when the GDR still existed. West Germans initially approached the consequences of unification with some guilt about their state of prosperity as compared to the relative deprivation of the GDR. They were also prepared to be generous. However, as the full extent of economic and social decay in the GDR was revealed and the full cost of social recovery became apparent, what remained of a West German sense of guilt nurtured less charity than resentment. East Germans were perceived as corrupted by the regime that they had had to endure—their work habits eroded by lack of reward and recognition for a job well done; their virtue compromised by accommodating too readily to the regime that oppressed them; and their needs so great as to defy the limits of the possible.

East Germans seem to have dreamed of the opportunity to share in the affluence of the other Germany without absorbing all of its perceived vices: selfishness, Americanized superficiality, and social injustice. When they realized that they had become lesser citizens of a single state committed explicitly to assisting them to adopt the ways of those whom they perceived to be their new masters, they tended to become outraged, internally, and sullen, externally. Their feelings of inferiority, induced by their earlier lack of freedom and material wealth, turned into dislike of those whom they saw as exploiters in the guise of Good Samaritans. And, in their case also, a sense of guilt about putting up with too much, too long nurtured less relief at the advent of freedom than bitterness toward those in the West who were better off, not because they were more deserving but only because fickle fate had been kinder to them. When the East Germans came to realize how long the process of social equalization would take, they became more embittered and depressed. Indeed, for those older East Germans who view forty years of the GDR as a blighting waste of their lives, and now perceive the remainder of their lives as worthless because social renaissance will flower only after their deaths, a mood of dejection is more than understandable.

It is obviously difficult to engender a strong and healthy sense of national identity from a basis of such lingering internal antipathy. On the other hand, however, perhaps nothing would overcome internal bickering more effectively than a new and increasingly self-confident unifying sense of national identity. The progress of unification will seem less onerous to all Germans when it is clear that the full costs have reached their maximum and that thereafter matters can and will only improve. The binding tie of common national sentiment and self-expression will become ever more desirable and potentially helpful. Germany's self-identity is, however, a matter of as much importance to her neighbors as to the Germans themselves, and must now in particular take account of the struggle for a new European identity as well. What kind of self-confident German sense of national self-identity is consistent with the larger European context?

GERMANY IN EUROPE

Until the end of the Cold War, there was occasional but increasing talk that the heyday of the nation-state was coming to its end. Not only did the stand-off between two nuclear superpowers and their allies severely restrict any single state's autonomy in international affairs, but the international flow of goods and currencies obliterated traditional economic autarchy and tied national currencies and markets inextricably into a larger economic community, which would soon attain global scope. There was also talk that nationalism itself was passé. Such talk was leavened by reminders—long before the disintegration of Yugoslavia—that the yearning for popular self-determination remained strong. In an effort to square this circle, the concept of a "Europe of Regions" was sometimes introduced: a vision of a European superstate, whose building blocks might devolve down to provinces or regions such as Bavaria, Brittany, Catalonia, Wales, Lombardy, etc. Less talk along these general lines has been heard since the collapse of the Soviet superpower and the disintegration of its Warsaw Pact bloc of satellites. The desire of Poles, Hungarians, Rumanians, Bulgarians, and others to manage their own national affairs gave new significance to the concept of the nation-state. What had been Czechoslovakia split into separate Czech and Slovak states; the Baltic states regained their separate autonomy; and the Soviet Union itself dissolved into newly separate nation-states. Indeed, the population of the GDR is the only population of a former Soviet satellite state that became part of another existing state rather than pursuing an autonomous national course.

This post-Cold War revival of the nation-state spared Germans the possible irony of at last peacefully regaining a unified national state just when the whole concept of the nation-state might have been going out of style. At the same time, it has already been noted that attempts by leading Germans to finesse the question of German national self-identity by invoking the vision of a European superstate are futile. These attempts do, however, point to the great dilemma of unified Germany—namely, how best to live with its neighbors. This is the very problem for which no predecessor German state had a satisfactory answer. It is also the problem whose solution will probably constitute the single most influential factor determining the character of German national self-identity. Nations do not entirely determine their own self-image. They are mirrored in the eyes of their neighbors, and, while they may accept or reject the validity of the perception of others, they invariably react to external perceptions. Unavoidably then, the Germans will look for positive reinforcement in their neighbors' perception of them. Such positive reinforcement will strengthen the self-confidence of a German national self-image that is attractive to Germans and acceptable to their neighbors; the absence of such external positive reinforcement will have a negative effect on a German national self-image.

The problem of Germany's relations with her neighbors involves two main issues, on which the German national interest is unlikely to correspond to the national interests of neighboring states. These divergences relate less to the purpose of German policy than to the size and power of the unified Federal Republic, and therefore appear unavoidable. Germany's neighbors, though accepting German unification, remain concerned about unified Germany's disproportionate size and power. In making every possible effort to reassure their neighbors, the Germans are likely instead to kindle rather than allay their neighbors' fears. The two main issues involved are the evolution of the European Union (EU) and the evolution of Central and Eastern Europe.

The European Union evolved primarily from the core of the linkage between France and the Federal Republic of Germany that began in the 1950s and whose great opening achievement was the European Coal and Steel Community. Because France, before 1871, had been identified as the archenemy of German unification, because that unification was achieved at French expense, and because Franco-German hostility had been a factor in three successive wars, the Franco-German partnership, and the EU rooted in that partnership, became the single greatest guarantee of the peaceful character of the Federal Republic, not only to its neighbors but also to itself. However, both the Franco-German partnership and the resulting EU evolved on the basis of a smaller Germany—not all that much larger than France, and not grossly disproportionate to the rest of Europe. Unified Germany is, quite simply, too large for the EU as it now exists. However, a large single Germany outside the EU is totally unacceptable to Germany's neighbors. The Germans understand this, but because their economic welfare sufficiently depends on the EU, they find no attraction in leaving it. On the contrary, Germany will not only cling to the EU with all her might but will also work with relentless diligence to increase the authority of the EU and tighten its bonds as much as possible—all for the purpose of proving to its neighbors that German national self-identity is so inextricably European as to be forever safe. However, every step the Germans take in this direction is likely to be perceived by other EU members as a transparently obvious German power play, designed to amplify and confirm the central power of the Union only so that the oversized Federal Republic can transform the EU and all its members into mere satellites of greater Germany. In fear of German domination, some EU member states will delay or defeat moves toward greater cohesion and authority of the EU. The Germans, aware that their size and power make them a threat within the EU unless there are procedural and institutional checks, will press for these checks so as to limit German power. However, these checks will also limit the power of all member states and, therefore, are apt to be perceived by those other members as but another attempt to weaken them so that the German giant can use its power more freely. This potential scenario of epic futility represents only half the problem.

The other half involves the nations of Central and Eastern Europe. This area is of essential importance to Germany, in terms of both its stability and its economic development. Absent stability, the area is likely to produce waves of refugees. Absent economic development, the area cannot become a major market for German goods, and a growing trade with Central and Eastern Europe is the key to German prosperity. Even for the old Federal Republic, the relatively small volume of East European trade made at least a marginal difference. The five new *Länder* began as an economic desert—the currency integration of 1990 priced everything made in the former GDR above the means of countries to the East—and thus with one stroke destroyed the only foreign market for East German goods. The future of the German economy, but especially the revival of economic productivity in the five new *Länder*, depends on finding new markets for German goods in Central and Eastern Europe because there is little hope of sufficiently increasing Germany's share of other world markets to absorb the new excess East German capacity.

Because of the economic importance of Central and Eastern Europe, the Germans cannot avoid doing all in their power to promote stability and economic development in the area. For the other members of the EU, however, Central and Eastern Europe are not as crucially important. If the Germans argue too strongly and impatiently for inclusion of these states in the EU, they will no doubt be suspected of diluting the EU with added members so as better to control it; of enlisting their economic satellites to further strengthen their power within the Union; and of grabbing the lion's share of these new markets for themselves at the expense of other EU members. However, should Germany pursue her goals in the area outside the EU, the criticism would be even stronger: the Germans would then be accused of establishing their own exclusive client states in Central and Eastern Europe, in violation of their commitments to the Union, and in order to pursue their own unilateral and self-aggrandizing course.

The point here is not to embark on a further excursion into German and European foreign policy, but rather to recognize as clearly as possible that it will prove to be difficult for the Germans to develop a stable and self-confident national self-image in the face of the suspicious doubts of their neighbors. Obviously, much will depend on the ability of the Germans to deal with their neighbors calmly, reasonably, and sensitively. A Germany unified without aggression, governed by a democratic constitution, chastened by a century of trauma, and profoundly interdependent in relations with her neighbors to the West has every chance of rising to this challenge. Enduring distrust among her neighbors, however, can frustrate and negate even the very best of German efforts. Europe has no satisfactory experience with a large, unified German state at its center. Having prevented the existence of a single German state for centuries, and having then suffered the consequences of an aggressive state created and maintained by the force of arms, Western Europe has more recently lived well with one of two German states; but neither the EU nor Europe as a whole has yet had long to live with a large, unified, and peaceful German neighbor. Understandably, then, Europe will for some time regard the new Germany with caution, mixed with suspicion at the least provocation. The risk Europe runs is that excessive and overt suspicion of Germany will create a self-fulfilling prophecy: perceived distrust from her neighbors is likely to undermine Germany's self-confidence; yet, even a tentative Germany—let alone a newly aggressive-defensive one—will exacerbate neighborly suspicions and fears.

In the face of so many difficulties, it would be all too easy to make pessimistic assumptions about the German future. But the fundamental situation is in fact positive. Europe—not only the European Union but all of Europe—has not only peacefully accepted a unified German state, but now cannot function effectively either without it or against it. Germany, for her part, can only survive in peace and prosperity within Europe, neither without it nor against it. Mutual love between Germany and her neighbors is not necessary. All that is necessary is mutual understanding and trust sufficient to sustain effective and increasing mutual interaction and partnership—and that level of mutual understanding already exists. To permit it to degenerate would have such obviously disastrous consequences as to guarantee that Germans and their neighbors have every reason to remain committed to each other.

As the Germans recover from more than a century of trauma, the challenge they face is also the finest opportunity in their history: to live among their neighbors in the heart of Europe as a people peacefully united in a German nation-state, seeking neither more nor less than common peace and prosperity. As the trauma of unification gives way to recovery, a new German leadership generation should emerge, capable—intellectually and politically—of enabling the Germans to rise above past torments: at long last to live as neither the victim of Europe's rivalries nor as Europe's curse, but as the key to the fugue of European harmony.

Heinrich August Winkler

Rebuilding of a Nation: The Germans Before and After Unification

A S WE HAVE KNOWN SINCE HEGEL, the owl of Minerva begins its flight only at dusk. The old Federal Republic of Germany (FRG) was already halfway into the fourth decade of her existence when she attained full self-consciousness. In 1976, in the fifth edition of his book *The German Dictatorship*, an analysis of National Socialist rule, the political scientist Karl Dietrich Bracher from the University of Bonn coined a concept that gained widespread notice ten years later, when the author repeated it in his contribution to the fourth volume of the *History of the Federal Republic of Germany*. Bracher called the Federal Republic a "postnational democracy among nation-states," a formula through which the West Germans, on both sides of the political center, could recognize their state and themselves.

The formula took hold. Bracher's postnational credo did away with the increasingly dubious doctrine that characterized the Federal Republic as only provisional. This idea of a "postnational democracy" contributed to that self-recognition of the Federal Republic that some rather conservative authors had already urged in the 1960s. Moreover, the designation of this stance by Bracher transformed a German deficiency into a European virtue: because the Federal Republic was not a nation-state she seemed particularly suited to promoting the supranational integration of Western Europe.

Bracher tied his 1986 verdict to the observation that in spite of the continuing meaning of the German question, the Federal Re-

Heinrich August Winkler is Professor of Modern History at Humboldt-Universität zu Berlin.

public was "not a special case which refers Germans to *Sonderwege* (special paths)."[1] The former Federal Republic had indeed developed over the years into something that the Weimar Republic had never been: a fully-functioning Western democracy. The historical German *Sonderweg* had reached both its climax and its demise in National Socialism. The collapse of the Third Reich and the division of Germany forced Germans to confront the consequences of what had been, until 1918, an authoritarian, then, after 1933, a totalitarian deviation from the democratic West, which therefore constituted a striking *argumentum e contrario* for democracy. This created the broad liberal consensus that, until 1990, was one of the factors that guaranteed political stability in the Federal Republic.

"Postnational democracy among nation-states" does not apply to unified Germany. The new Federal Republic *is* a nation-state — though clearly of a more postclassical than classical nature. From its inception, unified Germany renounced several possible attributes of sovereignty, including the possession of nuclear, biological, or chemical weapons, in its charter, the "Two-plus-Four-Treaty." Furthermore, Germany has agreed to a quantitative limitation of her military forces and is bound a priori to supranational alliances such as the European Union (EU) and NATO. This, however, does not change unified Germany's status as a nation-state. In a certain sense, Germany today is more of a "nation-state" than was the German Empire. Millions of German citizens lived in Bismarck's state who either were not Germans or did not want to be: Poles, Danes, and, certainly, a considerable number of Alsatians and Lorrainers. Since the Federal Republic of 1990 does not face such problems of nationality, she is a more homogeneous nation-state than was the Reich of 1871.

Naturally, the idea of a postnational identity has not been simply discredited now that it no longer applies to the Federal Republic. Indeed, there are recent authors who have stated this exact claim and who in retrospect brand all criticism of an uncompromising belief in reunification as national defeatism, if not as an apology for the communist dictatorship in East Germany.[2] But the problems with the postnational position begin where political polemics stop.

The political practice of the Federal Republic was already postnational under her first chancellor. From the beginning, Adenauer was concerned primarily with shaping the Federal Republic into a sovereign state inextricably bound to the West. Still, if only to gain a majority, Adenauer had to present political integration into the West as the only promising path to "unity in freedom." But for him reunification was not an immediate strategic goal.

Adenauer had good reasons for establishing these priorities. German unity would, at that time, only have been possible under the condition of neutrality, that is, by relinquishing integration into the West. No one who realistically assessed the danger of a rebirth of German nationalism and Soviet hegemony in Europe could have wanted that. Adenauer's strength lay in his realism, which paid off in domestic politics as well: integration into the West was much more relevant to West German security than was the goal of reunification.

Adenauer's assurance that integration into the West would eventually lead to reunification, however, was met with dwindling support, as the building of the Berlin Wall in August 1961 seemed to indicate: the division of Germany had deepened since 1949. From then on, *Realpolitik* could only mean one thing: the consequences of partition must be rendered more bearable through dialogue with the other German state, the German Democratic Republic (GDR), and the overall coherence of the nation must take precedence over the restoration of a German nation-state. The Social Democrats under Willy Brandt adopted this position earlier and held to it more consistently than did the Christian Democratic Union/Christian Social Union (CDU/CSU). Brandt championed this doctrine first in 1963 as mayor of Berlin when he negotiated the first agreement on travel passes, and later as Chancellor in 1972 through the framework treaty (*Grundlagenvertrag*) with the GDR—the next to the last of the East-West treaties of the social-liberal coalition.

The East-West treaties went hand in hand with a reversal of the domestic political fronts concerning the national question. During the Adenauer era, the moderate political Right had pursued a policy of supranational integration, while the moderate Left had proclaimed the primacy of German unity. Compared with the Empire and the Weimar Republic, this was a complete volte-face of position between the Left and the Right. In the second half of the 1960s, while the Chancellor still came from the ranks of the CDU, conservative publicists and political scientists such as Burghard Freudenfeld, Hans Buchheim, and Waldemar Besson demanded that the Federal

Republic develop her own national conscience and bid farewell to pan-German illusions. A few years later, the CDU/CSU attacked the framework treaty with national slogans, and in July 1973 the Bavarian state government obtained from the Federal Constitutional Court that famous verdict that prohibited all constitutional organs from giving up on the restoration of national unity and obliged them to pursue that goal. "Reunification" then converted more and more into a "right-wing" formula directed against social-liberal pragmatism. The traditional roles of the Left and the Right were, at least theoretically, restored.

Reality was much more complicated. Those who, eyeing the conservative constituency, swore by the restoration of Germany's national unity did not necessarily have to think or act "nationally." That held, first of all, for repeated public reference to the German Reich of 1937, which politicians of the CSU—not least its chairman, Finance Minister Theo Waigel, who attended the Germany meeting of the Silesians in Hanover on July 2, 1989—were not able to do without.[3] Conversely, there were nationalists who believed that the existence of two German states was an unalterable fact. In the 1980s, the interest of many Social Democrats in the stability of intra-German (and, bound up with that, German-Soviet) relations was pushed so much into the foreground that they lost sight of the other goal of their policy of détente: the broadening of human and civil rights. Seen from this perspective, the rise of the independent union, *Solidarnosc,* in Poland seemed downright dangerous for world peace. Thus, in 1982, Egon Bahr, one of the architects of the "Opening up to the East," affirmed without hesitation the Soviet Union's right to intervene militarily to prevent a possible Polish secession from the Warsaw Pact.[4] Suddenly, a model dating back to a much older German *Ostpolitik,* namely that of Bismarck, appeared to be reemerging: a Russo-German alliance in defense of the status quo against restless Poles.

The 1982 victory of the Christian Democrat Helmut Kohl over the Social Democrat Helmut Schmidt was a foreign policy break in so far as the new government coalition of the CDU/CSU and the Free Democratic Party (FDP) dispelled all doubts about the Federal Republic's political reliability—doubts that came about as the Social Democratic Party's (SPD) growing reluctance to a consequence of the "double resolutions" of NATO, arms modernization with midrange missiles, became visible. The transition in power did not, however, lead to a turning away from the social-liberal policy toward East Germany and the East in general. The East-West treaties were accepted by the new CDU-led government, just as they had been under the SPD since 1960, as the basis for the Federal Republic's policy regarding Western integration. Kohl frequently spoke of national unity, but already in the 1983 *Bundestag* elections, he added that it was his conviction that this did not mean a "return to the nation-state of earlier times."[5] The tenor of Kohl's policy vis-à-vis the other Germany remained the same as it had been under Chancellors Brandt and Schmidt: since national unity was not at the top of the agenda, intra-German relations had to be forged as satisfactorily as possible in the interest of the people.

In the 1980s, opposition to a sovereign German nation-state came more vocally from left-wing and liberal publications, from the Social Democrats and the Greens, than from government quarters. These positions were founded upon sound arguments. The first maintained that détente depended on the equilibrium between East and West, and that this equilibrium rested on the division of Germany. In the words of publicist Peter Bender in 1981, "The dual state of Germany has become a central element of European détente. The artificial construction of German division constitutes the basis for normalization in a divided Europe."[6] The second argument regarded a specific aspect of the German past: "Considering the role Germany played in the origins of both World Wars, Europe cannot, and the Germans should not, want a new German Reich, a sovereign nation-state. That is the logic of history, which is, as Bismarck noted, more exact than the Prussian government audit office."[7]

The first argument was in itself conclusive, even irrefutable. Human relief in a divided Germany, the quintessence of the "politics of small steps," could only exist in an atmosphere of détente, and thus, the Federal Republic had to respect the tacit assumption of the politics of détente: the existence of two German states. The flip side of German interest in détente was its distinct *étatiste* policy in relation to the Warsaw Pact countries, known first by *Solidarnosc* and then by other civil rights movements. The social democratic "inventors" of *Ostpolitik* were particularly consistent in this respect: for a long time they only accepted governments and governing parties as Eastern partners. Those who were left were the opposition groups, who were, to a certain degree, themselves children of détente, namely of the humanitarian "Basket 3" of the Helsinki Accords of 1975.

The thesis that division was, in the last instance, the result of Germany's own policy and therefore something that had to be endured by the Germans found advocates not only in liberal and leftist circles in the former Federal Republic but also in opposition groups in the GDR. For the latter, the repudiation of a German nation-state was indissolubly tied to the call for radical reforms in the GDR, a demand supported in the former Federal Republic by not all, but indeed many, critics of the "rhetoric of reunification":

> As long as human and civil rights are guaranteed only in the Federal Republic, but not in the GDR, the burden of German history is unevenly distributed. From this it follows that Germans in the Federal Republic are obligated to exhibit national solidarity with those Germans whose democratic self-determination is denied to this day. The order of the day is therefore not restoration of the German Reich, but the democratization of the German Democratic Republic.[8]

After the beginning of the Gorbachev era, this demand for democratization in the GDR gathered new momentum. The call for German national unity seemed counterproductive in comparison. Honecker and the Socialist Unity Party (SED) had always insisted on the alternative "Us or Reunification" and thereby found support beyond even the "socialist camp." Anyone who wanted a different, democratic GDR could not demand the abolition of that state. On the other hand, those who called for a unified Germany had to take into account that they were unintentionally strengthening the position of the opponents of reform in East Berlin.

The awareness of many Germans that the deeper causes for the division of their country lay in German history counteracted German nationalism, reduced foreign reservations about Germany, and, in the end, facilitated reunification. But that is only one side of the coin. In fact, the repudiation of one German nation-state has, in many cases, been merely an expression of West German indifference to East Germans.

Opinion polls from the second half of the 1980s show that feelings of national solidarity with East Germans developed less among young West Germans than among their older compatriots. In 1987, only 65 percent of West Germans between the ages of fourteen and twenty-nine (as opposed to 90 percent of citizens over the age of sixty) considered themselves members of *one* German people. Thirty-four percent of young West Germans started with the assumption that two German peoples existed. Between 1976 and 1987, an average of 15 percent of those over the age of sixty considered the GDR a foreign state; among young West Germans, the number was a good 50 percent. An evaluation of the corresponding data in the *Deutschland Archiv* in 1989 showed that the GDR was perceived by a large portion of the younger generation as a foreign nation with a different social order that was no longer a part of Germany. "This leads to a breakdown in the consciousness of a national common ground and makes room for constant mutual alienation."[9]

The alienation was by no means only a generational phenomenon. Many, even elderly citizens who might be labeled as "posthumous Adenauerian Left," perceived the division as a relief and the nation-state, at least the German variety, as the wrong path. Not all went so far as Günter Grass, who saw Germany's division as punishment for Auschwitz. But the overall course of German history seemed to confirm what Goethe and Schiller had already warned of as early as 1796:

> Your hope of shaping a nation,
> Germans, in vain;
> Instead shape yourselves ably
> into freer people![10]

The former Federal Republic, which defined itself as a postnational community, thought it was in harmony with the best traditions of German history. At the beginning of this century, the historian Friedrich Meinecke acknowledged that German development from cosmopolitanism to a nation-state was progress.[11] At the end of the century, German history seemed to have come full circle in the reversal of this process: from a nation-state to cosmopolitanism.

In a letter dated January 27, 1871, Heinrich von Sybel, a historian from Bonn, described the French capitulation and the founding of the German Reich to his colleague Hermann Baumgarten in Karlsruhe:

Why do we deserve the Lord's mercy? Why are we blessed with the experience of seeing such great and mighty things? And how will we live afterwards? What was for twenty years the aim of all wishing and all striving has fulfilled itself in such an infinitely glorious way! How should one at my age find new meaning and a new goal to live for?[12]

There is no sign that similar letters written by German historians in October 1990 will some day appear. The second German nation-state had not been the "aim of all wishing and striving." Even Kohl and Genscher only took advantage of the favorable conditions during and after the peaceful revolution in the GDR. What they did to push forward the process of reunification was, above all, crisis management on the highest level. Both had realized that, under the circumstances of 1990, only Germany's unity could guarantee what its division had previously ensured: relative stability in Central Europe. A stronger Soviet Union would have never agreed to unified Germany's military integration into the West, which made the above mentioned effect possible. In 1990, Gorbachev accepted Germany's membership in NATO because it was the only way to secure German aid in trying to stabilize the Soviet Union.

Of course, unity would not have come had the East Germans not wanted it. In the first phase of the revolution of 1989, no one spoke of reunification. Civil rights leaders strove for a radical democratization of the GDR; they demanded internal self-determination by East Germans, not national self-determination by the German people. Only after the fall of the Berlin Wall on November 9, 1989 were the democratic chants "We are the people" gradually subsumed by national slogans: the chorus of "Germany united Fatherland" was followed by the catchphrase "We are one people"—the slogan with which the conservative party alliance, *Allianz für Deutschland* (Alliance for Germany), entered into the East German parliamentary elections on March 18, 1990.

The civil rights leaders were representatives of an active, mostly intellectual minority. Demonstrators who shouted for German unity spoke for the hitherto silent majority. Everything the masses wanted to express could be neatly bundled in the demand for unity: "no" to the failed system of "real existing socialism" and to all attempts to merely reform this system or to find a "third way" between capitalism and socialism; "yes" to material equality with privileged Germans in the West.

The Federal Republic was not only obliged by the preamble of its Basic Law to complete Germany's unity and freedom. It also had a moral obligation to correct, through all available means, the unequal distribution of Germany's historical burden. Germans in the Soviet-occupied zone and later the GDR had to bear the consequences of World War II materially, in the form of reparations, much longer and more severely than did the West Germans. In contrast to the Germans in the Federal Republic, they had not enjoyed freedom and democracy; they had been forced to live for four decades under a communist dictatorship.

Since the beginning of 1990 there was no longer any doubt that it was too late for the stabilization of the GDR as an autonomous state. The decline of the East German economy had reached dramatic extremes. The potential of the reforming forces was weaker than Westerners had estimated; the masses' impatience grew daily. Only the prospect of prompt unification with the Federal Republic could safely maintain the peaceful character of East Germany's revolution. Consequently, national unity by means of an accession of the GDR to the Federal Republic under ARTICLE 23 of the Basic Law was the only way in which freedom for the East Germans could be secured. Another, theoretically possible, solution, a referendum on a yet-to-be-worked-out all-German constitution according to ARTICLE 146 of the Basic Law, would have required much more time and was, therefore, ruled out as a practical alternative to the agreement.

Reunification occurred on October 3, 1990 without false pathos and with the broad consent of Germans in the East and the West. The joy over unity did not last long, however. Only after national consolidation did many Germans realize the extent to which the two Germanys had grown apart during four decades of separation. Some West Germans felt that the East Germans were throwing them back into the world of the 1950s, a time they thought they had overcome. Unlike the West Germans, the East Germans had not had the chance to become "Europeans" and "cosmopolitans"; they had remained "German," if not "German National," in a way that deeply alienated intellectual Federal Republic citizens. Many East Germans found West Germans to be overpowering and superior, unsympathetic and presumptuous. Clichés of whining *Ossis* and arrogant *Wessis* spread quickly and were echoed in countless jokes.

Likewise, the extent of the "inherited costs" of four decades of the GDR entered only gradually into general awareness. Hardly any East German businesses were competitive. The decay of the old buildings and most inner cities, the downside of extremely low rents, had long ago turned into a social catastrophe. The ravages of the environment went even further than experts in the East and West had assumed. And the same was true of the moral destruction that the SED caused with help of the *Krake Stasi* (Octopus *Stasi*). The spying was so extensive that, in this field at least, the GDR belonged to the international top class.

Only after the collapse of the GDR was it possible to grasp what the migration of millions from the East to the West and the "building of socialism" had produced: a general reduction in the reservoirs of qualified workers, a social structure that was radically different from that of the old Federal Republic, as well as qualification and performance standards that strongly differed from Western patterns. A skilled and self-employed middle class was still only rudimentary in the East, and free enterprise in industry had completely disappeared. There were no independent farmers, no civil servants with tenure, and no "visible" unemployed. The GDR was an indiscriminate employee society with a highly privileged nomenclature that showed so many signs of being a "ruling class" that one could only apply the term "classless society" to the East German state with many reservations.

In the fields in which ideological reliability was the deciding criterion for professional access and performance, the deficiency, after 1989, of professionalism was especially great. Above all, this applied to party and security machinery and to justice and education. As a rule, the more "political" was a person's position before the "change," the lower would be his or her suitability for similar employment in united Germany.

After 1990, the workers who lost their jobs as a result of unification—an overproportional number of these being women—bore the main burden of radical social change. Dismissals and closings of businesses were primarily due to a lack of profitability and the extensive loss of Eastern European markets. But a Western obstacle stood also against the "upturn of the East": the principle of a "return before recompense" (*Rückgabe vor Entschädigung*), which had been stipulated in the reunification agreement and then later modified. Claims of ownership of countless pieces of land and buildings in the GDR were difficult to prove, in part because entries in land registers were deliberately falsified and because there was a lack of trained personnel to manage the flood of applications for returns.

High unemployment, rising rents, and a considerable difference in income between West and East contributed to the fact that very shortly after unification there was a swing in East German public opinion—from joy over unity to worry about the problems that were bound up with it. Similarly, the West Germans feared the high costs of unity.

A poll taken by the Opinion Research Institute in Allensbach in April 1993 made clear the depth of the gap between East and West Germans in the third year after the reunification. The question of the pollsters read, "Do you believe that West and East Germans feel solidarity with one another, that they feel together like Germans, or rather like West or East Germans with opposing interests?" Only 22 percent of West Germans and 11 percent of East Germans answered that they felt "together like Germans"; 71 percent of West Germans and 85 percent of East Germans saw themselves divided by "opposing interests."[13]

Already in 1990 it was clear that the process of psychological unification would be much more difficult than the physical one. The discrepancy of wealth between East and West and the collision of radically different world views opened the door for conflict and crisis. The dispute over whether Berlin or Bonn should become the center of government and thus the actual capital of unified Germany revealed an especially strong desire on the part of West Germans to leave everything the way it had been before unification. Protection of property was, and is, the unspoken motive underlying all attempts to shield the West from the concrete effects of unification. Few West Germans want to admit that the legacy of the second German dictatorship belongs to all Germans.

Unification was, from the beginning, burdened by the failings of the "political class" in the old Federal Republic. Chancellor Kohl promised the East Germans in the autumn of 1990 that within a few years the new *Länder* (states) would become "flourishing land-scapes." He did not say that the path to unity would be expensive, arduous, and long. There were no appeals to the West Germans to sacrifice and to the East Germans to be patient: first, because that sort of thing was not regarded as opportune in the 1990 election campaign; second, because the participants did not want to admit the seriousness of the situation in the GDR. The call for national solidarity would have been able to release moral and material energies; it had the greatest chances to gain a hearing as long as the laying of foundations of unity was being worked on. The pragmatism of the chancellor and foreign minister paid off, as long as the foreign policy of united Germany had to be managed. However, pragmatism was not sufficient for inner unity.

The social democratic opposition missed a historical chance in 1989–1990. The candidate for the post of chancellor of the SPD, Oskar Lafontaine, saw the economic problems of unification much more realistically than did the chancellor. However, he did not do anything to refute the impression that national unity was rather inconvenient for him. This impression was by no means false. Lafontaine, unlike the patriotically arguing honorary chairman Willy Brandt, stood for that part of social democracy that took not only the nation-states but also the nations for historically overhauled creations. Lafontaine could only see the unification of Germany as an intermediate stop on the way to the unification of Europe—a position that appeared confusingly similar to domestic disinterest in national unity.

The mistakes of the parliamentary Left corresponded to those of many intellectuals. Before 1989, the division of Germany had become a type of intellectual vested rights. This went so far that some political scientists and historians in the 1970s spoke of a "binationalization" of Germany, the forming of two German nations, a West German and a GDR nation—a theory that echoed the SED's assertion that the process of forming a socialist German nation would be carried out in the GDR.

Many have contradicted this thesis of the binationalization of Germany, holding on to the idea of one German nation, and at the same time believing that there could no longer be one German nation-state. Accepting that the division of Germany was a result of German guilt and, as such, part of the "logic of history" meant making some kind of sense of this history and thus making life under it more bearable. But who could be sure that the "logic of history" demanded the continuance of separation? After all, it was infinitely easier to "explain" Germany's partition historically from a Western than from an Eastern perspective. Nietzsche's dictum that the Germans would be Hegelians even if Hegel had never existed indeed holds some truth.[14] At least, there is a certain inclination among German intellectuals to accept as "reasonable" what seems to be "real." Perhaps even Luther stood godfather to the efforts to lift the experience of guilt to the level of a secularized theology of history.

The effects of everything Germans thought, said, and wrote about the German question before unification are still felt today. Not all, but much of this needed critical scrutiny. It was right to oppose the use of the unity slogan for purposes of the Federal Republic's domestic policy. Public declarations of a belief in reunification had become a kind of *Lebenslüge* (roughly, sham existence) for many citizens and politicians of the Federal Republic. However, was that not also valid for the "postnational" identity that many Germans had developed in the 1980s? Was the absolute denial of state unity a half-conscious attempt to escape the most terrible chapter of German history once and for all, to "dispose" of it definitively—a more subtle attempt than everything conservative apologists have done in this direction, but also too comfortable to be convincing? If that is so, is the most difficult part of the effort to learn from history still to come for the Germans?

The examination of the National Socialist past is in no way finished. The GDR has, indeed, through radical societal change, broken more completely with National Socialism than has the old Federal Republic. But the stereotyped rigid "antifascism" of the SED left fewer traces in the collective consciousness of the East Germans than the decades of discussion about the "question of guilt" left in the consciousness of the West Germans. One can say something similar about the "socialist internationalism" of the GDR: it was preached but not practiced. It hardly left its mark on the everyday life of the East Germans. Thus, the internationalist *Sonderweg* of the GDR differs fundamentally from the postnational *Sonderweg* of the old Federal Republic: the "internationalism" of the GDR was only a state doctrine; the "postnationality" of the Federal Republic was a way of life.

With the formation of the new, "postclassical" German nation-state on October 3, 1990, both *Sonderwege* came to an end. Their repercussions, however, will leave traces for a long time. Polls show that the East Germans are more "conventional," less "modern" than the West Germans. In response to the question, "Are you proud to be a German?," in 1992, 69 percent of West Germans and 71 percent of East Germans answered "yes." Twenty-two percent of West Germans, but only 13 percent of East Germans, answered "no." Even clearer is the East-West difference in national pride amongst the younger generation. Among West Germans between the ages of fourteen and twenty-seven, according to a poll by the Institute for Practical Social Research in Mannheim in February and March 1993, 47 percent were proud to be Germans, as compared to 68 percent of East Germans from a similar age group. Forty-eight percent of the young West Germans and 31 percent of the young East Germans did not feel any national pride.

Even more striking are the differences between the responses of West and East German youths and young adults when asked about the future status of Germany. In the old *Länder,* according to the poll cited above, a majority (52 percent) said that they would welcome merging Germany with other countries of the EU into a common European state; 44 percent believed that Germany should be and remain in the future an independent state. In contrast, in the new *Länder* 67 percent were in favor of Germany maintaining her national sovereignty; only 31 percent spoke in favor of a common European state.[15] The findings of the pollsters are not difficult to explain. Unlike the mobile and travel-enthusiastic West Germans, for the East Germans, "Europe" was not an experiential reality until 1989. Rather, it was what Metternich had once called Germany: a geographical term. For this reason, national orientation patterns have survived to a larger extent in the GDR than in the old Federal Republic.

What holds true for "Europe" also holds for the "West" as a whole. The idea of "West" has, for West Germans, an unequivocally positive meaning. In the eastern part of Germany, the renamed official party of the GDR, the Party of Democratic Socialism (PDS), is fighting for votes with the assertion that it wants no "Westernization of the East."[16] The electoral successes of the PDS, which in 1994 grew to be the third largest party in all the new *Länder*, represent the repercussions of such watchwords. It also allows us to recognize even more the division of Germany into two "political subcultures." In contrast to the "material" understanding of democracy in West Germany stands the rather "formal" understanding in East Germany. "Democratic" means in the West much the same thing as taking a stand for the free order assured by the constitution. In the East the relationship to democracy is frequently positivistic: In the view of many, a party is "democratic" if it calls itself so, is not outlawed, and in elections can get considerable shares of the votes.

Since there is only one political culture of liberal democracy, the Western one, the inner unification process can have as a goal only some kind of "Westernization of the East," which the PDS wants to prevent. On the other hand, in view of four decades of mutual alienation, it does not mean to unacceptably dramatize the joining together of the Germans if we describe it as the rebuilding of the German nation. This problem is not to be solved from a "postnational" outlook. The inner unification thus demands an "agonizing reappraisal" of self-assessments from both East and West Germans.

The most obvious expression of the postnational consciousness of the old Federal Republic was "constitutional patriotism," which oriented itself to the universal worths of Western democracy. In 1982, the rather conservative publicist and political scientist Dolf Sternberger coined the phrase; in 1986, the rather leftist philosopher Jürgen Habermas included it in the course of the *Historikerstreit,* the debate on the uniqueness of the annihilation of the Jews under National Socialism.[18] Constitutional patriotism was the inner counterpart to the bond of the Federal Republic to the West; it was not only an advance in respect to traditional German nationalism, but also a step toward overcoming it. The new Federal Republic cannot afford a reversal in this gain in political culture. It has to develop West German constitutional patriotism into a patriotism of mutual responsibility of all Germans. Only then can national solidarity be justified.

The special relationship between West and East Germans derives from their common history since the formation of the nation in the nineteenth century. The German nation, as it constituted itself in

1871, would be a closed chapter of German history had East and West Germany developed into autonomous nations after 1949. In the Federal Republic there were attempts at this that did not become "official." The GDR, on the other hand, officially defined itself as the new "socialist" German nation beginning in the early 1970s, but this view was not echoed by the population. Thus, the German nation continued to exist, and is now, since 1990 a *Staatsnation*—a nation united in one state.

The question, then, is not *whether* the Germans are a nation, but *how* they respond to it and *what* they make out of it. As the historian Hermann Heimpel once observed, "That there are nations is the historically European thing about Europe."[19] Seen in this way, the former Federal Republic's departure from a postnational *Sonderweg* can mean a step toward European normalization, a convergence with the self-definition of other Europeans.

There is, however, a historical burden linked to the German idea of nation, from which the Federal Republic has not freed itself. As defined in ARTICLE 116 of the Basic Law, the nation is an evolutionary community based on descent—supposedly the "objective" contrast to the "subjective" Western understanding of nation that is based on individual will. The traditional German conception of ethnic origin is still invoked today by those who deny naturalization to foreigners who have lived in Germany for decades and to their children who were born there, and thus refuse to acknowledge that Germany has become a country of immigrants. Xenophobia is nourished all too often by that ethnic, if not *völkisch*, idea of nation that has characterized German nationalism since the early nineteenth century.

The new formation of the German nation can only succeed if it coincides with a Westernization of the German understanding of nation. In the future, the term "German" will have to be defined not only by descent, but also by the will to belong to the German nation. That "unreserved opening up of the Federal Republic to Western political culture," which Jürgen Habermas rightly sees as *the* great intellectual achievement of the postwar era, will remain an unfinished project as long as the right to German citizenship does not follow the path of other Western democracies.[20]

The modernization of Germany's concept of nation belongs in the larger context of the critical reappraisal of the historical divergence from the West, or the German *Sonderweg*. Whenever German historians, philosophers, and authors spoke of a special German path before 1945, one that stood in contrast to Western Europe's path, they usually did so with a positive tone. They contrasted the allegedly shallow civilization of the West with the contemplative culture of Germany, and democratic majority rule to the strong state that Germany needed and would continue to need because of its threatened borders. The German *Sonderweg* appeared to many Germans in a new light only after World War II: it became the embodiment of the tradition that had paved the way for the "German catastrophe" of 1933 to 1945.

The starting point for the academic debate was why Germany was the only highly developed industrial country after the Great Depression of 1929 to give up its democratic system and replace it with a right-wing totalitarian dictatorship. Experts mostly agreed that, until 1918, Germany had been an authoritarian state ruled by preindustrial elites and that the Weimar Republic, Germany's first democracy, succumbed above all to this authoritarian legacy. According to this interpretation, the end of the German *Sonderweg* did not come until after the "collapse" of 1945: the manor holders east of the Elbe who had played a decisive role in the destruction of the Weimar Republic literally lost the ground from underneath their feet as a result of the loss of the East German regions and the "land reform" in the Soviet-occupied zone. For years there was no German military; the state of Prussia was formally dissolved in 1947 by a decree of the Allied Control Council; and German nationalism would be discredited, even made historically illegitimate, by National Socialism for years to come.

In more recent discussions, beginning long before reunification, a more complex picture of the German *Sonderweg* gained acceptance. In these discussions, emphasis is placed not only on authoritarian traditions but also on Germany's earlier partial democratization—particularly the male suffrage established by Bismarck in the North German Confederation in 1867 and in the German Reich in 1871. The coexistence of nonparliamentarian government and democratic suffrage before 1918 was one of the contradictions in the German process of modernization from which Hitler later profited. Since an authoritarian presidial system had taken the place of the failed parliamentarian Weimar democracy in 1930, he could appeal to *both*: to widespread resentment about the new, allegedly "un-German" parliamentarism *and* to the long attested, though practically ineffectual, right of the people to political codetermination. The deeper reason for the downfall of the first German democracy and for Hitler's triumph lay in Weimar's failure to master the conflicting legacy.

The German nation-state of 1990 differs fundamentally from the one that perished in 1945. In contrast to the German Reich, unified Germany is not a national power state, but an equal member of supranational communities. Unlike the Weimar Republic, it is a well-trained democracy with four decades of the experiences of the old Federal Republic behind it. Yet, there are also continuities between the second and the first German nation-state. As a federal, constitutional, and social welfare state, unified Germany shares a tradition with Bismarck's Reich and the Weimar Republic. The same applies to the democratic achievement of equal universal suffrage extended to women in 1918.

Striking, too, is the physical continuity of the area that the term "German nation" applies to: the *kleindeutsch* solution of 1866, which signified the exclusion of Austria, was reconfirmed in 1990. An even larger Germany would have been unbearable for the rest of Europe in 1871. In 1990, the written commitment to the national borders around a considerably smaller German area was one of the preconditions for the acceptance of Germany's unification by the four victorious powers of World War II.

After the end of all German *Sonderwege*—the anti-Western *Sonderweg* of the German Reich, the postnational *Sonderweg* of the old Federal Republic, and the internationalist *Sonderweg* of the GDR—Germany is, for the first time, a democratic nation-state integrated firmly into the West. Germans are only gradually realizing the consequences of that integration. As long as there were allied rights of reservation with regard to Germany as a whole, the Federal Republic could keep out of many world conflicts. The increase in sovereignty, which is bound up with unification, has taken away the foundations of this special role. As a member of the United Nations, unified Germany has to assume more military responsibility than did the old Federal Republic. More responsibility within the framework of the United Nations—for instance becoming a permanent member of the Security Council—also means more German activity.

Germany's Eastern neighbors aim expectations at united Germany that can only be fulfilled in close cooperation with her allies. Within the EU, Germany has to press for the democratization of the Union and its expansion toward the new democracies in East Central Europe. The expansion of the EU is necessary in order to give more stability to the new democracies. Democratization is indispensable as a means of strengthening the popular backing of the Union.

Germany can only play a constructive role in Europe and in the world if it finds constructive solutions for its inner problems. The alignment of living conditions in West and East Germany calls for an exertion that has not been demanded of the Germans since the reconstruction after World War II. The full integration of the foreigners living in Germany who want to become Germans makes turning away from deep-rooted traditions important, and thus will require a great effort. The Germans have to learn once again to be a nation and at the same time to fundamentally change their concept of nation. They have to take up these challenges at a time when the deepest recession of the postwar period lies behind them, but not by any means the crisis in the structure of the German national economy, which became visible simultaneously. There is no cause for fatalism or even for resignation. But this much appears certain: the second German democracy, which for four decades was only a West German democracy, still has its first real test ahead of it.

Translated by
C. Michelle Murphy, Cornelius Partsch,
Susan List, and Christine Ann Evans

ENDNOTES

[1]Karl Dietrich Bracher, *Die deutsche Diktatur. Entstehung, Struktur, Folgen des Nationalsozialismus,* 6th ed. (Cologne: 1979); also by Bracher, "Politik und Zeitgeist, Tendenzen der siebziger Jahre," in Bracher et al., *Republik im Wandel 1969–1974, Die Ära Brandt* (*Geschichte der Bundesrepublik Deutschland,* vol. V/1) (Stuttgart: 1986), 405.

[2]Jens Hacker, *Deutsche Irrtümer. Schönfärber und Helfershelfer der SED-Diktatur im Westen* (Berlin: Ullstein, 1992).

³*Frankfurter Allgemeine Zeitung* (150) (3 July 1989).

⁴Egon Bahr, *Was wird aus den Deutschen? Fragen und Antworten* (Reinbek: Rowohlt, 1982), 23.

⁵Karl Lamers, "Zivilisationskritik. Deutsche Identitätssuche und die Deutschlandpolitik," in Karl Lamers, ed., *Suche nach Deutschland. Nationalidentität und die Deutschlandpolitik* (Bonn: Europa-Union, 1983), 21–59.

⁶Peter Bender, *Das Ende des ideologischen Zeitalters. Die Europäisierung Europas* (Berlin: Severin and Siedler, 1981), 229.

⁷Heinrich August Winkler, "Auf ewig in Hitlers Schatten? Zum Streit über das Geschichtsbild der Deutschen," in *"Historikerstreit." Die Dokumentation der Kontroverse um die Einzigartigkeit der nationalsozialistischen Judenvernichtung* (Munich: Serie Piper, 1987), 256–63.

⁸Heinrich August Winkler, "Bismarcks Schatten. Ursachen und Folgen der deutschen Katastrophe," *Die Neue Gesellschaft/Frankfurter Hefte* 35 (2) (February 1988): 111–21.

⁹Silke Jansen, "Zwei deutsche Staaten—zwei deutsche Nationen? Meinungsbilder zur deutschen Frage im Zeitablauf," *Deutschland Archiv* 22 (1989): 1132–143.

¹⁰"Deutscher Nationalcharakter," in Johann Wolfgang von Goethe, *Poetische Werke, Gedichte und Singspiele,* vol. 2 (Berlin: Aufbau, 1966), 441.

¹¹Friedrich Meinecke, *Weltbürgertum und Nationalstaat* (Munich: R. Oldenbourg, 1907), in *Werke* (Collected Works), vol. V (Munich: R. Oldenbourg, 1962).

¹²"Die Sturmjahre der preussisch-deutschen Einigung 1859–1870. Politische Briefe aus dem Nachlass liberaler Parteiführer," in Julius Heyderhoff, ed., *Deutscher Liberalismus im Zeitalter Bismarcks. Eine politische Briefsammlung,* vol. 1 (Osnabrück: Biblio Verlag, 1967), 494.

¹³Elisabeth Noelle-Neumann, "Wird sich jetzt fremd, was zusammengehört?," *Frankfurter Allgemeine Zeitung,* 19 May 1993.

¹⁴Friedrich Nietzsche, *Die fröhliche Wissenschaft,* in Friedrich Nietzsche, *Werke in drei Bänden,* vol. 2 (Collected Works in 3 Volumes), ed. Karl Schlechta (Munich: Carl Hanser, 1977), 226f.

¹⁵"Jugendliche und junge Erwachsene in Deutschland," February/March 1993: report prepared by the Institut für praxisorientierte Sozialforschung (ipos), Mannheim, 1993, 70–72.

¹⁶Programm der Partei des Demokratischen Sozialismus, Berlin, 1993, 16.

¹⁷Helmut Willems et al., *Fremdenfeindliche Gewalt: Eine Analyse von Täterstrukturen und Eskalationsprozessen. Forschungsbericht,* submitted to the Ministry for Women and Youth and the German Research Council in June 1993, p. 15.

¹⁸Dolf Sternberger, *Verfassungspatriotismus* (Frankfurt: Insel, 1982); Jürgen Habermas, "Eine Art Schadensabwicklung" in *"Historikerstreit,"* 62–76.

¹⁹Hermann Heimpel, "Entwurf einer deutschen Geschichte," in Hermann Heimpel, *Der Mensch in seiner Gegenwart. Acht historische Essais* (Göttingen: Vondenhoeck and Ruprecht, 1957), 162–95.

²⁰Habermas, "Eine Art Schadensabwicklung," in *"Historikerstreit,"* 75.

Timothy Garton Ash

Germany's Choice

A HISTORIC MOMENT

THE GREAT FOREIGN POLICY DEBATE IN GERMANY has only just begun. In fact, the very nature of the foreign policy actor—Germany—is still disputed. Is this a new Germany or just an enlarged Federal Republic? After the first unification of Germany in 1871 it was clear to all that Europe had to deal with a new power. For all the underlying continuity of Prussian policy, the new German empire, or second Reich, was not just Prussia writ large.

Following the second unification of Germany, the change has been much less immediately visible. Externally, this unification was achieved by telephone and checkbook rather than blood and iron. Internally, the constitutional form of unification was the straight accession of the former German Democratic Republic to the Federal Republic. The larger Federal Republic continues to be integrated in the European Union (EU), NATO and other leading institutions of Western internationalism. Nor has much changed on the surface of everyday life in western (formerly West) Germany. Last but not least, there has been the emphatic continuity of government policy so massively embodied by Chancellor Helmut Kohl—in all senses one of the largest figures in European politics today.

This year Germany has no fewer than 19 elections, culminating in the national election on October 16. The present conservative-

Timothy Garton Ash is a Fellow of St. Antony's College, Oxford.

This essay, reprinted with the permission of Foreign Affairs, *originally appeared in* Foreign Affairs, *July/August 1994, Vol. 73, No. 4.*

liberal coalition—composed of the Christian Democratic Union, the Christian Social Union and the Free Democratic Party—is not certain to return to office. Yet Kohl's Social Democrat rival for the chancellorship, Rudolf Scharping, is going to extraordinary lengths to reassure German voters and the outside world that there will be almost no change in German foreign policy if his party comes into power.

In time, however, the deep underlying changes in the country's internal and external position must affect Germany's foreign policy. Even if foreign policy is not itself a major election issue, the elections will catalyze the process.

WHAT'S IN A NAME?

Within Germany, analysis and prescription are inextricably intertwined. Claims about what Germany is are also assertions about what Germany should be. The state in question continues to be called Bundesrepublik Deutschland, which is officially translated as "the Federal Republic of Germany," but is literally "Federal Republic Germany."

Some argue passionately that what really matters in the name is still the "Federal Republic": a post-national democracy with constitutional-patriotism in place of nationalism and state sovereignty devolved both downward to the federal states and upward to "Europe," meaning the EU. Others say that what really matters now is the "Germany," which should aim to become a "normal nation-state" like Britain or France, with all the traditional attributes of sovereignty, a great capital called Berlin, plain unhyphenated patriotism and the responsible but determined pursuit of national interest. Most fall somewhere in between, both seeing that Germany has and feeling that it should have a new mixture of the two, as the state name implies. But what mixture?

This Germany is larger, more powerful and more sovereign, and it occupies a more central geopolitical position than the old Federal Republic. Some German commentators have sweepingly asserted that Germany is now back in the old *Mittellage* of the Bismarckian second Reich: that fateful monkey-in-the-middle situation to which a long line of conservative German historians have attributed the subsequent, erratic and finally aggressive foreign policy of the Reich.

Others say that Germany is again a central European state, or even the center of Europe. Such striking claims need to be examined skeptically.

The leaders of the old Federal Republic were always deeply conscious of Germany's Cold War position as the divided center of a divided Europe and Berlin's position as the divided center of the divided center. The foreign policy of the Bonn republic was made under constant tension between its western and eastern ties. The Bonn government was vulnerable to blackmail from Moscow and East Berlin. Today Germany has no such dependency on the East. The last Russian soldier will leave Germany by the end of August 1994. In terms of its constitutional order and international ties, Germany is now more fully in the West than it was throughout the Cold War.

Many German politicians like to say that Germany's integration into the West, and specifically into Europe—that is, EU-rope—is irreversible. Since European history offers few examples of the irreversible integration of states into larger entities, and since the years following the end of the Cold War have been rich in examples of the opposite, this claim is bold, if not foolhardy. To observe that the West sorely misses the Soviet negative integrator has become a truism. Nonetheless, the single market and political institutions of the EU, the integrated command of NATO and all the associated habits of permanent cooperation are different in kind from earlier alliances between European states.

Geographically, this Germany also lies more to the west than did the Bismarckian Reich. A glance at the historical atlas shows Germany sprawling across east-central Europe, with Prussia stretching into what is now Lithuania and the Russian territory of Kaliningrad (formerly Königsberg). Today's political map shows a compact territory west of the Oder and Neisse rivers and the diamond wedge of Bohemia. Germany still faces sensitive special eastern issues, but the country's center lies westward.

In 1967 Federal Chancellor Kurt Georg Kiesinger observed that a reunited Germany would have a "critical size. . .too big to play no part in the balance of forces and too small to keep the forces around it in balance by itself." Exactly so. Germany is now the most powerful country in Europe. But it is not a superpower. It has great assets in each of the three main dimensions of power—the military, the economic and the social. But it also has special liabilities in each department.

Militarily, Germany has some of the largest and best-armed forces in Europe. However, in the "2 plus 4" unification treaty, the new Federal Republic solemnly reaffirmed the old Federal Republic's commitment not to acquire atomic, biological or chemical weapons. This may change. One cannot take post-Hitler public abhorrence for national military power as a permanent given. If Germany were not, in the longer term, to seek enhancement of this dimension of its power, to complement or buttress the other two, it would be behaving differently from most large states in history. But for the moment, several statements can be made with confidence. Germany is not in the world super league of military power. It is still virtually unthinkable that a German government would use force or the threat of force unilaterally to achieve a national goal, except the defense of its own territory. Any qualitative upgrading of its military power, including some form of control over nuclear weapons, would almost certainly come in a multilateral (probably European) context.

Economically, Germany is in the super league, and this power has been actively deployed, although in two distinct ways. First, economic instruments and incentives have been liberally and skillfully used by the German government to achieve its foreign policy goals. Second, the Bundesbank's single-minded pursuit of domestic monetary and fiscal policy objectives has had a direct impact on the economies of Germany's neighbors and trading partners, and hence on the country's foreign relations. The Bundesbank has, as it were, made foreign policy by not making foreign policy.

However, Germany is now afflicted by a double economic crisis. There is, obviously, the massive cost of incorporating and reconstructing the former East Germany. But there is also, less obviously, the crisis of the old West German "social market economy," which was already beginning to lose its competitive edge before unification.

Experts differ on how far and how fast Germany will surmount this double crisis, but for the next few years the consequences for foreign policy are clear. If Germany is still most unlikely to use guns as an instrument of foreign policy, neither will it be so ready to use butter. All decisions, including those inside the EU, will be scrutinized more closely for their impact on German budgets and competitiveness in European and world markets.

The third dimension of power has to do with the overall attractiveness of a particular society, culture and way of life. Its crudest measure is the number of people inside a country who want to get out compared to the number outside who want to get in. (One might call this the Statue of Liberty test.) In the 1980s this was a vital component of German power. Germany, seen in 1945 as a threat and a synonym for horror, had by 1985 become a model and magnet (West Germany, that is). When in 1989 people east of the Iron Curtain spoke of returning to Europe and normality, West Germany was a central part of the liberal, democratic, civil and bourgeois "normality" they had in mind.

But this achievement too is under stress. The exemplary openness and civility of the old Federal Republic have not yet been restored across its larger territory. This failure is not simply a case of easterners exhibiting the pathologies of post-communism. It is as much a problem of the condescending and at times frankly neocolonial attitudes of westerners toward easterners. There is more than a grain of bitter truth in the joke that when in 1989 the East Germans started chanting, "We are one people," the West Germans replied, "So are we."

The seemingly open, tolerant, civil society of the old West Germany has, in the last four years, too often looked like a spoiled, defensive consumer society, both demanding and assuming perpetual economic growth while yearning for the lost comfort of living with one's back to the Berlin Wall. Where easterners and westerners have found common ground, it has sometimes been in scapegoating the foreigners who have been admitted to the country in large numbers but given citizenship less liberally. At times, it seems as though the Federal Republic has grown in size but shrunk in spirit. These strains and the extreme voices they breed on the right and left will play into the political process through this year's elections. A nation still preoccupied with becoming one nation may have less time and patience, as well as less money, for foreign policy.

The Random House Dictionary of the English Language, published in 1968, memorably defined Germany as "a former country in Central Europe." Today Germany is a country in west-central Europe. In fact, together with Austria, it is west-central Europe. It is a Western state, but one directly confronting many of the problems characteristic of the former communist East. A troubled, medium-heavyweight power—and a nation in its perennial condition of becoming.

PROCESS, TRADITION AND CHOICE

What foreign policy will be made on these substantial but shifting foundations, and how will it be made? It is sometimes suggested that Germany lacks a political class or internationalist elite such as can be found in Paris, London or Washington. Yet Germany does not want for highly sophisticated, knowledgeable, multilingual practitioners and analysts of foreign affairs (including many of those who make this criticism).

It is true that a middle generation of politicians is coming into power with little experience beyond the professional party politics of the Federal Republic. But the same could be said of Kohl when he came to Bonn and of many American presidents. Some learn on the job. It is true that no one in Germany expected or was prepared for the quantum leap in Germany's power and responsibilities following unification. But neither were American elites prepared for the United States' quantum leap in the second half of the 1940s. They rose to the occasion.

Germany has a much less clear preponderance of wealth and power than the United States did a half-century ago, and a far more difficult geopolitical situation. But something of the human challenge for leadership, and the excitement that goes with such a challenge, is palpably there in Germany (and palpably not in France or Britain). Besides the question of personal qualities, however, there are those of process and tradition.

The foreign policy process in Germany labors under some disadvantages familiar to other Western democracies. As in all television democracies, German politicians often seem to be following public or published opinion rather than leading it. (It was this, and not any subtle or sinister calculation of national interest, that prompted Germany's initiative for the diplomatic recognition of Croatia in 1991.) The fact that responsibility for foreign policy is divided between a chancellor and a foreign minister from different political parties can on occasion make for more heat than light. And both the Bundesbank in Frankfurt and the constitutional court in Karlsruhe have become—rather against their will—important institutions in foreign policy.

Nonetheless, Germany has over the last 30 years pursued one of the most consistent foreign policies of any Western power. As a result, it has a well-formed foreign policy tradition. This tradition, a blend of Adenauerian Westpolitik and Brandtian Ostpolitik, has several distinctive features. Besides the renunciation of force and the pursuit of reconciliation with former foes, there is what one might call attritional multilateralism. German diplomacy has excelled at the patient, discreet pursuit of national goals through multilateral institutions and negotiations, whether in the European Community, NATO or the Helsinki process.

Closely related to this is the habitual conflation of German and European interests. In the German case, this policy has not merely been the familiar old European game of pursuing national interests in Europe's name. In postwar German politics there has also been a great deal of genuine idealistic commitment to the process of European integration. But for that very reason, German policymakers have sometimes found it difficult to distinguish between the one and the other.

At the same time, running like a leitmotiv through the history of the Federal Republic has been the effort, under all chancellors, to widen the bounds of German sovereignty and power. Certainly, German chancellors were at the same time busily and demonstratively surrendering elements of sovereignty to Europe. But the paradoxical effect of this readiness to surrender sovereignty was to convince Germany's key allies and partners that Germany could again be trusted with full sovereignty. It was by laying on the golden handcuffs that Germany set itself free.

Also ingrained in this tradition are the politics of *sowohl-als-auch*: not either-or, but as-well-as. The essence and great achievement of Genscherism was to maintain and improve Germany's ties with a wide range of states, which were themselves pursuing quite different and contradictory objectives. This complex balancing act involved saying somewhat different things in different places. Fudge was the hard core of Genscherism. This may not always have endeared Bonn to its more plain-spoken friends, but such an approach was well-suited to the achievement of Germany's aims in the last two decades of the Cold War.

This foreign policy culminated in a success beyond the dreams of those who made it. So it is not surprising that the first inclination of German policymakers was to stick with it. Even after the retirement of Hans-Dietrich Genscher in 1992, the motto of the foreign ministry was, "Herr Genscher is gone, long live Genscherism!"

Yet the policy that served the old Federal Republic so well is less appropriate for the new one. The state's external dependencies have been decisively reduced, but the external demands on it have significantly increased, and the resources to meet those demands have not grown commensurately. In the short term they have shrunk. The conclusion should be plain: the Federal Republic can and should make clearer choices than in the past. These are not absolute "either-or" choices—to some extent, all major states have to genscher—but choices of priorities: between the demands of its special relationship with the United States and those of its special relationship with France, between deepening the existing European Union around the Franco-German core and widening it to include Germany's immediate eastern neighbors, between relations with east-central Europe and those with Russia. Not all these things are compatible. Certainly not all can be done at once.

The obvious starting point for determining such priorities would be a definition of the national interest. However, the German national interest is particularly difficult to define when the nation itself is still in the making. Moreover, in Germany merely stating that one should define the national interest is controversial. Those who believe that the Federal Republic is or should be a post-national democracy on the path to a genuine European union regard the very notion of defining the national interest as suspect, retrograde, even reactionary. On the other hand, those who wish to see Germany become a normal nation-state use the idea of defining the national interest almost as a campaign slogan.

Yet this argument is itself a sign that a major foreign policy debate is slowly getting under way. In newspaper columns, speeches and Germany's ubiquitous television talk shows one can hear echoes of some of the great debates of the 1950s and 1960s—the Charlemagne school of West European integrationists, the German

Gaullists, the Atlanticists, the Ludwig Erhard economic *mondialistes*—
as well as snatches of much older tunes.

FOUR OPTIONS

To sharpen the debate let us consider four possible priorities for
German foreign policy after 1994, with several factors militating
for and against their adoption.

Carolingian Completion

For this school, the top priority would be a decisive further deepening of the existing European Union around a Franco-German core.
Germany, France and the Benelux countries would go ahead of
other member states, in the variable-speed Europe for which the
Maastricht treaty in fact allows. Monetary union would be achieved
in this core group around the end of the century, and prove a
decisive step—as it was in German unification—toward political
union. In ten years one would have, if not a United States of
Europe, then at least a Confederal Republic of North-Western
Europe—Charlemagne's empire in a new form.

For: This has been the personal top priority of Helmut Kohl and
seems to be high on the personal list of Rudolf Scharping. (Not
accidentally, both men have been prime minister of the western
state of Rhineland-Palatinate, a region with close historical ties to
France.) The Paris-Bonn axis has a 30-year track record and personal and institutional momentum. This simplistic version of Europe as an answer to the German question still has some appeal: it
looks like somewhere for Germany to go. Maastricht, wrote President Richard von Weizsäcker, offers Germany "the chance of being
delivered from the Mittellage."

Against: The Franco-German relationship has been rocky since
German unification. It is far from certain that the Euro-idealism of
the middle and younger generations in Germany is as widespread or
deep as that of the immediate postwar generation. In this respect
Helmut Kohl begins to look like a magnificent dinosaur. His likely
successors have a more hard-nosed view of the EU. So do many of
Rudolf Scharping's colleagues in the leadership of the Social Democrats.

More broadly, over the last two years Germany has experienced the popular reaction, also seen elsewhere in Europe, against the Messina-to-Maastricht model of functionalist, bureaucratic European integration from above. An appeal to the constitutional court against the Maastricht treaty meant that Germany was actually the last country in Europe to ratify it. The court produced a complicated judgment that nonetheless drew a clear line against any automatic progress to monetary union. As German budgets are squeezed, there is growing resentment of the outsize German contribution to the EU's budget. The outspokenly Euro-skeptical Bavarian Prime Minister Edmund Stoiber, sometimes jovially dubbed "Edmund Thatcher," is an extreme case, but not simply an aberration.

German banking and business circles are also far from enthusiastic about European monetary union. By and large, they think a single market can operate perfectly well without it. Further steps toward economic, monetary and social policy harmonization in the EU are not calculated to sharpen Germany's competitive edge in other markets.

Underneath, there is the deeper matter of sovereignty. It is one thing to surrender sovereignty in order to regain it. But has Germany now regained sovereignty only to surrender it? Even for the world's most dialectical nation, this may be a twist too far.

Wider Europe

Whatever anyone says, there is a day-to-day tension between concentrating on deepening or on widening the EU. This brings us to a second possible priority: widening the EU and NATO to include Germany's eastern neighbors. Germany would do everything in its power to ensure that within ten years the Czech Republic, Poland, Hungary, Slovakia and Slovenia would follow Austria, Sweden, Norway and Finland (the "EFTAns") into the European Union, the West European Union and NATO. Beyond this it would try to help the Baltic states, Romania, Bulgaria, Albania and, if they really became peaceful democracies, Croatia, Serbia and Bosnia, to prepare themselves to follow over the next decade. Europe would be built from EU-rope out.

Naturally, this approach would involve further derogations from the idea of the single *acquis communautaire,* with long economic transition periods for new member states and further special provisions of the kind seen in every earlier round of enlargement. Nonetheless, Germany would aim to preserve, in this Europe of more than 20 states and 400 million people, the present historically unprecedented level of permanent, institutionalized interstate cooperation, with major elements of economic and legal integration.

For: Germany has already shown a major interest in enlargement. Foreign Minister Klaus Kinkel was instrumental in pushing the negotiations with the EFTAns to a successful conclusion. Building on the achievements of a quarter-century of Ostpolitik, Germany has over the last four years played a leading and constructive role in east-central Europe (some problems connected with present or past German minorities notwithstanding). It has an obvious vital interest in having peaceful, stable democracies at its eastern frontier. Poland is now less than an hour's drive from Berlin—or a few minutes by fighter plane. It is no accident that the German defense minister, Volker Rühe, was the only senior Western minister to come out clearly in favor of a rapid enlargement of NATO to include Germany's eastern neighbors.

Perhaps there is still a little gratitude for what brave Poles, clever Hungarians and principled Czechs did to make German unification possible. The (exaggerated) fear of mass immigration from the east has also concentrated minds on this issue. Enlargement would expand the internal European market for German goods. German manufacturers are already taking advantage of the much cheaper skilled labor to be found just over the border by relocating production there. Last, but by no means least, Germany would be at the center of this wider Europe.

Against: This option would have substantial short-term costs. Unlike the EFTAns, these new members would definitely not be net contributors to the EU budget. Cheaper imports from east-central Europe could also undercut more expensive German products. In the short term, keeping industrial jobs in Bohemia could mean losing them in Bavaria. In the long term, such a bracing wind of competition would be good for the German economy, just as the North American Free Trade Agreement will be good for the American economy. But tell that to German trade unions and to voters already peevish about not getting richer.

Such an opening to the east would also be resisted by some of Germany's less economically developed EU partners. (Keeping agricultural jobs in Polish Galicia can mean losing them in Spanish Galicia.) As now constituted, the EU aggregates rather than transcends national, sectoral and regional special interests. Hence its continued overt and covert protectionism against eastern goods. Thus far, Germany's key European partner, France, has been extremely reluctant about enlargement, preferring to keep a smaller Europe with France still at its center.

There is no major lobby for this option in Germany. Less tangibly, there is not great tradition of Germany giving priority to its poorer and weaker eastern neighbors. Historically, when Germany looked east, it looked to Russia; this brings us to the third possible priority.

Moscow First

This is the classic eastern option of German foreign policy. The new-old great power in the center of Europe develops a new-old special relationship with what is still the most powerful state in eastern Europe. In doing so, over the heads of the peoples between, it argues that such a policy best serves the interests of Europe, indeed of the world. For what could be more important than a cooperative, peaceful or, at least, stable Russia?

For: Perhaps there is still gratitude for Moscow having agreed to German unification. Some may still see a grand symbiosis between Russia's abundant raw materials and primary energy sources and Germany's know-how (Germany as Ivan Stolz to Russia's Oblomov). There is also that part of German foreign policy tradition that puts order before freedom. Finally, there is fear.

Against: This is the great development that has not occurred over the last four years. In 1989–90 there was real German-Soviet euphoria. Germany's western and eastern neighbors looked anxiously for signs of one of Europe's oldest special relationships developing out of "Stavrapallo," as the Kohl-Gorbachev accord of mid-July 1990 was dubbed. Subsequently, Germany has given the lion's share of Western economic assistance to Russia (although much of the German contribution has been specifically related to unification or tied to trade promotion). Helmut Kohl has tried to establish with the Russian president, Boris Yeltsin, something of the personal rapport he had with Mikhail Gorbachev.

But, if anything, the Bonn government has privileged the relationship with east-central Europe over that with Moscow. And if anyone has had a policy of "Moscow First," it has been the Clinton administration. In one of those curious transatlantic role reversals that happen from time to time, the United States has played Germany to Yeltsin's Russia, while Germany has played America to east-central Europe.

If the Bill Clinton-Strobe Talbott gamble were to have paid off—that is, if Russia were set on course to become a cooperative capitalist democracy—then there would be a powerful case for Germany giving priority to its relations with Russia. But it has not, and it seems unlikely that it will in the foreseeable future. A strong but cooperative Russia would be a great partner for Germany. A weak but cooperative Russia could still be a partner. A strong but uncooperative Russia would be a sparring partner. But a Russia that is both weak and uncooperative?

World Power

Germany would give top priority to seeking both the rights and the duties of a world power, starting, of course, with a permanent seat on the U.N. Security Council. The Federal Republic would seize with both hands the United States' offer to be "partners in leadership." As once America was (reluctantly) prepared to "take up the White Man's burden" from Britain, to use Rudyard Kipling's disgracefully non-PC phrase, so now Germany would take up the GI's burden. This would mean enhancing its military power to match its economy, size and social magnetism. Thus equipped, Germany would be the captain of a great European trading bloc, dealing as an equal with the United States, the captain of the North American bloc, and with Japan and China, rival captains of the Asian bloc(s).

For: Such a prospect would appeal to many nations. The quiet widening of the bounds of German power has been a central purpose of the foreign policy of the Federal Republic for more than 40 years, and old habits die hard. The idea of Germany as a normal nation-state, taking its rightful place at the head table of world politics, is one of the two main visions of Germany currently being canvassed there.

The United States seems to have few qualms about German leadership in Europe; it has even pressed the role on it. This American encouragement is accompanied by the implied threat of a continued reduction of the American military commitment to Europe—an old familiar theme from the history of transatlantic relations, but more credible in the post-Cold War world.

This priority could find support among both the Atlanticist and the economic *mondialiste* tendencies in Germany. America, too, was historically drawn from being a continental trading state, protected by the military power of others, to doing its own protecting and power projecting.

Against: Germany is not like most nations. It has special burdens of history and self-doubt. Hitler and Auschwitz are less than a human lifetime away. For all the profound, historic changes in Germany, for all the trust in the liberal, democratic Federal Republic, many people around Germany and—quite as important—many Germans would be loath to see it even attempting to play such a role. Moreover, it is not big enough, not powerful enough, not rich enough. Germany does not even have that preponderance in Europe that America had in the world in 1945. If, however, the proposition were that of being junior partner to the United States, this policy would soon reactivate the complex but deep reactions known by the simplistic label of "anti-Americanism." The other three possible priorities seem closer to German concerns and better matched to Germany's means.

THE RIGHT CHOICE

What, then, will Germany choose? It will, I think, choose not to choose. True to its foreign policy tradition, the Federal Republic will try to do a little of all the above. *Sowohl-als-auch,* or, in the immortal words of Yogi Berra, "If you see a fork in the road, take it!" This tendency will be strengthened by any likely outcome of the 1994 elections.

Even without Genscher, Germany will genscher. To some extent this is inevitable for a major power in Germany's complex geopolitical position. But with increased demands on limited resources, the danger is that by trying to do everything Germany will end up achieving nothing.

Moreover, to choose not to choose does not mean you make no choices. It means only that the choices will be made reactively, as a response to the combination of unexpected external developments (especially in eastern and southeastern Europe) and internal pressures from political, published and public opinion. Again, this phenomenon is not peculiar to Germany. In a way, it is further proof of the Americanization of the Federal Republic. That may be small consolation.

In a probably vain attempt to make this prophecy self-negating, I shall now take the liberty of saying what I think Germany should do.

I am deeply convinced that Germany should pursue the second option: giving top priority for the next 20 years to building a wider Europe, extending the EU and NATO eastward step by step.

Of course Germany could not do this alone. It would need to win the agreement and active support of the United States, France, Britain, Italy and, so far as possible, other EU partners, for this priority. American support should and probably would be the easiest to secure. Although on present form one must seriously doubt the capacity of British politics to produce any coherent European policy at all, such a redefinition of European purpose—starting with the advance planning for the EU's intergovernmental conference in 1996—would be a way out of Britain's present hiding to nowhere. Britain could and should take it.

Italy has traditionally been a passionate advocate of deepening rather than widening the existing European Union, but with a new foreign minister who was a founding member of the Thatcherite Bruges Group, with its own interests in central and eastern Europe, and with scant likelihood of itself being included in a Carolingian inner core of European monetary union, Italy too might now be ready to embrace this priority. The most difficult partner to win for such a course is also the most important one: France. Helped by the United States, Britain and Italy, Germany would simply have to argue the case to its closest European partner, and even now there are signs of a revision of France's defensive little-Europe strategy.

In Germany, the argument for this priority is generally made negatively, in terms of the threat of mass immigration, the dangers of instability in eastern Europe, even the need for a *cordon sanitaire*. It can and should be made positively.

The voluntary westernization of what became West Germany after 1945 was a peaceful revolution for the better. (A revolution was proclaimed in the East, but happened in the West.) With all its faults, the old Federal Republic was a model bourgeois democracy and the best German state in history. But the job was only half done: West Germany's inner security and peace of mind came from its firm geopolitical and existential anchoring in the West; its insecurity, uncertainty and even schizophrenia came from the ghosts of the past and the fact of division.

Now it has a historic chance to finish the job. To recreate those virtues of the old Federal Republic across its larger territory, and find a lasting inner equilibrium, Germany not only needs to achieve the westernization of the former East Germany. It also needs to assist in the westernization on which the new democracies to its east have themselves embarked, and to bring them into the structures of Western and European integration to which the Federal Republic already belongs. If you really want to be a normal country like Britain, France or America, then you need Western neighbors to your east.

The strategic goal of German foreign policy in the 20 years after 1970 could be summarized in one sentence from the so-called letter on German unity: "to work toward a state of peace in Europe in which the German people regains its unity in free self-determination." The strategic goal of German foreign policy for the next 20 years should be to work toward a state of freedom in Europe in which Germany has Western allies and partners to its east.

This is not only a clear, positive goal. It is also a realistic one, proportionate to the country's size, resources and the limited readiness of its citizens to sustain larger external commitments. More would be less.

Kurt J. Lauk

Germany at the Crossroads: On the Efficiency of the German Economy

ERMANY'S SITUATION TODAY IS MARKED by two challenges that affect and influence each other economically and politically. Because they developed fully independently of each other, their chance crossing at the beginning of this last decade of the twentieth century is too rarely noted. Yet, it makes all the more imperative a fresh analysis of Germany's situation, one that departs from the conventional accounts that emphasize only how much unification is costing the nation, why the process is so substantially more arduous than predicted by politicians in or out of government.

The first challenge, growing out of the reestablishment of Germany's unity after forty years of division, requires that comparable living conditions and equal opportunities be afforded all who today live in Germany. The second challenge, much less commented on, requires that Germany pay close attention to its economic productivity, understanding that it is the only way for the country to maintain its prosperity, to be able to compete internationally. Too few acknowledge the seriousness of this latter problem, or indeed are aware that it has existed in some form since the mid-1980s. Lest it be thought to be simply a function of the recession that recently, although with some delay, held Germany in its grip, as it did much of the rest of democratic Europe, a very different argument needs to be considered.

The coincidence of these two major challenges occurring at a time when the market economy should be showing its superiority

Kurt J. Lauk is a Member of the Board of Management of VEBA Aktiengesellschaft, Düsseldorf.

precisely in those places where it was not allowed to operate previously, where the bankruptcy of socialist planning and organization is now fully revealed, makes this a unique moment in history. The possibilities for growth are enormous, but only if they are correctly perceived. Thus, for example, while the superiority of the West German economic system is no longer in question and while it is impossible for yesterday's communist mythmakers to continue pretending that the German Democratic Republic (GDR) was until very recently one of the world's leading economies, the discarding of these earlier fables does not give license for the creation of new ones. The issue today is whether, in Germany, but also in Central and Eastern Europe more generally, the world's economic problems and possibilities are correctly perceived. Is Germany, for example, in a position to play the role of pioneer and economic innovator? Does she, in fact, understand her own economic problems? Is she able to confront them? Does she know that the country's economic order has developed through various internal structural changes into something that makes change exceedingly difficult, but all the more necessary if an economic pioneering situation is to be achieved? Wilhelm Röpke, the distinguished German economist, defined what we would today call *Ordnungspolitik* as consisting

> of measures and institutions which impart to competition the framework, rules, and machinery of impartial supervision which a competitive system needs as much as any game or match if it is not to degenerate into a vulgar brawl. A genuine, equitable, and smoothly functioning competitive system can not in fact survive without a judicious moral and legal framework and without regular supervision of the conditions under which competition can take place pursuant to real efficiency principles. This presupposes mature economic discernment on the part of all responsible bodies and individuals and a strong impartial state.[1]

Germany today desperately needs to renew her doctrine of *Ordnungspolitik*, that is, her domestic framework, institutional and legal, for economic competition.

This cannot be said too often, and while the statement may appear to some to be hyperbole, that is not the case at all. It is not that the German economy at this moment is flat, or that any number of others are booming. It is true, however, that several others are growing more rapidly than Germany, and that there are structural reasons for this situation. The once effective values—autonomy and entrepreneurial creativity, set forth and made legal by the Federal Republic—threaten to be suffocated through excessive tutelage and overregulation. The dynamic state of the "economic miracle" has turned slowly into a static welfare state. This seriously threatens Germany's capacity to compete effectively in world markets. In these circumstances, it may not be irrelevant to ask whether Germany's vaunted industrial, fiscal, and political systems, so arduously and intelligently constructed in the years after the end of World War II, are not today in need of substantial revision.

While there is no adequate English equivalent for the German term *Ordnungspolitik*,[2] Germans will understand that it implies a consideration of the complex financial, legal, and social system, mandated by government, which helps to define the micro- and macroeconomic conditions that company directors and workers are expected to adhere to. In short, it creates the framework in which industrial and commercial firms operate. That previously effective system, which allowed for autonomy and entrepreneurial creativity, was dependent on various specific incentives legitimated by the state. That state is today strangely static, impeded by its own welfare legislation, which is no longer contributing to productivity, once known to be crucial both to social welfare and economic growth.

The current economic weaknesses are largely induced by the system itself. Reflected in one of the highest unemployment rates in the Federal Republic's history—2.6 million unemployed in West Germany and 1.1 million in East Germany—this represents a 8.5 percent rate in the West and a 14.2 percent rate in the former GDR.[3] What makes the situation even more serious is that there is no evidence that these figures are likely soon to be significantly reduced. The question, quite bluntly, is not whether the price of unification is proving to be too high, but whether Germany is aware that many of its economic problems antedated unification, that the first "early warning signals" were already beginning to be apparent almost a decade ago. While neither the arrival of Gorbachev in the Kremlin nor the dismantling of the Berlin Wall created Germany's productivity crisis, both helped create opportunities that are still not correctly perceived. Germany stands today before the question of whether it simply wants to expand or whether it wants to change as well.

If some expansion has occurred, there is still no consensus on the kinds of changes that are necessary. The contemporary discussion of both domestic and foreign policy marks the beginning of a search for that consensus, intended to produce both internal and external changes. A responsible repositioning of the country's foreign policy requires also a repositioning of the parameters of *Ordnungspolitik,* the domestic framework for economic competition. In the future, Germany will be obliged to redefine its role and assume greater responsibility as an actor in Europe and the world. To find this new position will be possible only when Germany's economic institutions and productive power have reached a higher, more internationally competitive level. This is too rarely said.

Yet, the connection is of fundamental significance for Germany and its partners. If the importance of military bargaining power has declined as a factor influencing foreign policy behavior, the economic dimension has grown, creating new possibilities and necessities for Germany. So long as its capabilities for economic performance are not greatly strengthened through improving the framework conditions required under the doctrine of *Ordnungspolitik,* the Federal Republic of Germany will neither be a reliable diplomatic partner nor will it have a coherent foreign policy of its own. It is in this sense that the Federal Republic's domestic economic order takes on great significance for its foreign policy. For the first twenty years of the postwar period, the Federal Republic's economic strength was marked and kept on course by a clear system of reference points, largely lost in more recent times. A partially excessive and badly supervised social policy, initially intended to temper a purely market-driven economy, has coated the state and the economy with a multitude of laws and regulations—with a thick layer of sweetener—which impedes productivity.

Selective state intervention in the affairs of the economy, in the manner increasingly common in recent years, will have to be reviewed. The forces essential for the dynamic growth of the economy need to be understood, indeed nurtured. The continued ability of certain powerful interest groups to exert pressure, to act in ways inimical to the country's economic interests, will have to be curtailed. It is unconscionable that these groups, often state-created, whose expenses are largely borne by others, should remain so powerful, making any number of others seem inconsequential.

Structural and organizational change is essential if the country's export capacity is to be significantly improved. In the 1980s, for a time, the Federal Republic led the world in exports. Automobiles, mechanical engineering, and the chemical industries gave Germany a considerable part of its preeminence.[4] The nations of the European Community (EC) became Germany's best customers. The Federal Republic's sales to France in 1988–1990 reached the astonishing total of 12.9 percent of all its exports; Italy followed with 9.3 percent, Great Britain with 9.0 percent, and the Netherlands with a remarkable 8.5 percent. The Soviet Union and the Communist states of Eastern Europe claimed a modest 4.8 percent in those years, while the United States accounted for 7.5 percent. The whole of Asia accounted for 9.4 percent of the Federal Republic's sales abroad.

Germany's strength in the European markets, particularly in those of the Community, was helped in some measure by the import restrictions fixed on many Japanese products in several member states, including France, Italy, and Spain. Germany's geostrategic position made trade with Central and Eastern Europe a very reasonable option, and the high technical quality of German goods guaranteed a continuous market there, which depended heavily on well-synchronized political support. Great advances were made in opening such markets, which in many instances had a long prior history. Today, these markets are largely lost. Given the economic dislocations in many of the new democracies and their capital shortages, there is an urgent need for Germany to consider loans and other forms of capital investment, and also to entertain petitions for every kind of technical assistance.

While all these provide obvious opportunities, they cannot blind anyone to the conditions that obtain elsewhere, that are much less favorable to Germany. In too many of the most important world markets, German industry has scarcely gained a foothold. While the United States occupies an important place as an export partner—it ranked third in 1993, sixth in 1991—analysis of that flow suggests that it was created principally by a few very strong positions in mechanical engineering and, obviously, by the continued popularity of German luxury automobiles. In the years 1981–1986, it was bolstered by a strong dollar; since 1987, with the weakening of the dollar, German exports have suffered and will continue to suffer. It is by no means certain that this situation can be quickly reversed.

In the Far East, a vast potential market, German industry has been successful principally with a number of specialized products. Only about 7 percent of all German exports go to the nations of the Pacific Rim, and the People's Republic of China remains a very small market, given the size of its population. The exports to mainland China are a tiny fraction of those that make their way to Switzerland. To alter this situation will require considerable effort. If Germany qualifies as a "world champion" exporter today, it owes that position principally to its capacity to sell to other members of the EC. At the core, it is a "champion" in exports only because of Europe. On close analysis, Germany's export strengths are structurally brittle and, on balance, very fragile.[5]

Why has there not been greater and more diversified export strength? The explanations are not to be found in the technical quality of German products, which is excellent. The same, however, cannot be said of German prices, which are today, for all sorts of products, exorbitantly high. Comparing the price relationship that exists between Germany and many of its industrial competitors, it becomes clear that Germany's costs of production greatly exceed those of many who wish to compete with her, and are increasingly able to do so. Also, internal bureaucratic regulations, having proliferated markedly in recent years, have not made it easy to manage a flexible, fast, competition-oriented economy of the kind required for success in world trade today. Furthermore, because Germany is still protectionist in certain sectors, including some of its old industries that date back to the nineteenth century— coal perhaps being the most conspicuous example—this also diminishes its competitive strength. Such industries are able even now to exert pressure on the federal government.

These internal circumstances are scarcely calculated to improve the productivity of key industries. The reasons for the deterioration of the relative strength of German industrial products lie mainly in those internal factors that weaken the productivity of industrial production. Germany risks losing her hard-won rank in worldwide competition. Indeed, there is a danger that Germany may soon begin to lose out even in those areas where she was recently preeminent. The recent cyclical downturn allowed the structural weaknesses in the German economy to come to light. These structural weaknesses exist even today, given the recent economic upturn. Their origin is in the imbalance of cost structure and productive capability, which has led to a decline in productivity. To exacerbate this imbalance, the burdens of reunification must be acknowledged. There is a danger, however, that reunification will be taken as the cause of Germany's structural problems, touching on her capacity to compete internationally, when it was in fact only the occasion by which these weaknesses became visible. While the economic recession came from the West, crisis and upheaval came from the East.

* * *

The reasons for these developments may be highlighted with examples from particular sectors of industry. The examples are intended to clarify the causes of the loss of relative competitive capability, and while each represents only one sector of the German economy, each has significance for the others.

Many argue, correctly, that the German automobile deserves its reputation for being technologically one of the world's best automobiles. Its success and superior competitive capability during the last forty years owes largely to its excellent technology. Technological perfection, however, is only one side of the coin. The other has to do with the price-performance relationship. In this, the German automobile has fallen behind, particularly in the much fought-over US market during the last twenty years.

The total market share of all Japanese automobile companies is now 29 percent in the United States. The total market share of all European companies is less than 4 percent in the same market. According to 1991 trade statistics, the rest of the market is divided among the several major American automobile companies. The production time per vehicle, according to a Massachusetts Institute of Technology study,[6] suggests that the figures in Europe and in the United States are approximately 80 percent higher than in Japan. For the introduction of new models, for example, the Japanese require four months, and the Americans five, to return to normal productivity; the corresponding time needed in Europe is approximately twelve months. Productivity measured by assembly hours per vehicle stands at seventeen in Japan, twenty-five in America, and thirty-six in Europe. Higher Japanese productivity is paired with higher quality; the defect rate is substantially lower in Japan than in either the United States or Europe. Indeed, it is highest in Europe.

The failure to win a larger share of the American market is linked to comparable failures elsewhere. In Scandinavia, for example, the purchase of automobiles is burdened both by high taxes and high tariffs. While this affects all producers equally, it is significant that Japanese producers have gained market shares there, which, almost without exception, stand at more than 30 percent, in some instances having reached the 50 percent mark. Twenty years ago, all these markets were dominated by German automobiles, next in importance only to those produced in Sweden.

The price-performance relationship in export markets, so important for German industry, has dropped off dramatically for potential customers. A German vehicle is within the economic means of an ever-decreasing circle of customers. The cause is not technological inferiority. To produce German automobiles today requires prices to be raised to a level excessively expensive for the average consumer. The decision of masses of automobile buyers sends a message that needs to be heeded: decreasing market shares in the United States and hardly any market share in Asia are signal proofs of competitive weakness.

The collapse in productivity relative to competitors is a result of several factors: the short thirty-five hour German work week; the high social benefits guaranteed contractually through negotiation with the trade unions or legally required by the state; the layout of factories and facilities, which allows for higher automatization but does not guarantee higher productivity.

In order to reach international competitiveness from a market-economy perspective, a successful production-oriented order will have to be restored in many of the larger corporations. This will enable a fast and flexible reaction to market trends; it will encourage even higher quality. This is clearly a management task. According to the German law on codetermination (*Mitbestimmungsgesetz*) and the law on workers' constitution (*Betriebsverfassungsgesetz*), however, management can only introduce and implement the necessary changes with the agreement of the factory committees, in accordance with the tariff treaties that have been negotiated. Thus, a change can hardly be introduced as a one-sided decision process by management alone; it calls for a lengthy consensus-finding process with the workers, necessarily accompanied by many compromises. Because the working-consensus criteria are oriented toward domestic concerns, and do not allow, as a practical criterion, an orientation toward the international competitive capability of the automobile industry, achieving any major change is an arduous task.

When we turn to German mechanical engineering we note that production rose to new heights in the 1980s. The retreat in the second half of the 1970s, mocked by many with the populist term "Eurosklerosis," was reversed because of the high technological quality of the machines but also because of the productive structure of the industry.

This is no longer true. The behavior of both labor and management has led to a situation where the wage level no longer corresponds to the productivity level. Because of this, the international competitive capability of the sector is endangered. For 1993, a decline of 2 to 2.5 percent in the gross domestic product (GDP) was expected. This would clearly have been an instance where a labor agreement was needed that corresponded to the situation, that stipulated that no more should be paid out in wages than can be gained in productivity.

This did not happened. The actual agreement for 1993 in this sector allowed for a total of approximately 6 percent in wage and salary increases.[7] A 3.2 percent rise in wages and salaries was negotiated, but the increase by one hour of the weekly work time, to thirty-six hours, adds approximately 3 percent to the wage package. In addition, a provision was made for an increase in Christmas bonuses for certain wage groups, particularly at the lower end. All these agreements, which carried the signatures both of the trade unions and the employer associations, were being implemented in a period of zero growth in the German economy. A social consensus mechanism, supposed to be free of state influence, has been erected, and is being used in a manner that takes no account of the actual conditions of Germany's competitive capability in world markets.

The strike in the metal industry in the spring of 1993 in the new states revealed a comparable unwillingness to confront certain stark realities. Despite the unfavorable situation, arising from diminished productivity and the consequent failure to remain competitive, a wage and salary increase of up to approximately 80 percent of the wages in the West was negotiated. As a consequence, the economic downturn was felt especially severely in this sector, resulting in significant job losses. The latest agreement clearly shows that structural reasons were not held responsible for those job losses. Cash payments corresponding to an increase of 3.46 percent in the first quarter will be followed by further increases in May and November 1995, of 3.4 and 3.6 percent respectively. The resulting average raises are above 5 percent in 1995 and 1996. Taking into account a further cut in weekly hours, the end of the year comparison of hourly wages shows a dramatic increase of more than 10 percent. This significantly offsets previous productivity gains.

The labor agreements in mechanical engineering reveal the kind of structural weakness caused by excessively high wage levels: such agreements can only lead to further burdens for mechanical engineering, assuming that it wishes to remain competitive, and to a rise in unemployment. These facts are indisputable, denied by no reputable economist. Through the numerous social benefits guaranteed by the state, the material effects are so diminished as to be scarcely felt by the individual worker or his family. In Germany in 1991, for a married working man with two children, unemployment benefits—including money for the children—came to about 71 percent of previous net income. The corresponding unemployment and social benefits in Japan came to 63 percent of the net income; in the United States, to only 55 percent.[8] The social consequences of this situation will inevitably lead to a modification of those values once recognized to be responsible for Germany's industrial prowess.

From the viewpoint of *Ordnungspolitik*, similar consequences can be found also in the machine tool industry, exemplary for many other branches of German industry. The state-provided social safety net artificially supports an overdrawn process of collective bargaining. Practiced in this manner by the social partners, the system of autonomous or nonregulated wage bargaining has failed. Free collective bargaining, when taken together with the generous state benefits, has had long-lasting negative results on the industry in general. The individual employee, protected to a great degree, is scarcely aware of what has been lost.

For decades, the German chemical industry enjoyed prominence, having a strong competitive international position. It is especially important for the structure of the German economy that this position be maintained, and indeed strengthened. Yet, certain conditions have developed in recent years that stand in the way of such progress. The chemical industry, being energy-intensive, is greatly affected by energy costs, which touch directly on its competitive capability. In Germany, the industry's electricity costs have reached an international high. For steady current from the public network, they are approximately twice as high as in the United States and about 20 percent higher than in France; the latter, together with the Scandinavian countries, boasts the lowest electrical expenses in Europe. The condition of a renowned German chemical company will suggest the dimension of the problem.[9] If its electrical costs were those of France, this company would save approximately DM 100 million per year. With Belgian natural gas prices, there would be a savings of approximately DM 70 million annually. The basic reason for the high energy costs lies not in an inefficient production structure, but in the fact that the mining of German coal is subsidized by an additional charge on every unit of energy. At present, German coal is around three times as expensive as the world market price. In addition, the expenses for environmental protection measures put into operation in Germany are about 1.5 times more than the EC average. This means that yearly overhead of DM 1 billion is about DM 340 million more than the average environmental protection cost level in the EC generally.

Through additional environmental protection laws already passed, this disadvantage in relation to the competition of others will almost certainly double in a few years. While there is no intention to disparage the principle of environmental protection costs, or of the necessity for environmental protection measures, "environment" ought to be understood less as a national than as an international responsibility. National solo efforts in this sphere bring progress neither to the environment—it generally transfers the problem from one country to another—nor to the industrial competitive capability of the national economy that is most fastidious in its policies.

An additional competitive disadvantage for the German chemical industry is created by the national legal regulations and technological rules that govern the licensing, building, and operation of chemical plants. These lead to significant additional expenditures; they raise the total investment risk. Because of frequently changing legal regulations, because of their complexity, planning security is impeded. As a result of complicated and sometimes scarcely comprehensible regulations, the licensing process for chemical plants is substantially longer than in other countries. While the average time it takes to authorize a chemical company in Germany is approximately thirteen months—the peak may be as long as seventy months—the comparable time in France is nine months, in Spain six months, and in Great Britain five months. If production is delayed because of the time taken for licensing, operation costs necessarily escalate, discouraging required investment in the new, complex chemical plants.

The interaction of these several factors threatens the German chemical industry at its core. The original international importance of the German chemical industry was sustained essentially by its strong position in basic and commodity chemicals. Specialty chemicals, with high value added, were derived from this stable foundation. Given the aforementioned conditions and the burdens created by excessive regulation, German basic and commodity chemical production is today challenged by the new industrializing countries, able to produce at lower costs. Without the basic and commodity chemicals, the production of speciality chemicals is scarcely viable over the long term.

It is obvious that a competitive renewal in the Federal Republic presupposes a willingness to set to work to contain the flood of state intervention, to recognize how regulation and licensing can hinder productivity. In many cases, such measures lead to excessive demands, inimical to the economic health of an industry. Unfortunately, they have been carried over to the new states, recently joined to the Federal Republic, and greatly complicate the problems of their economic reconstruction.

* * *

At a time when increasing internationalization of the market, major technological innovations, and the enormous challenges created by reunification and the opening of Central, East, and Southeast Europe demand greater adaptability from the German economy, the previously mentioned structural disadvantages diminish Germany's capacity to compete.

Increasing internationalization is linked with new markets, but even more with new competitors. The advantages of Germany's location—its infrastructure, educational system, worker qualifications, and technological production quality—are gradually being relativized by other industrial countries as well as those on the threshold of economic power. Japan, Taiwan, and Korea are only a few of Germany's new commercial rivals. At the same time, Eastern Europe is developing an economic dynamic that must, in the short term, offer new economic development opportunities for Germany. These opportunities, if taken, will greatly improve Germany's situation, but only if it is recognized that they will also increase the pressure on Germany's industries, making it even more imperative that quality be maintained at competitive prices. The expression, "Bohemia as the Korea of Europe," suggests the changed constellation of economic forces that must now be reckoned with.

The result of these developments is a greatly changed international division of labor. With a worldwide alignment of technical standards and quality requirements, the difference in productivity between individual countries will be an increasingly decisive factor. Recent studies indicate that German industry has a 20 percent lower work productivity than US industry. The German automobile industry and its suppliers, already forced into considerable cutbacks, are likely to eliminate two hundred to four hundred thousand positions in the next five years.[10] Similar processes will almost certainly be carried out in steel, coal, and textiles, and may even extend to banking. Some go so far as to suggest that there is a concealed unemployment rate of 20 to 30 percent in German industry. Competitive pressure will increase, and it is no exaggeration to say that that portion of Germany's industrial production with high international competitiveness appears to be in long-term danger. As a consequence, some say, industrial production will decline from 38 percent to approximately 30 percent of the gross national product (GNP).

Some minimize the explosive nature of this development by emphasizing the increasing importance of the service sector. They argue that the chances for Germany's position in the world lie in the nonmaterial realm—in the areas of education, creativity, and innovation. System competence is seen to be the key to Germany's continued prosperity. There is a dangerous error in the exclusivity of this argument. Even the so-called service society requires a productive industrial base; it is in great part tied to the logic of industry, and is dependent on it. In any case, the service industries cannot function competitively on a thirty-five hour work week.

It is absolutely essential that a wide and efficient industrial production base be maintained in Germany, that it be developed through successful international competition. German political leaders and society more generally must be made aware that international competition is essentially competition between more and less productive locales. Each country is required to measure its accomplishment not only in relation to its efficiency in maintaining a world standard; it needs also, and above all, to understand why flexibility in its structure is imperative.

There is much to suggest that, as often happens in saturated societies, a too rigid structure and a lack of willingness and preparedness to change hinder development. Exaggerated avoidance of risk, insufficient motivation to innovate, and a partially mismanaged training system are all expressions of a serious systemic malaise. In these conditions, the temptation to build trade barriers to protect one's own economy is certain to increase. Yet, it is the very vigor of international competition that calls for an open society, one that does not allow for isolationist elitism.

In the past, one of the principal factors that influenced Germany's production capability was its educational system. Today, there are signs that the system is gradually losing its function to select; there is a marked decrease in the traditional differentiation based on talent and ability.[11] An increasing number of pupils are crowding into high schools (into *Gymnasium,* as opposed to *Realschule* and *Hauptschule*), and an increasing number of high school graduates wish to study at the university level. This development would be welcome if it coincided with a higher level of qualification. In fact, the expansion of the educational system seems to be linked more to diminished performance requirements than to an explosion of talent.

The results are two: a devaluation of individual degrees, and a lack of direction for different educational paths. If a high school diploma (*Abitur*) and a university education become the standard for all, the value of vocational training will necessarily decrease. Because the number of students at universities is increasing, the already existing problem of "eternal students" is exacerbated, often leading to the flooding of those disciplines not protected by *Numerus clausus* (restricted entry). Encouragement is given to students to change into disciplines not protected by *Numerus clausus*; it is often the case that students enroll in these disciplines only as a last resort. These developments can be counteracted only by placing more value on quality. Also, in education and training, there is an obvious need for fundamental change, if a scientifically qualified younger generation is to be created, adequate to the needs of the country. Stronger competition among the existing universities, and additional pressure on all through an expansion of private education would be steps in the right direction.

The structural weaknesses that had always existed in the Federal Republic, that became increasingly apparent in the 1980s, were transferred to the new states after unification. Expansion took place; there was no renewal. This is too rarely acknowledged. If the difficulties of the construction process in the new *Länder* were created in part by the complex conditions encountered in a society that had no experience of a market economy, they were exacerbated through a universal underestimation of what a far-reaching systemic transformation would require. This miscalculation was common to all political parties and interest groups, though some choosing to look back today see themselves as prophets.

Instead of a dynamic new approach, the already existing model of the former Federal Republic was simply transferred to East Germany in one abrupt step. Unnecessary friction resulted, leading to exaggerated complaints on every side. For example, cumbersome and complex regulations and licensing processes were transferred to the new states. A complicated system of law, that had developed gradually over forty years, was transferred to the new states in one blow. Such detailed systems of regulation were wholly beyond the experience of men and women of the former GDR.

Just as seriously, the federal government chose not a straightforward productivity-oriented politics, but opted for an exchange rate of 1 to 1. While this was politically the right and necessary decision, economically it has had dire consequences: The citizens of the former East Germany were able to purchase goods and services with hard currency not previously available to them. While this led to a sales boom in the West, it ruined the economic structures in the East. As a result, there was an immediate transfer of more than one hundred thousand jobs to the West. Even though unemployment rates have somewhat recovered, the dependency on job-creation measures and on current infrastructure investments remains disturbing. A scaling down of the latter will cause further deterioration in East Germany's industrial base. Already, only 16 percent of the employed work in processing industries, as opposed to 30 percent in West Germany. Given this situation, it is not surprising that jobs are being dismantled only with great restraint in the public administration sector. If the need for service alone determined employment, unemployment would grow markedly, a recipe for even greater social unrest. This is recognized abroad, and has started to effect domestic policy.

Behind this lurks another disruptive potential that until now has not been sufficiently recognized. In order to prevent further fiscal deterioration, a highly indebted state must now sustain what remains of an unproductive system with transfer payments. Up to the beginning of 1995, debts of DM 340 billion have accumulated from the Treuhand, deficits of the old regime and of the former housing sector. This may not be the end. The winding down of what is left of the Treuhand will generate further debts. Given the magnitude of the indebtedness, help from the West is essential, but only if it is reconceived, put into a new framework.

Even if the people of the new states have the will to make something of their newly won freedom, their energy will be depleted by the detailed legal licensing and authorization processes, building permit processes, complex real estate administration rules, and the responsibility they are asked to assume for old deficits. All these processes, rules, and regulations were transferred to an economically underdeveloped region, a former socialist society denied any transition time, utterly unprepared to live by the procedures of the highly developed Federal Republic.

Given this background, it is not surprising that the population between Rügen and Plauen feels aggrieved. Very little remains of what they were accustomed to, what they had themselves erected. Much was discarded through the call for immediate products, without any concern for productivity. This was not economically viable. Forced to take over structures from the West even when they were unsuitable or outdated, the results have been less than what was originally hoped for. The success of the German economic model in both the new and old federal states cannot be guaranteed in the absence of far-reaching changes, but these are too rarely discussed.

The general fight over distribution in Germany and the habit of directing monies into consumer products rather than into investment has gone much too far. The individual's investment in leisure time rather than in productive work has reached a level that satisfies the current generation, but is certain to saddle succeeding generations with insuperable burdens. The agreed upon work week in the West German national economy in 1991 was 38.3 hours. In considering the guaranteed average of thirty vacation days, generous provisions for overtime and hours missed, the effective weekly work time is reduced to 29.9 hours. With thirty vacation days, twelve holidays, and twenty days allowable for sickness, accident, and the like, manufacturing industries accept that there are, in effect, sixty-two canceled days in the year. The Federal Republic holds the international lead in this regard. Neither Japan nor the United States provides comparable benefits (by comparison, the United States and Japan have thirty canceled days in the year).[12] At the same time, material compensation for sick days is prescribed by social legislation in such a way that there is hardly any net wage loss if the daily transport costs, not incurred during sickness, are counted in.

One of the many consequences of this is a dramatic change in the work ethic. The job is no longer seen as character building; the passion for free time is steadily increasing, even at work. Inner satisfaction is sought less at work and more in leisure time. The will to prove oneself at work has diminished. Social acceptance, formerly bound to a considerable degree to job and personal efficiency in the workplace, is no longer tied to such activity. Today, positions in leisure organizations, whether as chairman of the sport club, or president of the golf or tennis club, are perceived as more important than positions in job-related activities. Social acceptance depends increasingly on club and team participation. Because such activities require energy, effort, and personal engagement, it becomes important for many that their jobs not be too demanding. One does not wish to see one's energies, necessary for play, depleted by labor.

The work ethic is gradually developing into an ethic of leisure, the only meaningful prize for work. That productivity and quality of work suffer as a consequence is scarcely surprising.

The expense of the public budget for social security, whose portion of total expenditure was 27 percent in 1950, has since risen at an average yearly rate of 11 percent. This increase, out of proportion to other appropriations, has brought its portion of total expenditure to 47 percent. Implemented social security payments, a reasonable prognosis, could lead to a further increase of around 26 percent in the social expenditure between 1990 and the year 2000 without providing any additional services. To maintain the status quo, an average growth rate of the GNP will have to reach 2.3 percent per capita in the last decade of this century, if the portion of social expenditure is to be kept stable in relation to the GNP. Since the economy's growth was slow in the first half of the 1990s, the average growth rate of the GNP must be between 3 and 4 percent per annum between the years 1995 and 2000. When one considers that the average growth rate of real GNP per capita between 1950 and 1990—including the years of the German "economic miracle"—was approximately 3.8 percent, the prospect of a similar growth in the next few years is exceedingly unlikely, particularly when one considers the economic condition of the country, and its structural problems. It is only reasonable to expect that there will be an increase in expenditures on social programs as a percentage of the total GNP.

In order to finance these high costs of the welfare state in the 1990s, such expenses will necessarily create greater public indebtedness, which will in turn create pressure for higher taxes. Given that Germany's taxes as well as its indebtedness has increased to a higher level than the international average, this will certainly produce political dissension. When one considers that even today many taxpayers feel that their taxes are too high for what they receive from the state, not least because such a great portion of their taxes is sapped through the interest burden, the prospect of increased pressure to take on more of the state debt is more than disconcerting. Whether the German Bundesbank will be able to control all this through monetary policy is very questionable. Today's trend—to finance increasingly high levels of social welfare expenditures with new debts—is exceedingly hazardous. It must come to an end.

In Germany's budget today, the interest burden is second only to that created by welfare expenditures. The debts incurred through reunification, as well as the persisting debts of the rail and postal systems, add to the already heavy burden.[13] In 1994, more than DM 1,800 billion persisted as the national debt.[14] Interest payments are well above DM 130 billion.

The behavior of lawmakers, trade unions, and employers has led to a situation that imposes excessive demands on the state. Using fiscal policy as a state instrument to provide incentives for the economy will no longer work, given the high level of indebtedness. As a result of this high interest burden, there is almost no more latitude within the budget for redistribution. Yet, the politicians go on promising additional social benefits.

Because fiscal policy leaves hardly any room for political measures, politicians tend to concentrate on interest politics, on monetary questions. Until now, monetary policy has functioned relatively well because of the independence of the Bundesbank. With increasing indebtedness, there are growing political pressures on the Bundesbank. In these circumstances, it becomes all the more important that it pursue a course of monetary stability, resisting inflationary pressures.

This, however, leads to another dilemma. For a long time, the Deutsche Bundesbank conducted a European monetary policy heavily oriented toward national goals. This led to a dangerous contradiction that strained the European monetary system greatly. Up to now, the Deutsche Bundesbank has been able to pursue its course. It is one of the few countries complying with the criteria set up by the Maastricht Treaty. However, increasing pressure from European partners is limiting what the bank is able to do. The postponement of Monetary Union has led to serious differences between the countries concerned, and contributes to the current upheaval in several of the European currencies. In the long run, there can be no coordinated monetary policy without coordinated economic policies in the participating countries.

European integration is endangered through a lack of economic growth and insufficient coordination of separate national economic policies. European union and the Maastricht Treaty suffer from an imbalance between economic and political vision; there is a failure to bring them into a sound coordination.[15] Popular acceptance of the Maastricht Treaty was only achieved with very slim majorities.

No matter how essential further progress toward European integration may be, the benefits of integration to the individual citizen must not be left purely abstract. Owing to the continuing migration of peoples, the opening of Europe's borders is increasingly perceived as a threat. By comparison, the new economic order remains heavily theoretical. In terms of the comprehensive framework for economic competition implied by *Ordnungspolitik*, Maastricht pushed economic union too far while leaving political union underdeveloped. The European citizen is concerned to find out what kinds of enduring jurisdiction the national parliaments will have, what kind of jurisdiction the European parliament will assume. Without a broad political component, the process of European union will be led by the innumerable small steps of economic policy to what can only be a dead end.

Of course, it is always easy to be wise in hindsight. Yet, it is important to mention that new and far-reaching structural requirements will be necessary if there is to be significant further European integration. A comprehensible balance between European executive and legislative branches, acceptable to its citizens, needs to be devised. The reduction of the European idea to economic and monetary questions alone must fail in the end. It is obvious that the economic-political core of the Maastricht Treaty must be redefined.

The rapid introduction of a hard currency in economically weak regions with lower productivity was linked in the German case to an inappropriately rapid adjustment of wages and salaries. This inevitably led to massive unemployment. As a result, the economic reunification of Germany cannot provide a model for the economic unification of Europe. The danger is that such a process must be linked to high transfer payments—unless only a small number of economically strong countries are included. If this is to be avoided for political reasons, it will require substantial transfer payments from wealthy to poorer regions. These large transfer payments, which may be politically desirable and necessary, are in the long term neither politically supportable nor economically sensible. They are not capable of generating political consensus when cuts in social entitlements have already been anticipated and are being argued over in the most prosperous countries. Further burdens for additional transfer payments to poorer European regions are not likely to be tolerated. They lead to a subsidized transfer to areas that would not be economically competitive on their own strengths.

In the face of these great demands, and the simultaneous burdens pushing the German economy to its limits from every side, not to speak of the need for Germany to find a new political identity both domestically and abroad, many fear that the strain on the Federal Republic's model, which has functioned smoothly until now, will prove to be excessive. One may legitimately wonder whether the Federal Republic's traditional model of interaction between employees, employers, state, and society can function in a time of economic restructuring. Consensus has until now only proven itself in a regulated labor market. Its efficiency in establishing a framework for lasting improvements in German competitiveness has yet to be shown. More importantly, will this principle support a political restructuring? Tied to those questions are others that ask whether the political parties will be able to articulate political analyses and provide concepts that will compel real sacrifice. Also, will they be able to integrate the many special interests? Today there is no answer to these questions. The need for deeper cooperation and a new consciousness of the framework for competition from all economically active groups must not be overlooked.

SUMMARY

The quality of Germany as a production site has declined. The combined power of foreign investment in Germany has greatly subsided. While the stock of foreign direct investment in Germany increased approximately 10 percent annually in the 1960s, it declined to 1.5 percent annually in the 1970s and 1980s. Meanwhile, German investments abroad rose, from under DM 10 billion annually in the first half of the 1980s to approximately DM 30 billion annually in 1991 and 1992.[16]

It is evident that a vast array of structural economic and sociopolitical problems remain to be solved. Germany is today the nation with the shortest work hours and the longest vacations; Germans spent almost DM 70 billion on travel in 1994. It is also the country of the oldest students and the youngest retirees. This goes along with a protected system of very high wages and large social benefits. If there were only twenty-three vacation days and holidays, as in the United States, real German GNP would be around DM 160 billion, 7 percent higher than it is today. Deep cuts in the welfare net, immediately influencing the standard of living for all citizens, are necessary. Further sacrifices, as essential for the continuing adjustment of living standards in the new federal states as for the unification of Western Europe, are required, but they have become much more difficult. Their acceptance can be achieved only with difficulty, given the heavy burdens they are likely to impose.

In the last ten years of the former Federal Republic, potential growth in productivity was sacrificed in favor of an increase in the standard of living. This provided a much increased real personal income, a reduction of work hours, and greater social benefits, but a price was paid. Germany was no longer able to compete internationally, even in those industries where she traditionally enjoyed great strength.

Following on reunification, rifts in Germany's social fabric have become visible again. The vision of Germany's role as a partner in the world needs to be defined anew. The Germans are being closely observed from abroad, sometimes mistrustfully. It has once again become difficult to be German. What many believed had been overcome through forty years of West German good conduct is once again being debated; what was put aside and laid to rest in the status quo produced by the Cold War has been stirred up again. The fear of uncertainty is felt both at home and abroad. The dream of not upsetting the status quo through good conduct, with the wish to appear exclusively as a stable element of European and Atlantic integration, has been rendered less important through unanticipated developments in all of Europe. No appropriate new political vision has emerged in Germany, either for the country or for the continent.

In the public mind, there is no separation of the problems created by reunification and those that became increasingly characteristic of the economic system of the former Federal Republic. Both, in fact, developed independently, though their effects coincide. Only when they are seen as two distinct phenomena will there be a basis for restructuring the system. Until then, severe cuts in social benefits in Germany cannot possibly gain consensus; they will be viewed as the unacceptable price brought on by reunification alone.

Against this background, the Solidarity Pact, initiated and realized by Helmut Kohl, is a first, important, and necessary step. The Solidarity Pact of March 1993—a joint agreement between federal and state authorities, between government and the opposition—is important because it aims to dismantle those *Ordnungspolitik* weaknesses in the West that have contributed so considerably to stagnation in the new states. At the same time, its goal is to decrease the transfer payments to the new states, making room for a uniquely dynamic and self-sufficient boom. Among the most important elements of the Solidarity Pact is the Federal Consolidation Program,[17] which mandates, among other things, the transfer of all the debts from Treuhand, together with loan payments and East German housing finance funds by January 1, 1995 into a pool for inherited debts, to be financed and paid off solely by the federation within thirty years. In addition, the new states are promised additional financial assistance from the federal government. To finance this, cuts in expenditures were called for, together with the dismantling of tax breaks and an increase in income and corporate taxes across the board (a so-called "solidarity income tax increase"), by January 1, 1995.

Further essential elements of the Solidarity Pact are measures taken to insure Germany's appeal as a production site. Included in this category are the Law for the Assurance of Germany as a Production Site (*Standortsicherungsgesetz*), legislative measures for the acceleration of planning and licensing procedures, the privatization of the rail and postal systems, and changes in working hours. Corporate taxes were reduced from 50 to 45 percent for retained profits, and from 36 to 30 percent for distributed profits.

Some of the central obstacles that burden Germany's appeal as a production site, including the necessary reorientation of public finances, have thus been taken up. Still, the Gordian knot of the existing welfare state order has not yet been chopped through. The initially intended intervention into social benefits was not able to draw upon the consensus required within the parameters of the Solidarity Pact. The planned reduction of social benefits was intended to finance the additional burdens of the economic construction program. Instead, the tax and duty burdens were increased by the "solidarity" tax proposal. Still, the Solidarity Pact may be seen as the beginning of a new social discussion, if it is recognized to be also the beginning of a new political process, in some measure created by a deepening economic crisis.

Such a process must not shy away from carrying out further significant cuts. From today's perspective, we still lack a comprehensive and consistent management plan for the process of change, taking into consideration economic, legal, and political factors. Along with the general underestimation of the management needed for an effective transition, the existing economic-political model of the Federal Republic was greatly overvalued. This has been slowly revised in the last few months. It has become clear that the maximum economic capacity of a highly differentiated economy overloaded with regulations is hardly in a position to handle the kind of special burdens inherent in rebuilding a socialist command economy. The suitability of the current system for restructuring and generating a new building dynamic is much narrower than had once been thought. It works more often as a braking than as an accelerating mechanism.

If there is a need for new thinking in politics and administration, there is also a desperate need for a new orientation in many business corporations. Consistent decentralization and a greater concern with the consumer are clearly required. These things are already being pursued by many corporations and are vital to the recovery that will again make Germany competitive in world markets. Solutions to these problems are possible if indeed the Solidarity Pact provides the impetus for the much needed structural discussion. If the price-performance relationship in Germany and of German products abroad is to be improved, the expenses of state programs must be reduced.

If, as is implied by *Ordnungspolitik*, the market is to be appropriately emphasized as a proper framework for competition, then it would be disastrous to have structural weaknesses perpetuated in particular sectors through a protectionist trade policy. The opening of markets needs to be extended; herein lies the opportunity for structural adjustment. This is particularly valid for the newly opened markets of Eastern Europe. The German economy is in a position to take advantage of opportunities in the adjacent countries with lower factor costs through a more active concept of production siting. Through an effective division of activities within an association of producer countries, the German economy can concentrate on those elements that have a higher value-added component. Every state subsidy in Germany must be a one-time and time-limited measure, so that the positive restructuring process can take effect. These limits would allow corporate taxes to drop to levels comparable to those of other countries and would thereby encourage a needed increase in foreign investment in Germany. The latter is desirable for political as well as economic reasons.

An increase in investment activities certainly presupposes that cuts in certain social provisions take place. Fringe benefits in Germany have become higher than anywhere else in the world. Cuts are especially necessary where the possibility of abuse is evident. This, originally a provision of the Solidarity Pact, did not win federal consensus. The social entitlement laws must be adjusted to the new situation; reunification has left the Federal Republic poorer in economic terms. A great deal of social welfare legislation must be adjusted to this fact. At the same time, the individual incentives for claiming social benefits must be reoriented so that there is a more responsible use of legal entitlements.

The necessary increase in domestic and foreign investment requires new yardsticks for the practice of collective bargaining, which will in the future have to be closely oriented to the international competitive strengths of German industry. Plant-level flexibility in the arrangement of wage negotiations and plant-specific hours have to be rendered possible if the international competitiveness of firms in particular product markets is to be guaranteed. Similarly, working hours ought to be flexible at the individual level; they may be longer or shorter. Some headway was made in increased flexibility under the impression of the worst German economic recession. Recent agreements with trade unions, however, significantly overcompensate for improvements made to overcome the recession.

Among the necessary changes in the framework conditions of competition, licensing procedures ought to be firmly decided, ended within a reasonable period of time. Only under these conditions can a project be successfully planned. In the field of environmental protection requirements, the Federal Republic has taken an active role. The gap with other countries, however, has become too large. Further agreements can only be meaningful in the context of international negotiations.

In this sense, the Solidarity Pact offers numerous possibilities for establishing new and more appropriate reference points for the framework of competition implied by the term *Ordnungspolitk*. In retrospect it seems curious that the need for a new framework of social and economic conditions, while recognized in the early 1980s, was obscured and overturned through the cyclical upturn later in that decade. The positive economic development in the advanced industrial countries not only accelerated the disintegration of the Eastern bloc, but also delayed the new orientation that was required in the Federal Republic. Only after experiencing the consequences of Eastern Europe's collapse did the need for a new alignment of the competitive framework in the West become clear. Now, the meandering structures of the satisfied and prosperous society in the older parts of the Federal Republic have to be changed so that they guarantee a prosperous future for the whole of united Germany.

The virtues of *Ordnungspolitik*, responsible for the first economic upturn in the middle of this century, are deeply anchored in Germany's social and economic systems. They are available—but in too many areas submerged. In order to make a successful beginning in the new century, they need to be made effective once again.

ENDNOTES

[1]Christopher S. Allen, "The Underdevelopment of Keynesianism in the Federal Republic of Germany," in Peter A. Hall, ed. *The Political Power of Economic Ideas: Keynesianism across Nations* (Princeton, N.J.: Princeton University Press, 1989), 281.

[2]In particular cf. *Volkswirtschaftspolitik* (macroeconomic policy) in Dr. Gabler's *Wirtschaftslexikon,* Wiesbaden, 1972.

[3]See labor market statistics for March 1995 as published by Bundesanstalt für Arbeit, press information no. 24, 1995.

[4]Cf. *Statistisches Jahrbuch 1994 für die Bundesrepublik Deutschland* (Statistical Yearbook 1992 for the Federal Republic of Germany), Wiesbaden, 1992.

[5]Also see the study "Service Sector Productivity," McKinsey & Company, Washington, D.C., 1992.

[6]See James P. Womack, Daniel T. Jones, and Daniel Roos, *The Machine That Changed the World* (New York: Rawson Associates, 1990), chap. 5.

[7]Compare Gesamtverbandes der metallindustriellen Arbeitgeberverbände e.V. (National Association of the Metal Industry Employer's Federation) press conference no. 12, 1992 from 18 May 1992.

[8]Compare the study, "In search of a post-Maastricht Socioeconomic Order," McKinsey & Company, Washington, D.C., 1992.

[9]See Wolfgang Jentzsch, *Chemiestandort Deutschland—Kriterien für Investitionsentscheidungen* (*The Chemical Position in Germany—Criteria for Decisions to Invest*), lecture given on 8 May 1993 at the delegates' conference of the Verbandes Angestellter Akademiker and Leitender Angestelleter der Chemischen Industrie e.V. (Association of Nontenured Academics and Exccutives of the Chemical Industry), Frankfurt.

[10]Compare Nikolaus Piper, *Wege aus der Krise* (*Ways Out of the Crisis*), installment 1, *Die Zeit,* March 1993.

[11]See Hubert Markl, *Bemerkungen zum Standortfaktor "Ausbildung und Grundlagenforschung"* (*Observations on the Locational Factors "Training and Pure Research"*), Constance, 1992.

[12]Cf. Institut der deutschen Wirtschaft Köln, *Internationale Wirtschaftszahlen* (*International Economic Statistics*), 1992.

[13]Cf. "Finanzbericht 1995" ("Financial Status 1995"), Ministry of Finance, 1994.

[14]Cf. "Deutschland-prognose," West LB, 1995.

[15]On the text of the Maastricht Treaty, see Presse- und Informationsamt der Bundesregierung (Department of Press and Information of the Federal Government), *Europäische Gemeinschaft/Europäische Union: Neufassung der europäischen Vertragstext* (*European Community/European Union: Revised Version of the Text of the European Treaty*), Bonn, 1992.

[16]Cf. *Statistisches Jahrbuch 1994 für die Bundesrepublik Deutschland,* chap. 25.

[17]Cf. Deutscher Bundestag pamphlet 12/4401, 4 March 1993, from the twelfth session of the parliament, *Gesetzentwurf zur Umsetzung des Föderalen Konsolidierungsprogramms* (*Bill on the Changing of the Federal Consolidation Program*).

The "Competing Nation." A subtly different version of "positive nationalism" recognizes that capital is mobile, that companies are increasingly global, that governments have little talent for "picking winners," and that competition occurs, essentially, between companies rather than countries. Nonetheless, a sense of national economic purpose can be created around the idea of "competitiveness": creating a pool of highly educated and flexible workers, an efficient infrastructure, sound money, and a good quality of life. Such a "competing nation" is then well placed to operate as an open economy, attracting mobile financial and human capital. At the same time, some areas of discretion are still open to governments—migration control for example. This is the "Singapore model," now being intentionally or unconsciously adopted by large numbers of small states, others which are not so small (Britain is a major country trying to position itself to be as attractive as possible to foreign investors), and some of the reforming economies of Eastern Europe, like Hungary and Czechia.

Vincent Cable

From "The Diminished Nation-State: A Study in the Loss of Economic Power" *Dædalus* 124 (2) (Spring 1995)

Klaus J. Bade

Immigration and Social Peace in United Germany

U NITED GERMANY AS A DESTINATION FOR immigrants raises hopes and fears. Dreams and nightmares collide at its borders: those who are outside dream of entering; those who are inside fear outsiders will indeed come and demand a share of the imagined fortune at the center of the continent, which, it is said, lies in Germany.

AGGRESSION AND VIOLENCE

At the start of the 1990s, public discussion in united Germany is marked by fear of a growing, aggressive xenophobia, acceptance of violence against foreigners, and, correspondingly, a growing number of perpetrators and victims. Young people are especially well represented among the aggressors, under the influence of the radical Right.[1] After unification (in 1990), first in the Eastern and then also in the Western parts of Germany, foreigners were openly attacked and hunted down in the streets, with the slogans "foreigners out" and "Germany for the Germans."

In the beginning, the victims of such violence were primarily asylum seekers hoping to find refuge from political, racial, or religious persecution, from war, poverty, and destitution in the crisis areas of the world. Soon the daytime encounters became arson attacks at night: first, and still, mostly on shelters for asylum seekers, but also on domiciles of ethnic Germans from Eastern Europe. In addition, since 1992, attacks have increasingly been

Klaus J. Bade is Professor of Modern History and Director of the Institute for Migration Research and Intercultural Studies, University of Osnabrück.

aimed at the Turks—the largest group of "local foreigners," originating from the former population of "guest workers," living in united Germany. "Hoyerswerda" (September 1991) and "Rostock-Lichtenhagen" (August 1992), where attacks on asylum seekers were applauded by the public, have become worldwide known catchwords for the new terror in Germany. Arson attacks on Turks, long-term residents of Germany, in Mölln and Solingen have been similarly commemorated.[2] Aggression has also been directed against the Romanies, who already in the darkest epoch of German history were victims of government-organized crime. Since the 1980s, they have immigrated to Germany in large numbers.[3] In addition, a growing number of anti-Semitic offenses have been noted, including attacks on memorials of the Holocaust and Jewish cemeteries.[4] The increase in offenses does not, however, include physical attacks on Jews who have lived in Germany all along or who returned after the Holocaust or on those who immigrated from the former Soviet Union during the past few years. Even the homeless and the handicapped have become victims of right-wing aggression.[5]

This is more than "simple" hostility toward foreigners and outsiders. It is xenophobic violence originating from a lack of perspective, a lack of orientation, and social fear, as well as frustration and aggression. The search for the sources of this new threat to society has become a focus of social science research and of public and published discussion in united Germany.[6]

The new xenophobia is neither "fascist" nor distinctly "German." It also exists in other European countries with similar problems. But in Germany it exists in the shadow of a history that makes brutality against minorities seem even more gruesome. This fact and pronounced media interest in xenophobic aggressiveness have led to distortions and misinterpretations.[7] Normal peaceful coexistence in united Germany is thus overlooked, as are the "foreigner friendly" countermovements and helpful initiatives: the human chains of candle light in the winter of 1992; the vast numbers of organized and spontaneous offers for help in daily life; the taking in and caring for refugees; and the provision of illegal hiding places for asylum seekers whose applications have been denied and who are to be extradited.

This highly complex set of problems is usually discussed in only partially accurate, and therefore highly simplified catchwords such as "hostility toward foreigners," "xenophobia," "right-wing extremism," or "youth violence." Apart from the socioanthropological, bioevolutionary, and even sociobiological assessments diagnosing as a "natural" state of social behavior fear of that which is foreign,[8] which sometimes legitimize xenophobia in the simplistic and coarse versions of public discussion, a variety of more or less broad attempts at explanation and interpretation of the causes are in circulation. Of those, only a few can be mentioned here. An important motive undoubtedly lies in the continued disorientation of the population about social problems relating to immigration and integration. The reason lies in a kind of emphatic political denial that the Federal Republic has become a new kind of country of immigration—not in a legal but in a social and cultural sense.[9]

Apart from that, there are indications of a development away from spontaneous aggressiveness of a diffuse nature to a new formation of right-wing extremism under neo-Nazi subversion.[10] The thesis has been proposed that a collective mental overload exists as a result of the rapidly changing political culture since the late 1980s, with special regard to the psychosocial collective problems and crises of disorientation of the people in Eastern Germany.[11] There are pedagogical social science models that explain far-Right protest behavior of young people as the search for authoritarian guidelines following a period of "antiauthoritarian upbringing and education."[12] And there is a critique of civilization that points to deeper causes in society, to the process of "social paralysis," including the disintegration of social ties, growing mental dissolution, and desolidarization as a result of progressive individualization in the process of modernization. Combined with this are warnings about the dangers of removing aggressors from the context of these social causes by focusing only on their obvious criminal profiles.[13]

Each of the various, frequently overlapping, interpretations claims to provide an explanation. But a unified model continues to be absent and with it the framework for solving the problems. Federal antiviolence initiatives, such as the DM 20 million annual "Action Program against Aggression and Violence (AgAG)" for the pacification of skinheads in Eastern Germany, put into effect in response to the events of Hoyerswerda, reduce the damages on a local and concrete level. Generally, however, they will remain merely cosmetic social remedies as long as their objective is the reduction of acts of aggressive xenophobia rather than the elimination of its social roots.[14]

One thing remains certain: xenophobia has become a major social problem and has contributed decisively to a crisis regarding political legitimacy in united Germany. It reached its high point when the fear of many citizens regarding the evermore obvious situation of immigration, denied by the government, collided with the lack of concept that lay behind that emphatic denial. In the end, the collision of fear "from below" and helplessness "from above" triggered a devastating chain reaction in the realms of political culture and political orientations. For years migration and integration researchers had warned of it in vain.[15]

HISTORICAL EXPERIENCES

At the center of public discussion about migration in united Germany, and the fear of it, are the two interrelated concepts of "locals" versus "foreigners." "Locals" regard immigrating "foreigners" as a threat, but many Germans are themselves descendants of immigrants, and in the nineteenth and twentieth centuries, millions of Germans were "foreigners" in other countries.

In the course of history, Germans and foreigners in Germany have experienced all imaginable forms of cross-border migrations: labor migration of Germans into foreign countries and of foreigners into Germany; refuge and the forced movement of Germans into foreign countries and of foreigners into Germany; and migration of Germans as victims and as perpetrators within and outside German borders. German history is also familiar with borders moving over people and isolating "strangers"—Jews, Romanies, and others— inside those borders. And, there were interior migrations over long distances, whereby locals could themselves become foreigners: the long distance East-West migrations of the "Poles of the Ruhr" and the "Mazurcs of the Ruhr" out of the Prussian East into the coal and steel regions of the Ruhr and Emsch; and the refugees and displaced persons from East Germany at the end and as a result of World War II.[16]

Before the transatlantic emigration of almost eight million Germans to the United States in the early nineteenth century,[17] continental emigration took hundreds of thousands of people from

German speaking areas to Eastern and Southeastern Europe.[18] But since the late nineteenth century, the transnational movements and the problems related to them have been reversed: Germany, once a country of emigration, is today a country of immigration, albeit an unwilling one.[19]

Since World War II, this development has accelerated dramatically in Western Germany. Between the end of the war in 1945 and German reunification in 1990, almost fifteen million people immigrated to the Federal Republic: refugees and expellees after the war, refugees from the Soviet occupied zone, Germans from the German Democratic Republic (GDR), and ethnic Germans from Eastern and Southeastern Europe.[20] On the eve of unification in 1990, this influx of new citizens accounted for more than one-fourth of the inhabitants of the Federal Republic. Taking into account the 4.8 million foreign minorities in 1990, the total number of people who immigrated since 1945 corresponded to one-third of the West German inhabitants in 1990. No comparable situation exists among Western industrialized nations in the second half of this century. Since 1987, the Federal Republic has absorbed more immigrants annually than the two classic immigration countries, Canada and Australia, combined. Yet, government declarations insist that Germany is not an "immigration country."

Overall, three different processes of integration of foreigners can be distinguished in West Germany since World War II: *1)* the integration of refugees and expellees; *2)* the evolution of the "guest workers issue" into an immigration problem; and *3)* the new immigration situation in united Germany.

Refugees and expellees from East Germany and from Eastern Europe fled or were expelled primarily because of National Socialist politics, the war initiated by Germany, and the horrors of German occupation.[21] Many were still foreigners in their new homeland when the German-Italian treaty of 1955 gave the signal for the officially organized recruitment of a foreign work force for the labor market of the Federal Republic.[22] In contrast to the "foreign migrant workers" of the German Empire [23] and the "foreign workers" in National Socialist Germany,[24] those affected by the treaty of 1955 were publicly called "guest workers." A "guest," however, is someone who does not stay permanently.

At no time in the history of the Federal Republic has a comprehensive and long-term concept existed for the permanent integration of an immigrant population. For decades, the "politics concerning foreigners" were characterized by reactive social repair work without long-term organizational principles. Foreign workers, in the 1960s, established residence for increasingly longer periods. This led to a full fledged immigration problem, unsuccessfully "denied" by the government. After the construction of the Berlin Wall on the Western border of the GDR, and in conjunction with the related termination of a steady influx of workers from East to West Germany, the number of foreign workers in West Germany quickly rose into the millions. Approximately fourteen million people came during that time, of which eleven million returned to their home countries. The official recruiting process lasted until the worldwide economic crisis of 1973. Of the foreign population in West Germany, numbering approximately 4.8 million in 1990, almost three million were guest workers (or descendants thereof) from former recruitment countries.[25]

The guest worker period ended with the "Recruitment Stop" of 1973. It had a boomerang effect on German politics regarding foreigners: for a short time it decreased the numbers of foreigners, but by lowering the transnational flux of migrant workers, it further strengthened the already growing tendency toward permanent residence. Foreign workers who did not want to be separated forever from their families still living in the country of origin were faced with the alternative of permanently returning to the homeland or moving their families to the Federal Republic. Most remained in Germany, and by 1979, the migration of their families raised the foreign population in the Federal Republic beyond the level of 1973.

With the increasing length of residence came the transition from guest worker to immigrant. At the start of the 1980s, a significant part of the foreign minority already derived from the former guest worker population. They lived in the paradoxical situation of being permanently integrated immigrants without an immigrant country. Even at the start of the 1990s, the declaration "The Federal Republic is not a country of immigration" continued to be the common denominator transcending all party lines regarding not "immigration politics" but "politics concerning foreigners."[26]

CURRENT PROBLEMS

Since unification, Germany is confronted with a third process of integration, even more complex than those occurring since World War II.[27] It encompasses several immigrant groups, the largest of which is "domestic foreigners," a minority originating from the former guest worker population.[28] The second group consists of ethnic Germans from Eastern Europe who immigrated by the hundreds of thousands every year since the late 1980s. They come from former Communist areas and, according to the passports they receive shortly after arriving in Germany, are Germans. Like other immigrants, they face sociocultural problems that have long gone unrecognized by the government.[29]

The number of refugees from Eastern Europe and the Third World seeking asylum in the Federal Republic has strongly increased since the 1980s. As of July 1, 1993, a new, restrictive German asylum law is in effect. Those coming from "persecution-free" countries or entering Europe via "safe third countries" have, as a general rule, no chance of being granted asylum. This could increase the already high number of illegal immigrants and the periods of residence of those who have not filed an application for asylum.[30] A relatively recent phenomenon in Germany is the immigration of Jews from the former Soviet Union. It is skeptically watched by Israel and in early 1993 already included an estimated fifteen thousand people.[31]

In addition to immigration across German borders, there are two major problems of internal integration in united Germany. First, those who came to the West in great numbers at the end of the 1980s as GDR refugees still suffer identity problems. Once in the West, many of them suffered culture shock—evidence of how great the distance had become not only in terms of life-style and material culture, but also in ways of thinking.[32]

Second, there are special problems of mental integration in East Germany since the unification of Germany. Many in East Germany live in an imaginary, imported situation of integration: they did not leave for a foreign country, but the familiar environment turned into a foreign country. During the rapid social, economic, political, and ideological changes in the early 1990s, they were confronted with the alternative of unconditional adjustment or progressive estrangement.[33]

The ordeals related to these processes diminished any readiness to accommodate foreigners. Instead, they led to xenophobic attacks even before the riots in Hoyerswerda in September 1991. However, they were insufficiently noticed at the time because the media had not yet "discovered" this new topic.

In the GDR, there had been government sponsored isolation and even ghettoization rather than integration of foreigners. In 1989, the GDR still had a foreign population of approximately 190,000, not including members of the Soviet army and their families. By far the largest group was the foreign work force hired on the basis of government agreements. Workers were housed in separate group accommodations and thus kept at a social distance. Closer contact had to be cleared through permissions and reports. Officially, there were no foreign workers in the GDR; their presence was covered up or only alluded to, even at professional conferences about foreign worker employment.[34]

Foreigners in the GDR—like the guest workers in the Federal Republic—worked mostly in those areas of employment least favored by German workers. The social vacuum, brought about by official isolation of foreigners and taboos surrounding their existence, caused rumors and suspicions, and mistrust, fear, and hatred became rampant. Once latent xenophobic tensions were openly displayed after the collapse of the Socialist Unity Party (SED) regime and the simultaneous termination of its totalitarian order.

Foreign workers from the Third World who had entered the country primarily in GDR-times were the first to be affected by the growing xenophobia. According to estimates, the largest remaining groups in 1990 were from Vietnam (approximately 53,000) and Mozambique (approximately 35,000). Their numbers fell drastically as they returned to the homeland or sought asylum in West Germany, fleeing the threat of growing xenophobia. Groups of asylum seeking refugees, assigned to the new *Länder* in accordance with the unification treaty, soon became victims of assaults. Although such assaults were, at first, more aggressive and more brutal in the East, xenophobia was neither "typically East German" nor solely a matter of marginalized social groups threatened by social decline, and it soon spread across united Germany.

XENOPHOBIA AND POLITICS

At the beginning of the 1990s, Germany still lacked a concept for a definite solution to the social problems of migration, integration, and minorities. Meanwhile, xenophobic defense mechanisms were triggered by the polemics of party politics, election campaigns, and the media: polls taken at the start of the election campaign showed "the problem concerning foreigners" and "the asylum issue" to be of medium importance; at the height and at the end of the elections such issues were of the utmost importance. In 1991, the topics of foreigners and asylum ranked second in the public mind, after the problems of German unification. In October 1992, the "problem of foreigners" was ranked highest in West Germany and third in East Germany, after issues of unemployment and economic growth.[35] This change occurred in the face of increasing numbers of asylum seekers, among biting party conflicts concerning policies regarding foreigners and asylum, and alongside a rapid decline into recession, rising unemployment, and growing poverty of marginal social groups.

The situation of integration in united Germany has created a multitude of new and changing "pecking orders" between "locals" and "foreigners." In West Germany, it is not unusual for citizens of the West (*Wessis*) to be positioned against the immigrant citizens of the East (*Ossis*). In East Germany, on the other hand, there is often a combination of curiosity and fear, of social envy and hatred of *Wessis* who frequently march in with the posturing attitude of conquistadors. Germans leaving the East are suspicious of German speaking ethnic groups who emigrated from Eastern and Southeastern Europe (i.e., Romania and Transylvania). Those groups are skeptical of German ethnic groups speaking other languages (i.e., Russian). Germans from East Germany and German ethnic groups show common defense behavior vis-à-vis "foreigners," particularly Turks. Most immigrant groups and a growing majority of Germans in the East and the West are distrustful of asylum seeking refugees from the Third World and from Eastern Europe, but especially of the immigrating Romanies ("gypsies") from Romania.

There is also joint opposition between Germans and "domestic foreigners" toward the newly immigrated "foreign Germans" from the East. "Domestic foreigners" even participated in violence against other foreigners, especially in attacks on domiciles of asylum seekers.[36] These are but a few of the tensions and "hierarchies of foreigners and strangers" in the new situation concerning immigration and integration. Immigration history contains the lesson that, within such a situation, "ethnic stratification" (class formation) is particularly dangerous—with regard to social consensus and likewise with regard to multiethnic coexistance and multicultural lifestyles.[37]

The pressure of immigration from the outside grew into a "new mass-migration," an "invasion of the poor," an "onslaught on Europe,"[38] and was frightfully exaggerated in sensational reports by the media and in widely distributed horror publications. The fear of foreigners grew accordingly, in an immigration situation without guidelines. In the summer of 1991, the government deputy in charge of immigration affairs, Liselotte Funcke, resigned, thereby protesting the continued absence of political direction. The government blatantly ignored the resignation and seemed in no hurry to replace the person in charge of this important, but insufficiently funded, office.[39]

The unrest continued to grow in large parts of the population, inflamed by the demagoguery of press reports during the "summer doldrums." Responses by the government, primarily concerned with problems of unification, showed continued helplessness on issues of immigration and integration. But the polemic rebuttals between government and opposition signaled an ability, on both sides, to take action. The tension grew from day to day, while the fear-producing topics "migration" and "asylum" became talk-show hits. Within party politics, the lack of direction was replaced by the noise of such polemical invectives as "Social Democratic Party (SPD) asylum seekers," "hypocrites," "agitators," and "multicriminal society." The office of the administrator for immigrant affairs remained vacant in the autumn of 1991.[40]

"We are warning of the danger of further neglecting the central political concern regarding immigration and integration of immigrant minorities," a committed professoriat from various sciences stated in an appeal at the end of August 1991. "The problems. . .must finally be understood as a decisive task for the future of German and European politics and must be determined by encompassing concepts. The situation will worsen if future oriented political action is not forthcoming."[41] There was no political answer. Suddenly the repeated warnings, which had been ignored by the political parties, turned into a terrifying reality. It started with the attacks on an apartment house for foreigners in Saxon Hoyerswerda in late September 1992 and raged through Germany like an infernal wildfire. The events in the autumn of 1991 brought to the surface the xenophobic undercurrents of which experts had warned for a long time. They produced a worldwide reaction of horror, disgust, and memories of the darkest epoch in German history.

A second wave of xenophobic violence ensued following the terror-nights in Rostock in August 1992, where the withdrawal of a police without guidelines at the height of the riot could have been taken to be an invitation to escalate the attack. The flames of Rostock-Lichtenhagen sparked similar attacks; at various places in the East and the West, shelters of asylum seeking refugees went up in flames. Many arson attacks could be countered and the flames put out before it was too late, but in Mölln in Schleswig-Holstein in November 1992, two houses inhabited by Turks went up in flames. Three people burned to death and nine escaped with serious injuries.

Only then did a united front emerge throughout the country against the xenophobic aggression from the Right. In this country of highly nervous consternation, many intellectuals and other well-intentioned people had initially reacted with shock and helplessness. After the arson attacks in Mölln, human chains of light gathered in stunned protest against xenophobia, right-wing extremism, and violence. At that point, the well established government monopoly on force against the Left went into motion, after appearing, until then, all-too hesitant toward the Right; far-Right organizations, well known for years, were forbidden; house searches followed. The danger from the Right had become unmistakable and impossible to ignore.

The fact that the government was reacting much less systematically to the extremism of the Right than it had years ago to the extremism of the Left did not have to do with the frequently raised argument that state and law in Bonn, as in Weimar, was "blind in its right eye," although it is true that the far-Right danger had indeed been underestimated. Rather, it had primarily to do with the fact that the perpetrators were a large and growing number of poorly educated, unorganized individuals and small groups whose actions were less strategically planned than spontaneously executed, in contrast to the highly intelligent, tightly organized conspiracy of the "Red Army Faction" (RAF) of the Left. Evidence in 1992–1993, however, pointed to an increasingly tighter organization of numerous factions of the far-Right.[42]

The fact that the people killed in Mölln had not been asylum seekers but had lived in Germany as domestic foreigners was a shock to the German public—as though physical and spiritual attacks on one group were more offensive than on others. This attitude became part of a fatal development: it began, on the one hand, with the presumptuous isolation and collective denunciation of asylum seekers ("fakes," "economic refugees"), and, on the other hand, with sympathetic solicitations for ethnic German immigrants from the East with the well-meaning but formulaic slogan "Ethnic Germans Are Not Foreigners." It reached its peak with the notion that foreigners who lived and worked in Germany were surely not asylum seekers. This inhuman measurement, widely used by the media, which employed a differentiating evaluation for misanthropic acts based on the victims, figured even in the minds of the victims themselves. The day after the arson attacks in Mölln, German television showed a Turkish mother who had been seriously wounded during the attack on her child. Not yet aware of the death of her child, she delivered two messages: first, a desperate plea for peaceful coexistence between Germans and Turks, and, second, the statement that the victims in Mölln were "not asylum seekers" and also "not Kurds," but "real Turks." In this respect too, things came full circle in Mölln.

After the murder in Solingen at the end of May 1993, after the eruption of violence in the streets at the scene of the crime, there was growing concern that an immigration situation in which many lines of tension overlapped would give rise to scenarios reminiscent of civil war.[43] Germany is as ill-prepared for such problems now as before. This has much to do with the political delays in dealing with migration issues. It is not, however, a matter of having been right and blaming others, but of learning from the omissions of the past.

POSSIBLE ACTIONS AND OVERALL PERSPECTIVES

Researchers and professionals working with immigrants, the government deputy for immigration, church and welfare institutions, unions, and a variety of other initiatives had repeatedly warned of the dangers of political avoidance and defensive attitudes. This was the case particularly with regard to the asylum discussion concerning ARTICLE 16 of the Basic Law (Constitution). The discussion frequently took on the character of an open war, while all matters concerning the social problems of immigration and integration remained the same. Guidelines for a comprehensive policy with clearly established long-term planning and perspective, as well as the institutions necessary to carry them out, such as a federal office for migration and integration, were not developed for over a decade. Instead of enlightening the public and soliciting understanding, there was only a feeble attempt to cast a spell on that specter "immigration" with the outdated and unrealistic incantation "The Federal Republic is not a Country of Immigration!" Only the shock caused by the incidents of xenophobic violence since the autumn of 1991 gave the push for political rethinking. Until then, political discussion had focused on the legal rights of foreigners, not reformed until 1990 even though announced more than a decade ago, and on the polemic asylum debate.

Many of the problems politicians complain of today are the result of misjudgments and neglect concerning the issues of immigration, integration, and minorities. They are largely self-imposed and had been repeatedly warned of and predicted. This was one reason why "political disgruntledness" was chosen as the expression of the year 1992.[44] The result provides a dangerous opportunity for the great simplifiers of the radical Right, whose political platform is based on fear and xenophobic slogans. In 1994, with a total of almost twenty elections on European, Federal, state, and local levels, there could be dangerous results for the political culture in united Germany.

Not until 1992 did the open discussion urgently encouraged a decade earlier concerning an overall sociopolitical conceptualization of issues about immigration and integration begin in the Federal Republic.[45] For issues of immigration, however, the Federal government wanted to see only European solutions, not national ones. At the beginning of 1993, the European Market became a reality, but, apart from defensive measures, correlated European concepts were mere points of inception. But a European policy would be just as insufficient as a national perspective. What had been neglected in Germany for almost a decade cannot be delegated to Europe.

Europe cannot simply be designed from the top down, but must also be constructed on the national level.

In 1993, a hesitant beginning was made in the political discussion concerning an encompassing legislation for immigration, particularly citizenship, immigration law, and immigration policies. It was forced by leading representatives of the Social Democratic Party and the Free Democratic Party (FDP), including the president of the Ministry of Lower Saxony Gerhard Schroeder (SPD), the new party chairman and president of the Ministry of Rhineland-Palatinate Rudolf Scharping, the deputy of foreigners of the Federal government Cornelia Schmalz-Jacobsen (FDP), and the FDP party chairman Klaus Kinkel. Leading representatives of the Christian Democratic Union/Christian Social Union (CDU/CSU) fraction, however, continued to dismiss the "phantom discussion" concerning immigration law. They used the usual arguments, which have their roots in an almost classic misunderstanding of political debates surrounding migration issues in Germany, namely that politics of immigration and promotion of immigration are one and the same.[46]

Although there had been, for many years, directive starting points in the political discussion in Germany, they were not translated into action. This was especially true for the "Refugee Related Considerations of the Federal Republic of Germany" presented in September 1990. It was the first formulation of an "interdepartmental policy" and was thereby suitable as an official framework for a comprehensive answer to the challenge of the worldwide refugee problem. Foreign and development policy, asylum policy, the causes of the refugee problem, the acceptance of refugees, and assistance in returning the refugees to their homelands were emphasized. The objectives of these "Considerations" were accepted nationally and internationally. But taken as a "foundation for an international approach concerning the issue of refugees," it was only a theoretical step in the right direction.[47]

After the mid-1980s in Germany, as elsewhere, the pros and cons of a "multicultural society" were debated more intensively.[48] Such debates were often a forum for those who felt too embarrassed to talk with clarity on matters of immigration legislation and policies in this context of the unavoidable immigration quotas that were considered inhuman. Not until 1991–1992 did the idea slowly penetrate that immigration legislation and policy need not be opposed by multiethnic coexistence and multicultural life-styles.[49]

Yet, in the debates in Germany about opportunities and limits of multicultural coexistence, immigration legislation, and immigration policies, the dramatic catchwords of 1992, "Los Angeles" and "Sarajevo," and increasingly the events in Germany, have contributed to the suspicion that multicultural perspectives are ideological, and that plans for immigration legislation and policies were discussed by their opponents as, at best, a means for the prevention of immigration ("legislation for immigration limitation"). But in the background lurked that European dichotomy of the end of another era: supranational structures were being built and the formation of a multicultural European Community was being discussed, while the fragile and, at least since World War II, explosive multicultural consensus in the southeast of Europe was falling apart. The bloody specter of ethnic nationalism, long since assumed to be buried in history, returned to the present.

CONCLUSIONS AND CHALLENGES

All the more urgent is the need, on the worldwide, European, and national level, for the solution of the pressing problems of immigration, integration, and minorities. But immigration policies without radical development strategies are as insufficient as humanitarian acceptance of refugees without the, by now much praised and to an extent fossilized, political formula, "control of flood causes." This is much more than conventional "development aid"; rather, it is assistance for attaining a new and self-sustaining level of development, because, in the end, it is a problem of global distribution. In this developmentally oriented control of flood causes, there is no escape from the issue of an "international equalization of burdens" between North and South, but also between East and West, in a world that is increasingly less divided by political and ideological differences and evermore by differences in economic development, in which "a human right to development" must also exist.[50]

A single country like Germany, likely to long remain heavily burdened with the economic and social problems resulting from the unification process, would be greatly overtaxed by such global tasks. But as a preferred country of migration in Europe, Germany has a special responsibility to help in developing appropriate plans. First, however, it must cope with the internal problems of a united Germany.

Discussions about German migration and asylum, emotionalized and neuroticised through political polemics and demagoguery, must be put into a proper perspective. In evaluating the changes of the rights to asylum, which went into effect in the summer of 1993, it is important to remember that the offer of individual asylum for the politically persecuted, like the Basic Law itself, was the historical reply of the West Germans to the experience of National Socialism. Thus, the debate about changing the asylum policy carried not only humanitarian but historical and political weight. What is needed in addition is international agreement and coordination of a collective, generally limited regulation of contingents for refugees from areas of war and crises.

The asylum crisis in Germany, however, was the flip side of political helplessness and a lack of guidelines in immigration affairs. Therefore, the increasing pressure of problems did not only result from the asylum hysteria of the 1980s and early 1990s. It was primarily the result of more profound omissions made a long time ago concerning immigration issues. Basically, the asylum debate only took people's minds off those issues. The price of this became evident when, in the beginning of the 1990s, many additional problems arose due to the unification process. Among the population, a diffuse fear of foreigners was growing; among the politicians, a fear of the attitudes of citizens towards foreigners as well as towards domestic politicians was increasing.

Disorientation and fear among the population, coupled with the helplessness of politicians, had a decisive influence on the political credibility crisis, warnings of which had been sounded in vain for many years. For a brief period, this crisis even seemed to endanger the parliamentary democratic system. In autumn 1992, Chancellor Kohl spoke of a "state of emergency" ("*Staatsnotstand*") in migration affairs, which even led some opinion leaders of public debate to recall the political instability, governmental powerlessness, and ultimate rejection of parliamentary democracy at the end of the Weimar Republic.[51]

In November 1993, sixty scholars issued the "*Manifest der 60*," a manifesto confronting the topic of "Germany and the Immigration." According to these scholars, silent xenophobia, violent hostility towards strangers, and acceptance of violence in this context during the unification process of the early 1990s were "not inevitable consequences of immigration and integration, but rather, avoidable results of a lack of political structuring of these processes" as well as "an aggressive response to the lack of migration policies."[52]

In united Germany, stronger efforts are needed for the integration and protection of immigrants and minorities. Comprehensive guidelines with long-term perspectives are required for the development of population and economy, society and culture. Experts agree that Germany is a country that fears an excess of immigration but which continually and for some time needs a minimum of immigration. Otherwise, there might well be the frightening scenario at the turn of the century of a central European bunker with a shrinking and aging crew, causing innumerable problems for the development of the labor market, the stability of social security systems supported through the "contract between generations" as well as for the entire social welfare state. Without such guiding principles, immigration politics would remain aimless or would be condemned to remain merely defensive.[53] Answers must be sought not just for periods of legislation but for generations. Most importantly, a public discussion must no longer develop the mistaken notion that the pressure of immigration at the German borders can be remedied with changes to the Basic Law.

Today, we are facing the danger of a shift from "alarmism" to indifference. In the late 1980s and early 1990s, political debate and the media coverage of asylum issues resulted in a sort of Titanic hysteria. In the election year of 1994, however, political parties and the media, fearing a resurfacing of violent offenses against foreigners, avoided the explosive topics of migration, integration, and minorities.

In the end, there still remains the paradoxical issue of de facto immigration in a nonimmigration country. Currently there are some cautious attempts at structuring and many open questions for the future. But one thing is certain: migration policy cannot be limited to regulations for transnational movements or to foreign security politics. It requires corresponding internal policies for integration and minorities. Therefore, the internal side of migration politics falls essentially under the category of domestic social politics.

However, such migration policies can only be successful if they are based on a large fundamental consensus. In a liberal democracy, such an agreement must be carried through with the will of the majority. It cannot be pushed through against the will of the majority without severe consequences, from which the immigrant minorities and the political system as a whole could suffer. Therefore, migration policies must be properly promoted. Social coexistence, cultural tolerance, and social peace depend on whether and to what extent society and the political elite in united Germany are willing to respond to the challenges of migration with the development of integral programs and far-sighted perspectives.[54]

Germans must come to realize that they will have to live with the continued pressure and the resulting problems of immigration for decades to come; that it is a lasting and constantly changing political problem that cannot be "solved" with pat legal-technical solutions.[55] It is all the more important to denounce scare tactics and horror visions in public discussions and to contribute to a positive, or at least a more relaxed attitude toward the problems of immigration, integration, and minorities. In coping with these problems, political consulting based on multiethnic studies and research on migration and conflicts in multicultural societies can no doubt make an important contribution.[56]

Translated by
Lieselotte Anderson

ENDNOTES

[1] An evaluation of police records initiated by the federal government showed that 39 percent of the suspects in violence against foreigners were between the ages of eighteen and twenty. Thirty-three percent were between fifteen and seventeen, 3 percent were younger than fifteen. Documentation by the Saxony criminal justice department showed that only a third of the suspects was over eighteen years old. An investigation by the Berlin police department indicated that 45 percent of the suspects were between fourteen and eighteen years old. Cf. Kurt Reumann, "Jung und schuldfähig?, *Frankfurter Allgemeine Zeitung* (FAZ), 7 August 1993, 8.

[2] Documentation by Gabriele Nandlinger, "Chronik der Gewalt," in Klaus Henning Rosen, ed., *Die zweite Vertreibung. Fremde in Deutschland* (Bonn: J. H. W. Dietz, Nachf., 1992), 119–158.

[3] "Die Zigeuner: Asyl in Deutschland?," *Der Spiegel,* 3 September 1990, 34 –57; "Einwanderung: Bürgerhaß auf Roma und Sinti," Ibid., 7 August 1992, 30 –36.

[4]"'Der Holo ist beendet:' Jugendliche Nazis verwüsten jüdische Friedhöfe, sprengen Denkmäler und brennen KZ-Gedenkstätten nieder," *Der Spiegel,* 16 November 1992, 65–73; Raffael Seligmann, "Die Juden leben," Ibid., 16 November 1992, 75–78; "'Dann bin ich weg über Nacht': Die jüdischen Gemeinden und der wachsende Antisemitismus in Deutschland," Ibid., 14 December 1992, 48 –56.

[5]"Menschliche Bomben. Terror gegen Behinderte," *Der Spiegel,* 1 February 1993, 67.

[6]Cf. Jürgen Fjialkowski, *Aggressive Nationalism, Immigrant Pressure, and Asylum Policy Disputes in Contemporary Germany,* German Historical Institute Occasional Paper no. 9, Washington, 1993.

[7]Armin Pfahl-Traughber, *Rechtsextremismus. Eine kritische Bestandaufnahme nach der Wiedervereinigung* (Bonn: Bouvier, 1993); cf. Armin Pfahl-Traughber, "Unter dem Vergrößerungsglas: Wie man den Neonationalsozialismus stärker macht als er ist," *FAZ,* 26 July 1993, 23.

[8]Irenäus Eibl-Eibesfeldt and Christa Sütterlin, *Im Banne der Angst. Zur Natur-und Kunstgeschichte menschlicher Abwehrsymbolik* (Munich: Piper, 1992); Dieter E. Zimmer, "Die Angst vor dem Anderen: Über die Anthropologie des Fremdenhaßes," *Die Zeit, 9,* 16, 23 July 1993; Berhard Verbeek, "Fremdenhaß: biologisch verwurzelt?," *Universitas* 48 (7) (1993): 642–54.

[9]Klaus J. Bade, *Vom Auswanderungsland zum Einwanderungsland? Deutschland 1880 –1980* (Berlin: Colloquium, 1983); Klaus J. Bade, ed., *Auswanderer— Wanderarbeiter—Gastarbeiter: Bevölkerung, Arbeitsmarkt und Wanderung in Deutschland seit der Mitte des 19. Jahrhunderts,* vol. 2 (Ostfildern: Scripta Mercaturae, 1984); Klaus J. Bade, ed., *Population, Labour and Migration in 19th and 20th Century Germany* (Oxford: Berg, 1987).

[10]Bernd Sigler, *Auferstanden aus Ruinen. Rechtsextremismus in der DDR* (Berlin: Klaus Bittermann, 1991); Pfahl-Traughber, *Rechtsextremismus;* Claus Leggewie, *Druck von rechts. Wohin treibt die Bundesrepublik?* (Munich: C. H. Beck, 1933).

[11]Hans Joachim Maaz, *Der Gefühlsstau: Ein Psychogramm der DDR* (Berlin: Argon, 1990); Hans Joachim Maaz, *Das gestürzte Volk oder die verunglückte Einheit* (Berlin: Argon, 1991); Hans Joachim Maaz, "Gewalt in Deutschland— eine psychologische Analyse," *PZG,* 8 January 1993, 26 –32.

[12]Claus Leggewie, "Ursachen der Gewalt rechtsextremer Jungendlicher," *Die Woche,* 9 June 1993; cf. Tilmann Moser, "Die Enkel der Nazi-Zeit. Beschädigte Biographien und jugendliche Gewalt," Ibid., 24 June 1993.

[13]Wilhelm Heitmeyer et al., *Die Bielefelder Rechtsextremismus Studie* (Munich: Yuventa, 1992); Wilhelm Heitmeyer, "Gesellschaftliche Desintegrationsprozesse als Ursachen von fremdenfeindlicher Gewalt und politischer Paralisierung," *PZG,* 8 January 1993, 3–13.

[14]Frank Drieschner, "Glatzenpflege auf Staatskosten: Hilft Geld gegen Gewalt?," *Die Zeit,* 13 August 1993, 50; Wilhelm Heitmeyer, "Die Maßnahmen gegen Fremdenfeindlichkeit gehen an den Ursachen vorbei," in Berhard Blanke, ed., *Zuwanderung und Asyl in der Konkurrenzgesellschaft* (Opladen: Leske & Budrich, 1993), 151– 62.

[15]Cf., for example, Bade, *Vom Auswanderungsland zum Einwanderungsland?*, 106–24.

[16]In this context, cf. Klaus J. Bade, ed., *Deutsche im Ausland—Fremde in Deutschland: Migration in Geschichte und Gegenwart* (Munich: C. H. Beck, 1992).

[17]Mack Walker, *Germany and the Emigration, 1816–1885* (Cambridge, Mass.: Harvard University Press, 1964); Wolfgang Helbich, Walter D. Kamphoefner, and Ulrike Sommer, eds., *Briefe aus Amerika: Deutsche Auswanderer schreiben aus der Neuen Welt 1830–1930* (Munich: C. H. Beck, 1988); Walter D. Kamphoefner, *The Westfalians: From Germany to Missouri* (Princeton, N.J.: Princeton University Press, 1987); cf. the contributions "Weströme: überseeische Auswanderung," in Bade, ed., *Deutsche im Ausland-Fremde in Deutschland*, 135–230.

[18]Related to this topic are the contributions "Ostströme: kontinentale Auswanderung," in Bade, *Deutsche im Ausland—Fremde in Deutschland*, 29–134; Alfred Eisfeld, *Die Rußlanddeutschen* (Munich: Langen Müller, 1992); Barbara Dietz and Peter Hilkes, *Rußlanddeutsche: Unbekannte im Osten. Geschichte—Situation—Zukunftsperspektiven* (Munich: Olzog, 1992).

[19]Klaus J. Bade, "Vom Export der Sozialen Frage zur importierten Sozialen Frage: Deutschland im transnationalen Wanderungsgeschehen seit der Mitte des 19. Jahrhunderts," in Bade, eds., *Auswanderer—Wanderarbeiter—Gastarbeiter*, vol. 1, 9–17; cf. Klaus J. Bade, "Immigration and Integration in Germany since 1945," *European Review: Interdisciplinary Journal of the Academia Europea* 1 (1) (1993): 75–79.

[20]Marion Frantzioch, *Die Vertriebenen: Hemmnisse und Wege ihrer Integration. Mit einer kommentierten Bibliographie* (Berlin: Dietrich Reimer, 1987); Klaus J. Bade, ed., *Neue Heimat im Westen: Vertriebene—Flüchtlinge—Aussiedler* (Münster: Westfälischer Heimatbund, 1990).

[21]*Dokumentation der Vertreibung der Deutschen aus Ost-Mitteleuropa,* reprint (Munich: dtv, 1984); Wolfgang Benz, ed., *Die Vertreibung der Deutschen aus dem Osten: Ursachen Ereignisse, Folgen* (Frankfurt a.M.: Fischer, 1985).

[22]Ulrich Herbert, *A History of Foreign Labor in Germany 1880–1980. Seasonal Workers—Forced Laborers—Guest Workers* (Ann Arbor, Mich.: University of Michigan Press, 1991, German original 1986).

[23]Klaus J. Bade, "'Preußengänger' und 'Abwehrpolitik': Ausländerbeschäftigung, Ausländerpolitik und Ausländerkontrolle auf dem Arbeitsmarkt in Preußen vor dem Ersten Weltkrieg," *Archiv für Sozialgeschichte* 24 (1984): 91–283.

[24]Ulrich Herbert, *Fremdarbeiter: Politik und Praxis des "Ausländer-Einsatzes" in der Kriegswirtschaft des Dritten Reiches* (Berlin: J. H. W. Dietz, Nachf., 1985).

[25]Johannes Gerster, "Illusion oder realistisches Ziel? Ausländerintegration als wichtige Zukunftsaufgabe," *Die Neue Ordnung* 42 (4) (1988): 272.

[26]Friedrich Heckmann, *Die Bundesrepublik: Ein Einwanderungsland? Zur Soziologie der Gastarbeiterbevölkerung als Einwandererminorität* (Stuttgart: Klett-Cotta, 1981); cf. Bade, *Vom Auswanderungsland zum Einwanderungsland?*, 59–124.

[27]In this context, Klaus J. Bade, *Ausländer—Aussiedler—Asyl in der Bundesrepublik Deutschland,* 2nd ed. (Bonn: Bundeszentrale für politische Bildung, 1992).

[28]Karl-Heinz Meier-Braun, *Integration und Rückkehr? Zur Ausländerpolitik des Bundes und der Länder, insbesondere Baden-Württembergs* (Munich: Chr. Kaiser, 1988); Wolfgang Benz, ed., *Integration ist machbar. Ausländer in Deutschland* (Munich: C. H. Beck, 1993).

[29]Barbara Malchow, Keyumars Tayebi, and Ulrike Brand, *Die fremden Deutschen: Aussiedler in der Bundesrepublik* (Reinbek: Rowohlt, 1990).

[30]Blanke, *Zuwanderung und Asyl in der Konkurrenzgesellschaft*; Philip L. Martin, "The German Case," *Controlling Illegal Immigration: A Global Perspective* (Research Workshop, Center for U.S.-Mexican Studies, UC San Diego, La Jolla, Calif., 18–20 March 1993).

[31]"Invaliden des 5. Punkts: Mehr als 15.000 jüdische Emigranten aus den GUS-Staaten leben in Deutschland—für viele Israelis ein Ärgernis," *Der Spiegel,* 29 March 1993, 77–81; cf. Irene Runge and Detlef Steinberg, *Vom Kommen und Bleiben: Osteuropäische jüdische Einwanderer in Berlin*; Klaus J. Bade and S. Illan Troen, eds., *Zuwanderung und Eingliederung von Deutschen und Juden aus der früheren Sovietunion in Deutschland und Israel* (Bonn: 1993).

[32]Dieter Voigt and Lothar Mertens, eds., *Minderheiten in und Übersiedler aus der DDR* (Berlin: Duncker & Humbolt, 1992).

[33]In connection with this are the investigations by Hans-Joachim Maaz.

[34]Bade, *Ausländer—Aussiedler—Asyl,* 38f.; Andrzej Stach and Saleh Hussain, *Ausländer in der DDR: Ein Rückblick*; *Miteinander leben in Berlin* (Berlin: Ausländerbeauftragte des Senats, 1991); Siegfried Grundmann et al., "Ausländer in Ostdeutschland," *Wissenschaftliche Mitteilungen des Berliner Instituts für Sozialwissenschaftliche Studien* 3 (1991): 6–75.

[35]Matthias Jung and Dieter Roth, "Politische Einstellungen seit der Bundestagswahl 1990," *PZG,* 1 May 1992, 3–16; "Spiegel-Umfrage: Asystreit entscheidet Wahl," *Der Spiegel,* 16 October 1992, 58–65; Horst Becker, "Einstellungen zu Ausländern in der Bevölkerung der Bundesrepublik Deutschland 1992," in Blanke, *Zuwanderung und Asyl in der Konkurrenzgesellschaft,* 141–49.

[36]*FAZ,* 7 August 1993, 8.

[37]Roland Tichy, *Ausländer rein! Warum es kein "Ausländerproblem" gibt* (Munich: Piper, 1990), 37–53, 145–52; Lutz Hoffmann, *Die unvollendete Republik: Zwischen Einwanderungsland und deutschem Nationalstaat* (Cologne: PapyRossa, 1990); Paul Bernhard Hill, *Determinanten der Eingliederung von Arbeitsmigranten* (Königstein i.Ts.: Hanstein, 1984); Friedrich Heckmann, *Ethnische Minderheiten, Volk und Nation. Soziologie inter-ethnischer Beziehungen* (Stuttgart: Ferdinand Encke, 1992).

[38]Cf., for example, Manfred Ritter, *Sturm auf Europa: Asylanten und Armutsflüchtlinge. Droht eine neue Völkerwanderung?* (Munich: von Hase & Koehler, 1990); Jan Werner, *Die Invasion der Armen: Asylanten und illegale Einwanderer* (Munich: von Hase & Koeher, 1992); cf. Beate Winkler, ed., *Zukunftsangst Einwanderung* (Munich: C. H. Beck, 1992).

[39] In this context, Bade, *Ausländer—Aussiedler—Asyl*, 20ff.

[40] Ibid., 125–41.

[41] "Aufruf" in *Frankfurter Rundschau (FR)*, 8 August 1991; *FAZ*, 30 August 1991; and *SZ*, 31 August/1 September 1991; also in Bade, *Ausländer—Aussiedler—Asyl*, 92ff.

[42] During the presentation of the 1992 report by the Bavarian Court of Constitutional Protection on 30 July 1993, Bavarian Interior Minister Beckstein (CSU) declared that "internal security" was "seriously endangered" by the increasingly "more organized right-wing extremism," *FAZ*, 31 July 1993, 1; cf. Pfahl-Traughber, *Rechtsextremismus*.

[43] "Die deutschen Türken: Opfer des Fremdenhasses," *Der Spiegel*, 7 June 1993, 16–31; Hans Magnus Enzensberger, "Ausblicke auf den Bürgerkrieg," Ibid., 21 June 1993, 170–75.

[44] "'Politikverdrossenheit' ist das Wort des Jahres," *FAZ*, 18 December 1992.

[45] Most recently, Dieter Oberdörfer and Uwe Berndt, *Einwanderungs- und Eingliederungspolitik als Gestaltungsaufgaben* (Gütersloh: Bertelsmann-Stiftung, 1992); Helmut Rittstieg and Gerard C. Rowe, *Einwanderung als gesellschaftliche Herausforderung. Inhalt und rechtliche Grundlagen einer neuen Politik* (Baden-Baden: Nomos, 1992); Forschungsinstitut der Friedrich-Ebert-Stiftung, ed., *Einwanderungsland Deutschland: Bisherige Ausländer-und Asylpolitik. Vergleich mit anderen europäischen Ländern* (Bonn: Forschungsinstitut der Friedrich-Ebert-Stiftung, 1992); Bade, *Ausländer—Aussiedler—Asyl*, 163–74.

[46] "'Die Fahne des Blutes.' Edmund Stoiber (CSU) und Gerhard Schröder (SPD) über Einwanderung und doppelte Staatsbürgerschaft," *Der Spiegel*, 5 April 1993, 11–122; Rudolf Scharping, "Zwischen Heimat und offener Republik: Herausforderungen der Einwanderungspolitik," *FR*, 25 June 1993, 16; Cornelia Schmalz-Jacobsen, *Einwanderung—und dann? Perspektiven einer neuen Ausländerpolitik* (München: Droemer Knaur, 1993); for Kinkel (FDP) and the counterargument of the CDU/CSU, cf. *FAZ*, 5 August 1993, 4.

[47] Bundesministerium des Innern, ed., *Flüchtlingskonzeption der Bundesrepublik Deutschland. Ansätze für eine Ressort übergreifende Politik*, Bonn, 25 September 1990.

[48] Heiner Geißler, "Die multikulturelle Gesellschaft," in Heiner Geißler, *Zugluft—Politik in stürmischer Zeit* (Munich: C. Bertelsmann, 1990), 177–218; Claus Leggewie, *Multikulti: Spielregeln für die Vielvölkerrepublik* (Nördlingen: Rotbuch, 1990); Axel Schulte, "Multikulturelle Gesellschaft: Chance, Ideologie oder Bedrohung?," *PZG*, 1 June 1990, 3–15; Jürgen Micksch, *Deutschland—Einheit in kultureller Vielfalt* (Frankfurt a.M.: Otto Lemback, 1991); Daniel Cohn-Bendit and Thomas Schmidt, *Heimat Babylon: Das Wagnis der multikulturellen Demokratie* (Hamburg: Hoffmann und Campe, 1992).

[49] Micha Brumlik and Claus Leggewie, "Konturen der Einwanderungsgesellschaft: Nationale Identität, Multikulturalismus und 'Civil Society'," in Bade, ed., *Deutsche im Ausland—Fremde in Deutschland*, 430–42; Bade, "Politik in der Einwanderungssituation: Migration—Integration—Minderheiten," in Ibid., 442–55.

[50]Franz Nuscheler, "Menschenrechte und Entwicklung—Recht auf Entwicklung," in Franz Nuscheler and Dieter Nohlen, eds., *Handbuch der Dritten Welt,* 3rd ed. (Bonn: J. H. W. Dietz Nachf., 1992), 269 – 86; Peter J. Opitz, ed., *Weltprobleme* (Munich: Bayerische Landeszentrale für politische Bildungsarbeit, 1990).

[51]Klaus J. Bade, *Ausländer—Aussiedler—Asyl: Eine Bestandsaufnahme* (Munich: C. H. Beck, 1994), 122.

[52]Klaus J. Bade, ed., *Das Manifest der 60: Deutschland und die Einwanderung* (Munich: C. H. Beck, 1993), 13, 20.

[53]Bernd Hof, "Arbeitskräftebedarf der Wirtschaft, Arbeitsmarktchancen für Zuwanderer," in Forschungsinstitut der Friedrich-Ebert-Stiftung, ed., *Zuwanderungspolitik der Zukunft* (Bonn: Forschungsinstitut der Friedrich-Ebert-Stiftung, 1992), 7–22; Wolfgang Klauder, "Deutschland im Jahr 2030: Modellrechnungen und Visionen," in Bade, ed., *Deutsche im Ausland—Fremde in Deutschland,* 455– 64; Horst Afheldt, "Sozialstaat und Zuwanderung," *PZG,* 12 February 1993, 42– 45.

[54]Claus Leggewie, "Das Ende der Lebenslügen: Plädoyer für eine neue Einwandersungspolitik," in Bade, ed., *Manifest der 60,* 55–60, 213–225; Cornelia Schmalz-Jacobsen et al., *Einwanderung—und dann? Perspektiven einer neuen Ausländerpolitik* (Munich: Knaur, 1993); and Werner Weidenfeld, ed., *Das europäische Einwanderungskonzept* (Gütersloh: Bertelsmann Stiftung, 1994).

[55]Peter Opitz, *Flüchtlings- und Migrationsbewegungen: Herausforderungen für Europa* (Munich: Forschungsstelle Dritte Welt, 1993); Heiko Körner, "Wanderungsbewegungen und ihre Ursachen: Süd-Nord-Wanderungen," in *Zuwanderungspolitik der Zukunft* (Bonn: Forschungsinstitut der Friedrich-Ebert-Stiftung, 1992), 33 – 40; Elmar Hönekopp, "Ursachen und Perspektiven: Ost-West-Wanderungen," Ibid., 23–32; Volker Ronge, "Ost-West Wanderung nach Deutschland," *PZG,* 12 February 1993, 16 –28; Manfred Wöhlcke, *Umweltflüchtlinge, Ursachen und Folgen* (Munich: C. H. Beck, 1992).

[56]Klaus J. Bade, "Von der Ratlosigkeit der Politik und der Sprachlosigkeit zwischen Politik und Wissenschaft," *Themen. Vierteljahreszeitschrift der Stiftung Christlich-Soziale Politik* 6 (4) (1991): 20f; Wilhelm Heitmeyer, "Multikulturelle Konfliktforschung als Beitrag zur Rechtsextremismus-Bekämpfung," in *Zusammenleben in einem multikulturellen Staat: Voraussetzungen und Perspektiven. Aufsatzsammlung zum Carl-Bertelsmann-Preis 1992* (Gütersloh: Bertelsmann-Stiftung, 1993), 39 – 49; Alois Wierlacher, ed., *Kulturthema Fremdheit. Leitbegriffe und Problemfelder kulturwissenschaftlicher Fremdheitsforschung* (Munich: Ludicium, 1993).

Throughout the 1980s, while the conservatives remained in power, the West German Left maintained its principled resistance to liberalism in the name of antinationalism. Even the Green Party's entrance in parliament had a dreamy, "apolitical" feel to it, as did the Euromissiles debate. While the German population was growing ever more attached to the institutions of liberal government, and therefore ever more comfortable expressing national feeling, left intellectuals drew further away. However understandable this reaction was, it had the unfortunate consequence (as Ernst Nolte, alas, rightly put it) of opening a chasm between the *pays légal* of German intellectuals and the *pays réel* of the German population. Hence the profound sense of shock in the aftermath of the events of 1989. The moment West and East Germans descended into the streets to march under common banners proclaiming *"Wir sind ein Volk,"* the illusion that East Germans had been happily pursuing a "third way" was shattered. Many Europeans expressed misgivings about such scenes and had reasonable reservations, mainly geopolitical, about unification. But a number of prominent West German intellectuals campaigned against unification on openly antinationalist grounds, Günter Grass first among them. And when Christa Wolf and Stefan Heym published their petition (*"Für unser Land"*), calling for the preservation of East Germany as a workshop for building the "third way," it evoked surprising sympathy among prominent West German intellectuals.

The difficulties facing the German state since unification are real enough, but left intellectuals continue to see in them nothing but the German past, not the new challenge of incorporating a formerly communist population into a legitimate liberal state. At some level they still consider that state to be illegitimate. A good example of this ambivalent attitude towards the Bundesrepublik, and now towards unification, is the work of Jürgen Habermas. Habermas remains the single most influential political thinker in Germany.

Mark Lilla

From "The Other Velvet Revolution: Continental Liberalism
and its Discontents"
Dædalus 123 (2) (Spring 1994)

Anne-Marie Le Gloannec

On German Identity

G ERMANY'S REUNIFICATION OR UNIFICATION—as the Germans prefer to call it—took place at a time when, following eight years of sound economic growth, the Federal Republic of Germany (FRG) seemed able to bear the anticipated financial burden. It also came after more than forty years of estrangement. Two states and two bureaucracies, two economic and social systems—two kinds of Germans—had developed, rendering more difficult the merging of Eastern Germany into the Western mold. While state authority had stifled individual initiatives and social organization in the former German Democratic Republic (GDR), making the East Germans dependent on West German imports and influences, the Federal Republic had become one of the liveliest democracies in the world, open to worldwide trends, largely closed to influences from the East. While East Germans yearned for a greater Germany, most West Germans forgot their Eastern brethren.

Nations, past and present, were and are the product of mobilization from above or from below, violent or pacific. Today, in Germany, little mobilization is at work, and the very notion of common interest seems to split up into a mosaic of particular interests. Is the lack of a clear German identity responsible for this?

Questions about a German identity are not new; they were pondered by nineteenth and twentieth-century intellectuals and politicians. In a country where borders and institutions changed dramatically over time, the *Volk* (people) became a mythical element of permanence, purportedly defining identity. In postwar Germany, divided into two states, questions about identity were common:

Anne-Marie Le Gloannec is Senior Researcher at Centre d'Etudes et de Recherches Internationales, Fondation Nationale des Sciences Politiques, Paris.

East Germans longed for a reunited nation; West Germans wavered between a European identity as a makeshift for Germanness and a quest for identity, for roots and things German. The West German identity could be described as markedly democratic and open, an intertwining of identities: local, German, European, predemocratic, democratic, and postmodern. Will German unification alter this combination? Will the addition of the East German *Länder* to the Federal Republic increase fragmentation, and will this open the door to a *völkisch* definition of identity? Or will it blend into a *Verfassungspatriotismus*, a democratic identity made up of various elements?

A NATIONAL REVOLUTION?

The revolution that brought down both the East German regime and the state in the autumn of 1989 founded a single German identity in two ways. First, on a symbolic level, it happened under the banner of unity, particularly after the Wall was opened on November 9, 1989. Whereas those who had called for democracy during the ceremonies celebrating the fortieth anniversary of the GDR in October sought to transform the regime while preserving an East German state and identity, those who took to the streets in November and December demanded nothing less than the demise of the GDR and Germany's unification. The former, democrats, claimed to be the people, the *Volk*: "*Wir sind das Volk*"—the demos, the *volonté constituante,* those peasants and workers whose state the GDR was supposed to be. The latter, also democrats, wanted to become citizens of the Federal Republic. For them, however, democracy was to be achieved through national unity, through the re-creation of a German entity embodying one German people, one *Volk*—"*Wir sind ein Volk*"—stressing ethnic filiation.

Second, the East German revolution brought about German unity not only symbolically but actually; unification took place with the demise of communism and of the East German state. Once the Wall was opened under the pressure of those who wanted to reform or transform the state, to establish democracy in this part of Germany,[1] the GDR as an independent entity was doomed. The East German elites, the so-called communist reformers or opponents of the re-gime, did not provide any sensible political program to revamp politics, economics, and society; the East German population did not structure itself into an independent body.

The East German revolution, as the founding element of German unity and of a single German identity, appears today a highly ambiguous event. Four years after unification, the German nation—the body politic, society, political culture—remains divided; unity, especially in the economic realm, only slowly bears fruit. Moreover, the nature and purpose of the East German revolution is a subject of controversy, dividing intellectuals and politicians, the Right and the Left, both in the East and in the West.

Ever since the opening of the Wall and the first demonstrations in favor of reunification, Germans, particularly German intellectuals, have wondered whether Germany's national revolution and unity were the product of nationalism, understood as an ethnic and cultural bond, or a strategy designed to catch up with Western standards of living: in other words, whether the yearning for national identity was of a "primordial," fundamentalist quality or of a "situational," utilitarian one.[2] For a number of politicians, mostly conservatives and a few Social Democrats such as Walter Momper, the Mayor of Berlin, and Manfred Stolpe, Minister-President of Berlin-Brandenburg, the East German revolution betokened the Germans' will to live together. Meanwhile, many intellectuals, including radicals like Bärbel Bohley, one of the principal actors in the October revolution in the East, or Otto Schily, a former member of the Green party in the West, looked down on the November revolution as a search for goods—for the deutsche mark and for bananas, the quintessential symbol of consumption. Disdaining the German revolution both for its national features—unity—and its practical purposes—consumption—they showed contempt for those who approved of unification.

Most advocates and opponents of unification erred, however, in the same way: instead of contrasting national and liberal options, they should have taken heed of the close interconnection. Unity was supposed to provide the means to achieve a better world, both at the micro- and the macrolevels: liberalism, economic and political, was to be extended to the Eastern part of Germany, thereby improving the living conditions of its inhabitants. Those, both in the East and in the West, who scornfully criticized the East Germans' lust for riches—for consumption—ignored the fact that wealth and democracy often do go hand in hand. The so-called economic miracle of the 1950s ingrained democracy in West German minds, opening up minds and spirits, providing for social mobility and integration in a Western, cosmopolitan world. Some West German intellectuals, critics of the critics, like Brigitte Seebacher-Brandt or Thomas Schmid, argued that those who despised the East Germans' reach for wealth shunned the very nature of the West German democracy.[3] Both Seebacher-Brandt and Schmid resented in particular the expression "*DM-Nationalismus*," which did no justice to the unification process.

Jürgen Habermas, who coined the phrase, did not ignore the twin character of unification: as a prepolitical process, it aimed at the reconstitution of national unity; as a democratic process, it allowed the East Germans to take part in a "politically happier and economically more successful development."[4] The expression "*DM-Nationalismus*" misled some because it focused on a kind of libidinal lust for the deutsche mark, passing over in silence its democratic component. Nonetheless, it pointed to the twofold nature of the East German revolution: national *and* democratic.

The quest for national unity and the assertion of national identity were not simply strategies intended to improve conditions. National unity and identity had been sustained for more than forty years in the Eastern part of Germany. In communist Germany, surrounded by the Wall, the Federal Republic became the obsessive measure of all things—acts and ideas. As the East Germans were made prisoners of their restrictive borders, the Federal Republic was the only foreign country to provide them with visitors, goods, news, and values. As a public space, a civil society was not allowed to emerge, stifled as it was by Party control on the one hand and privacy on the other (the so-called *Nischengesellschaft*[5]); West German images, information, values, and standards invaded East Germany. They nurtured both the culture and the counterculture. The latter would not have existed without West German support, both material— books and photocopy machines—and immaterial—standards and values.

Paradoxically, the counterculture could not flourish because of West German pervasiveness. A broad opposition could not take shape so long as those who opposed the regime were expelled to the Federal Republic and those who simply disagreed with the regime either sought to emigrate or continued to dream of reunification. Those opponents of the regime who managed to gain strength in the 1980s could only build upon West German foundations or withdraw into a bastion of socialist creed, the last one in Central Europe. In the absence of a structured civil society, the East Germans reacted in two ways when the Wall opened in the autumn of 1989. A majority wanted to appropriate those West German structures that had pervaded their lives. A tiny minority rejected this approach and pleaded for a socialist Germany, imagining that the only way to withstand West German standards lay in socialism.

As a result, the national question and the constitutional question became intimately intertwined.[6] As the communist regime had aimed at creating a *new* state and a *new* man, it had tried to sever the political and national ties that had linked the two parts of Germany. But by surrounding its subjects with a wall, stripping them of their rights, it undermined the independence both of state and society, and East Germany relied increasingly on a West German contribution. The Federal Republic became East Germany's exclusive opening to the world. Instead of consolidating an independent state, the Wall kept the national question afloat.

Most German intellectuals did not perceive the dialectic relation between the national question and the constitutional question. This misunderstanding reflects the aversion most German intellectuals have for such categories as nation, national identity, and national unity. For them, the "nation" is to be understood solely as a prepolitical phenomenon, not as a democratic one.[7] This perception is rooted in the fact that national reunification puts into question the very premises on which the two German states were based, as political and ideological constructs. In the case of the GDR, because it lost its legitimacy, according to a majority of East Germans, it had to disappear as a state. And even though the Federal Republic acquired over time a strong legitimacy of its own, its ideological foundations—from 1949 till 1990—were necessarily premised on the existence of a second German state: it was not and could not be a nation-state.[8]

As the unification process continues, the national question is again raised. The new Republic has to redefine its future as a nation-state *and* recover both the East German past and the past common to both states. In other words, unification entails the coupling, however uneven, of two ideological visions, two political and cultural projects, two different kinds of legitimacy and logic. It requires also the recovery of a common past. If the constitution of a national identity involves a common past and a common culture shared by those inhabiting a common territory, Germany's unification brings with it the need to redefine German identity.

TWO PASTS THAT NEVER DIE

The two German states were created as mirror images of each other, though both rested on ambiguous foundations. The Federal Republic, in claiming to embody the Reich from a legal point of view, sought to recover the territories lost to the communist regimes; politically and constitutionally, it wished to break with the Nazi past. The East German regime pretended to be an entirely new state, though it claimed to embody all the progressive forces in German history. Both, in fact, became the opposite of what they were supposed to be. The Federal Republic broke more radically with the past than did the GDR; it opened itself to liberal, cosmopolitan influences. The East German regime surrounded its society with a wall and anchored itself in illiberalism. With the disappearance of the GDR, the project, or the vision it was supposed to achieve, foundered. Yet, it lingers in certain ways.

First, the socialist ideal is still cherished by those few, mostly East German intellectuals, who deem socialism reformable. They continue to entertain an opposition between socialism and capitalism, between *Kultur* and *Zivilisation*, believing in a better German state even if their dream clashes with the reality of the GDR as it once existed. Heiner Müller, the famous playwright, epitomizes those for whom

> the so-called German "reunification". . .happens to be a colonization process. The former Federal Republic—a civilization economically overdeveloped and culturally underdeveloped—attempts to eradicate, by means of contempt and of bureaucracy, the culture which once flourished in the former GDR in opposition to Stalinist colonization.[9]

Second, the GDR existed as a counterproject, a reality outside rather than against the official political project, an apolitical

Nischengesellschaft, a *Gemeinschaft* (community) rather than a *Gesellschaft* (society). This GDR is thought to have drawn its virtues from a certain modesty of those who lived in that community, from a certain equalitarianism, a kind of moral superiority that echoes virtues that the socialist project was supposed to embody.[10] Its raison d'être as an apolitical community, protecting individuals against state control and providing them with necessary goods—material and immaterial—is vanishing in the new, open, competitive Germany. Still, it provides a kind of self-protection, even if only temporary, against the harshness of open competition.

One may wonder what remains of the political past: the socialist dreams, the societal reality. "This greatest sham on earth," as one prominent writer and opponent of the regime put it, may well have been all pretense and lies.[11] Eventually, the political heritage of the communist regime may require a tracking down of lies if the past is to be understood. *"Begreifen, was gewesen ist"* ("To understand what happened"): this is the plea a number of former opponents of the regime put forward in asking for a tribunal to be set up, to evaluate not only the nature of the regime but also the role of its victims, of all the ambiguous relations that existed.[12] A parliamentary commission, under the leadership of Reiner Eppelmann, was established to serve this end. Yet, as different pasts linger on in Eastern Germany, the task threatens to tear the former GDR apart, opposing, for instance, those who today support Manfred Stolpe, a former consistory President of Berlin-Brandenburg, who played a key role in defining church policy in the 1980s, and those who accuse him of having collaborated with the *Stasi.* Those who would distinguish between the regime and its victims confront those for whom such distinctions are blurred. To track down lies, to look for truth, may turn out to be impossible, at least in this generation.

In these various East German realities, past projects and present memories, the national dimension remained—and still remains—more or less unreflected while looming large on the horizon. The so-called socialist regime appealed to national feelings after the partition of Germany: in the 1950s, it sought to mobilize all national forces in both parts of the country to promote its own version of reunification. Later, it aimed at creating a new German nation, socialist as opposed to the capitalist one of Western Germany. In both cases, its purpose was to alleviate the rigors of socialism, to rally the East German population, appealing to such notions as *Heimat, Vaterland* or *Patriotismus*. Despite these efforts, many East Germans saw reunification as an alternative to partition and socialism, either because they deemed geopolitical transformations still possible, or because they considered individual emigration as a makeshift reunification.

In any case, the notion of nation had a positive connotation in the GDR. The regime certainly meant to break with fascism, but not with nationalism. Most communists who fought against German fascism did so under the banner of the German nation. They did not hold the nation responsible for Nazi crimes; Nazism, a mere variant of fascism, was dehistoricized (*enthistorisiert*).[13] Its essence was never revealed to the East German population. They felt exculpated, all the more so as they were themselves victims to history, to the arbitrary partition of the country, having been on the wrong side of the Iron Curtain. In the eyes of most, a socialist present was seen as a redemption from a Nazi past. For all these reasons, an undemocratic past survived in Eastern Germany; the country recalled a previous Germany that the West had more or less erased. Many in both East and West Germany, and elsewhere, felt it to be "the more German" of the two states.

Far from being considered as the source of evil, the nation was looked upon as a panacea, a cure for all miseries. For those who thought themselves prisoners of a regime they rejected, the nation was the road to democracy and the free market, the chief symbols of the West. National reunification and Westernization became synonymous. Surrounded by a Wall, some East Germans enjoyed their national dream; it served as an escape from a dreary reality but it also meant that most East Germans chose not to confront the past—an undemocratic past that still lingered on.

In the Federal Republic, a new political culture crystallized after the War under the influence of the victors and of those Germans, like Adenauer, who meant to ingrain democracy in the Western part of the divided country. They more or less discarded nationalism, brushing aside the very notion of nation. Though the FRG pretended to embody the Reich, its successive governments claiming to be the sole legitimate power on German soil, committed to recovering territories lost to communist regimes, it was also recognized to be a departure from the past. This contradiction was tenable so long as reunification seemed within reach, and democratization and reunification did not oppose one another. As reunification vanished from the realm of probabilities, the contradiction became obvious. Lest a united Germany follow a *Sonderweg*, shunning democracy, Adenauer chose to anchor the Western part of the divided country in the Atlantic alliance and in the European Community, opening German minds to Western influences. As a result, the Federal Republic became a "system" rather than a nation-state, a democratic state, not a nation.[14]

While reunification certainly remained a possibility, though a remote one for some West Germans, others increasingly discarded it. West Germans, living in an open and mobile society, part and parcel of the Western world, subject to democratic influences and global trends, looked upon the GDR as another world, closed and stale, with which they had few affinities, if any. In the early 1960s, the celebrated author Hans-Magnus Enzensberger stressed that "our identity is so irremediably lost that one may wonder whether we can still speak of a German nation. For someone who lives in Frankfurt am Main, New York is close whereas it is a psychological, political, and geographical expedition to go to Frankfurt an der Oder."[15] More than twenty years later, Patrick Süsskind, a member of the younger generation of West German writers, echoed his elder's remarks: "Otherwise we looked towards the West or the South. What could we be looking for in Leipzig, Dresden or Halle? Nothing, and for everything in Florence, Paris or London."[16]

Yet, a number of West Germans traveled to the GDR, searching for familiar roots, hoping to recover a German past, especially after the establishment of quasi-diplomatic relations between the two states, as the question of German identity came to the fore.[17] They saw the antiquated industrial and urban landscapes dating back to the beginning of the century which were, for them, ointment on a "wound named Germany."[18] A greater number, however, looked away, seeking comfort in the Western world. The East could never provide the sources of excitement available in the West. At best, it offered a hint of the past, precisely what some West Germans searched for, but what most shunned.

The West forged a counterpoint to Auschwitz, offering a modern and flawless present, a democratic and cosmopolitan social and political body, removed from the national past. The new Germany—

the Federal Republic—was devoid of asperity and national celebrations; it was smooth, odorless, colorless. In the 1950s, 1960s, and 1970s, many of the young claimed to be European; intellectuals toyed with the idea of emigrating. Hans-Magnus Enzensberger and Peter Schneider took up residence in Italy, Lothar Baier in France. Later, postmodernism and postnationalism became fashionable. Radical intellectuals came to believe that a postnational era was making headway in Europe, in the Federal Republic first and foremost.[19]

For both the general public and intellectuals, there was a denial of historical continuity, though the Federal Republic claimed to embody the Reich, and even though some historians and politicians sought to establish a continuity beyond the parenthesis of history, as the *Historikerstreit* proved. As a new democratic state, the Federal Republic offered more than a guarantee against the past; it provided, in a new sense, an escape from it. The past was confronted through reeducation programs and self-questioning. Public opinion rejected the past, pushed it aside to the periphery, but for most intellectuals, and not only Habermas and Günter Grass, the new Republic was the sole conceivable answer to Auschwitz, calling for a radical departure and the founding of a new state.

OLD QUESTIONS SET ANEW

Reunification must alter the nature of the Federal Republic. The united state is no longer a system, another form of government on German soil. It is a nation-state. Hence, its exceptional character as a radically new construct is mitigated. This change raises two questions. First, what is the nature of the new Germany? If it is not a system, is democracy now at risk? Second, what kind of filiation links the new state to any number of former German constructs? Is historical continuity being restored?

These questions, which shake the security progressively installed in forty years of division and bipolarity, are disconcerting to many intellectuals, but also to those West Germans who fear the consequences of unification. It is a mistake to imagine that West German public opinion resents unification only because of the economic costs involved. A part of West German public opinion—certainly among the better educated members of the middle class—shares some of the fear advanced by leftist intellectuals: that democracy will be endangered, or at least altered, that Germany as a Western, open, modern (or postmodern) society will change its character. Because of their undemocratic past, East Germans are likely to be tempted to tamper with it. The problems they confront are redolent of questions that the West Germans imagined they had resolved decades ago.

Unification is a merging of a community whose sole aim is to become a modern society, economically and politically, with a society that believed, to some extent at least, that it was postindustrial and postmodern.[20] The comfortable expectations of yesterday—of a West German middle class and of its intellectuals—are questioned: unification brings the Federal Republic back to the 1950s and 1960s when it was a less democratic society, striving to modernize. To put the matter bluntly, the East Germans appear to be the West Germans of yesterday. Yet, according to certain prominent intellectuals, democracy may itself be endangered, principally because of what they perceive to have been the undemocratic character of the unification process itself. While some East German writers—Heiner Müller and Christa Wolf, for example—see the process as sheer colonization, Jürgen Habermas, in the West, deplores the failure to sanction the change by a new constitution. A vote of all Germans, East and West, would have signaled the democratic will; it would have symbolized a democratic departure.

The fear of the traditional democracy being tampered with points to certain ambiguities in the attitude of some West Germans who, paradoxically, are reconciled with their own (Western) state at precisely the moment when it is being altered. As Seebacher-Brandt stresses:

> Those very commentators who did not know what to do—at least what to do in a positive way—with the Federal Republic as late as September 1985, discovered in September 1992 that they had a liking for this "dull, small, unloved, and practical state, the Federal Republic of Germany."[21]

Intellectuals who decry unification may be weeping, however discreetly, over the GDR. Though that regime never represented another reality for most West Germans, including West German intellectuals, it symbolized the fact that some other form of government might exist on German soil, that the Federal Republic was not the ultimate answer.[22] For those, in the East and the West, who deplored its death, the GDR was regretted less for what it was and more for what it might have been. Its demise symbolized the end of utopia, the end of other possibilities, the end of that "other, better Germany" that haunts German history. The Federal Republic became in a way the *real existierendes Deutschland*.

Unification raises questions also about historical continuity and discontinuity. For such a prominent opponent of unification as Günter Grass, the constitution of a single, national state means the return—"*eine Neuauflage*"—of history, the reemergence of a threatening power at the core of Europe:

> There would be no gain apart from an excess of power swollen by an increasing desire for more power. . . .A reunited Germany would be a complex colossus which would stand both in its own way and in Europe's way.[23]

Curiously, the Grass argument echoes one made by conservative historians; he appears to blame Nazism on geopolitics, choosing to ignore how institutions and ideology played their part in the rise of illiberalism. There is no mention of the fact that the new, democratic nature of the Federal Republic may provide a guarantee against the "return" of history.

Inevitably, the question of how to deal with the Nazi past again comes to the fore with the Federal Republic's incorporation of the GDR. Germans in the Eastern part of the country are obliged to confront it for the first time in fifty years. Yet, they risk overlooking it as they tackle the complex issues of unification. The Ravensbrück affair—the decision to build a supermarket on land bordering a former concentration camp—showed insensitivity. The rooting out of *Stasi* collaborators is, for many, taking precedence over denazification. In their desire to overcome or erase forty years of communism, Germans in both parts of the country may be tempted to establish a continuity between precommunist and postcommunist times, however questionable that may be. Some, for instance, who favor the reconstruction of the Berlin castle, blasted by the communists after the war, resort to arguments that ignore history. The publisher and essayist Wolf Jobst Siedler advocates its reconstruction on the ground that other cities and buildings—Warsaw and the

Campanile in Venice, for example—are mere trompe-l'oeil (*"Die Baugeschichte Europas ist eine Geschichte von Falsifikaten"*), putting on the same level natural catastrophes, the destruction of Warsaw by Nazi invaders, and the course of German history.[24]

While East Germans have to reflect on their past, communist and Nazi, the West Germans face a double, contradictory task. They have to stay aloof *and,* at the same time, incorporate the East German past into their own. Allowing the East Germans to ponder the nature of the communist regime and of East German society, without interfering, while at the same time putting their own history into question on the ground that both federal institutions and West German society shaped the course of East German evolutions, will prove a daunting undertaking. Though West Germans ought to refrain from judging East Germans, they have given the East Germans the means to understand and judge themselves, not least in (West) German courts. Inevitably, they intervene in the process. Yet, wishing to avoid painful self-doubt may lead them to behave as spectators, to skew their attitude towards East Germans, failing to question their own past attitudes and policies.

Thus, *Ost-* and *Deutschlandpolitik* remain, to some extent, a taboo subject: the West German public debate comes down to very little. There is an unwillingness to bare the ambiguities of a policy that relied on proximity to communist regimes, thereby fostering changes within both East German and East European societies and political systems (according to the formula *"Wandel durch Annäherung"*), while consolidating the status quo.[25] A parallel debate raging in East Germany on whether the Church stabilized the regime or promoted gradual changes, whether Manfred Stolpe, for example, or a prominent writer like Christa Wolf collaborated too closely, does not trigger self-analysis among the principal political parties in West Germany. Instead, there is a kind of cheap revision of history. The East German regime is denominated a dictatorship, a notion that all but vanished from the West German vocabulary after 1960. It is a way of pretending that the West German government and opposition always kept their distance. The West German political parties would rather not ponder the premises of their former policies towards the GDR: The Left wishes to blur the fact that it lost sight of reunification as the ultimate aim of

Deutschlandpolitik; the conservatives pretend that they always believed in reunification as a historical necessity.

DOES GERMANY NEED A NATIONAL IDENTITY?

As long as different pasts, real or imaginary, linger in Germany, there will be no single national identity. As long as the present and immediate futures do not merge, an East German identity will continue to loom large. While it seemed to vanish in the wake of the national revolution, it reemerged very quickly. Though 76 percent of East Germans looked upon themselves as such in November 1989, about the same percentage (73 percent) subscribed to the idea of there being a single German identity in April 1990.[26] Monetary, political, and legal unification produced surprising results. A year after the deutsche mark was introduced in the GDR, nine months after unity was proclaimed, 51 percent of those interviewed claimed to be East German while a minority (40 percent) proclaimed their German identity, though few regretted the demise of the GDR.[27] According to a 1993 poll, only 22 percent of West Germans and 11 percent of East Germans say they have a common identity.[28] As a rational strategy and an emotional construct, the idea of German identity, as opposed to East German identity, seemed initially to open access to West Germany and its goods, material as well as immaterial. As this perspective receded into a more or less distant future, as it became obvious that two types of Germans had been molded by forty years of democracy in the West and communism in the East, a greater number of East Germans insisted on their difference.

An East German identity became a symbol of defiance hurled at the West Germans; "*eine Trotzidentität*," an identity of defiance, as Jens Reich, one of the fathers of the East German revolution, put it.[29] As East Germans could not instantly become (West) Germans, they fell back on what they had been, stressing their differences from other Germans. Prominent East Germans, Manfred Stolpe and Katrin Krabbe, for example, rallied others; their previous actions, right or wrong, seemed irrelevant. An East German identity may be looked on as a sort of refuge, an illusory compensation, one might say "*eine Trostidentität*," an identity by default, an apolitical nostalgia, a utopia, what West Germany had been as a dream for over forty years. The difference, however, is that West Germany was a social and political reality that structured East German aspirations; East Germany is the past, and an East German identity is not today politically articulated. A "committee for justice," created in 1992, which assembled politicians from various groups, does not seem to have taken root for many of the same reasons that a structured opposition could not develop in the former GDR.

In the old *Bundesländer*, a comparable, though different, process has been taking place. Some West Germans, like Patrick Süsskind, for example, became fully aware of their attachment to the Federal Republic at the very moment it was subjected to change through unification. Was it a kind of West German patriotism, gratitude for the state and its institutions that had provided a democracy, or was it an attachment for things German? Was it a democratic preference or a prepolitical affect? Did it refer to a West German or to an all-German identity? It may have been more complex: West German and German, prepolitical and democratic, and, among the Left particularly, postnational, at least rhetorically.[30] In any case, it is a stable identity compared with the East German one; it is politically structured. Defiance, however, is not totally absent, both towards Germans in other parts of the country and towards foreigners, inside and outside Germany.

In both parts of the country, identity channels hatred, particularly among those who feel excluded from the political, economic, and societal system. In their eyes, a prepolitical notion of German identity becomes synonymous with a kind of national preference: as Germans, they feel that they ought to enjoy the benefits now shared with foreigners. They turn against Gypsies and Turks—and against those democrats who support the latters' rights—to underscore the fact that they are not the Gypsies and Turks of the better-off brethren. For them, bonds of kinship must prevail over the political, economic, and social links that the Federal Republic has made with immigrants. A *völkisch* notion of nation is preferred to the democratic principle of de facto integration.

While violence has flared up against foreigners less as a consequence of unification itself than of the social upheavals and redefinitions that the merging of two asymmetrical social bodies has produced, one may wonder whether Germany's role in Europe and in the world at large is indeed affected by this process. There is a danger in pointing too quickly at what is thought to be a revival of German nationalism in world affairs.[31] The Germans' understanding of their role is, nevertheless, colored by their understanding of their past and their identity. For a number of conservatives, unification is a return to normalcy: united, Germany is no longer exceptional; it is a country, like others, which has to fulfill obligations, including those prescribed by the UN Charter. Some intellectuals such as Arnulf Baring, Hans-Peter Schwarz, or Rainer Zitelmann even prescribe self-assertion.[32] Others, on the Left, deny such normalcy, which they fear would erase the exceptional character of Auschwitz.[33] The greater part of the political establishment, both Left and Right, interpret German history as a *Sonderweg*, the very particular path Germany is said to have taken from the middle of the nineteenth century till 1945.[34] The consequences flowing from this interpretation do not, however, oppose Left and Right; rather, they draw a dividing line within both Left and Right. For moderate conservatives as well as for some Social Democrats and Left intellectuals, such as Wolf Biermann or Hans-Magnus Enzensberger, the rejection of a *Sonderweg* requires the Federal Republic to integrate within the Western community, to fulfill its international obligations, including military ones. For national conservatives, however, self-assertion is said to take precedence over integration. For a greater part of the Left, the Federal Republic is asked to stay away from all military involvement: Germans are said to know what war means.

In order to ease Germany's integration of all Germans into a single society and the integration of the country in the post-Yalta world, some say that a new patriotism is needed. As the historian Christian Meier puts it, "What is at stake is the constitution of a broad *volonté constituante* which cannot be left to politicians alone." He goes on to ask, "How is it possible to create a new nation at the end of the twentieth century? What is meant by that?"[35] While nationalism as an ideology papers over differences among people it seeks to unite, the kind of enlightened patriotism that Christian Meier, Dieter Buhl, or, in a somewhat different way, Jürgen Habermas advocate may not be powerful enough to promote the kind of integration fostered, for example, in the nineteenth century.

In any case, patriotism cannot be thrust upon a people if it is not to remain a dead letter or become antidemocratic, denying popular sovereignty. For an identity to emerge in a united Germany, all Germans will have to share a common past and future. This will take time. The past will need to be analyzed and its present consequences reinterpreted, in accordance with a future vision, which will be democratic. The law on German citizenship, for instance, will have to be revised, since it is presently based on a historical rationale that is no longer valid. The jus sanguinis prevailed, first, because Germany over many centuries was a country characterized by uncertain borders and ever-changing institutions; second, because it had to include German populations fleeing communist regimes after World War II. It lost all relevance in post-1989 Europe because borders opened up, because the democratic bonds that linked German society to foreigners living on its soil were thought to have precedence, a request actually put forward by all those who demonstrated in Germany's major cities in the second half of 1991.

As democracy strengthens, past and future will be seen to be both one and multiple. They cannot be linear, deprived of all asperity and controversy. Different interpretations of past and future will coexist, just as there will be numerous circles of complex identities, German and East German, regional and European. Germany will be integrated when most Germans are recognized to have access to multiple choices. The task is more daunting than it was a century ago; democracy today is certainly not the mobilizing force nationalism was. The aim—the pursuit of democracy—makes the effort both worthwhile and necessary.

ENDNOTES

[1]And once, of course, the international situation—i.e., the evolution in the Soviet Union, Poland, and Hungary—allowed it.

[2]On the concept of national identity and its different meanings, see Anthony D. Smith, *National Identity* (London: Penguin Books, 1991), especially 20.

[3]Brigitte Seebacher-Brandt, *Die Linke und die Einheit* (Berlin: Corso bei Siedler, 1991), 27. One should note that Seebacher-Brandt, an academic and the last wife of the late Willy Brandt, is a maverick within the Left. In this pamphlet, she harshly criticizes the Social Democratic Party (SPD) for ignoring the national question. See also Thomas Schmid, "Die Eingeschlossenen von Jalta," *Kursbuch: Deutschland, Deutschland* (Berlin: Rowohlt) (109) (September 1992): 149–60.

[4]"*Nachholen will man, was den westlichen Teil Deutschlands vom östlichen vier Jahrzehnte getrennt hat—die politisch glücklichere und ökonomisch erfolgreichere Entwicklung*," in Jürgen Habermas, "Nachholende Revolution und linker Revisionsbedarf. Was heißt Sozialismus heute?," in Jürgen Habermas, *Die nachholende Revolution* (Frankfurt am Main: Suhrkamp, 1990), 181. See also Jürgen Habermas, "Citoyenneté et identité nationale. Réflexions sur l'avenir de l'Europe," in Jacques Lenoble and Nicole Dewandre, eds., *L'Europe au soir du siècle. Identité et démocratie* (Paris: Editions Esprit, 1992), 19.

[5]Günter Gaus, *Wo Deutschland liegt: eine Ortsbestimmung* (Hamburg: Hoffmann und Campe, 1983). Günter Gaus was the first representative of the Federal Republic to the GDR after the signing of the German-German treaty in 1972.

[6]Few have underlined this interconnection as clearly as the philosopher Dieter Henrich who stated that "*Die Forderungen nach der Einigkeit und nach der einen Währung gehen nämlich in ungebrochener Motivationslinie auf den Ruf nach Freiheitsrechten zurück.*" In Dieter Henrich, *Eine Republik Deutschland* (Frankfurt am Main: Suhrkamp, 1990), 21. See also Seebacher-Brandt, *Die Linke und die Einheit* and Schmid, "Die Eingeschlossenen von Jalta."

[7]As Jürgen Habermas puts it, "*...die nationale Frage (gerät) wieder einmal in Gegensatz zu Fragen republikanischer Gleichheit und sozialer Gerechtigkeit.*" Cf. Jürgen Habermas, "Nochmals: Zur Identität der Deutschen. Ein einig Volk von aufgebrachten Wirtschaftsbürgern?," in Habermas, *Die nachholende Revolution,* 215.

[8]All the more so as the Federal Republic was supposed to be a transitory state, a *Provisorium*, to disappear in a greater, reunified Germany.

[9]Heiner Müller, "Bautzen oder Babylon," *Sinn und Form* (4) (1991): 664; quoted by Horst Domdey, "Feindbild: BRD," *Kursbuch: Deutschland, Deutschland* (109) (September 1992): 67.

[10]As the West German historian Christian Meier correctly underlines: "*Da berief man sich auf die eigene Bescheidenheit, die relative Gleichheit, die 'Abschaffung der Macht des Geldes'. . .die bessere Moral, die Überlegenheit der Leidenden; oder man berief sich gut deutsch darauf, dass im Osten der Geist, im Westen dagegen nur das Geld sei. . . .Dazu gehört der—ja nicht unberechtigte—Stolz auf das Leseland DDR,*" in Christian Meier, *Die Nation die keine sein will* (Munich: Carl Hanser Verlag, 1991), 56.

[11]Günter Kunert, "Das Gespenst auf der Schulter," *Die Zeit* (21) (17 May 1991).

[12]Cf. J. Gauck, F. Schorlemmer, W. Thierse, W. Ullmann, R. Höppner et al., "Begreifen, was gewesen ist: Plädoyer für ein Tribunal," *Frankfurter Allgemeine Zeitung,* 23 January 1992.

[13]Domdey, "Feindbild: BRD," 68.

[14]"*Beide deutsche Staaten definierten sich, wenn auch gegensätzlich, so doch auf der Grundlage politischer und gesellschaftlicher Wertbezüge. Jedenfalls nicht national. . . .Die Bundesrepublik—das in der Bezeichnung des Gemeinwesens nachfolgende 'Deutschland' entfiel im politischen Vokabular des Alltags nicht zufällig—war vor allen Dingen ein Verfassungsstaat.*" Dan Diner, *Der Krieg der Erinnerungen und die Ordnung der Welt* (Berlin: Rotbuch Verlag, 1991), 51–52.

[15]Hans-Magnus Enzensberger, *Deutschland, Deutschland unter anderm. Äußerungen zur Politik* (Frankfurt am Main: Suhrkamp, 1967), 9.

[16]Patrick Süsskind, "Deutschland, eine Midlife Crisis," *Der Spiegel* (38) (1990): 116–25.

[17]Cf. Anne-Marie Le Gloannec, *La nation orpheline: Les Allemagnes en Europe* (Paris: Calmann-Lévy, 1989 and Pluriel, 1990), chaps. 2 and 3. See also Karl-Rudolf Korte, *Über Deutschland schreiben: Schriftsteller sehen ihren Staat* (Munich: Verlag C. H. Beck, 1992).

[18]*Die Wunde namens Deutschland: Ein Lesebuch zur deutschen Teilung* is the title of a book edited by Hedwig Walwei-Weigelmann (Freiburg: F. K. Kerle, 1981).

[19]As the philosopher Peter Sloterdijk puts it: "*Es wollte aussehen, als sei die deutsche Frage für immer suspendiert; eine Endform von Vorläufigkeit schien erreicht; die Stabilität in der Abstumpfung fand den Konsens der meisten.*" In Peter Sloterdijk, *Versprechen auf Deutsch, Rede über das eigene Land* (Frankfurt am Main: Suhrkamp, 1990), 11.

[20]As Michael Weck puts it: "*Dem Westen drohe unter dem Druck des autoritären Ostens die 'Verwilderung' seiner durch Verwestlichung 'gezähmten' politischen Sitten.*" Cf. Michael Weck, "Der ironische Westen und der tragische Osten," *Kursbuch: Deutschland, Deutschland* (109) (September 1992): 133.

[21]Seebacher-Brandt, *Die Linke und die Einheit*, 65. See also the exemplary article by Süsskind, "Deutschland, eine Midlife-Crisis," to which Seebacher-Brandt explicitly refers.

[22]Seebacher-Brandt again correctly underlines this point: "*Mehr noch, die Ressentiments gegen das eigene westliche Deutschland gediehen erst vor dem Hintergrund des Gegenbildes. Warum sonst wäre, als das Ende eingeläutet war, auf der Linken so sehr nach Hinterlassenschaften der DDR gesucht worden.*" Seebacher-Brandt, *Die Linke und die Einheit*, 64. See also Thomas Schmid, "*Ich glaube, man ist rücksichtsvoll, nachsichtig und milde mit der DDR umgegangen, weil man sie als imaginären Fluchtpunkt brauchte....Sie stand für die exterritoriale, im Wortsinne u-topische Idee des staatlichen Strebens nach dem Guten,*" in Schmid, "Die Eingeschlossenen von Jalta." On Germany as a utopia, see Le Gloannec, *La nation orpheline*, chap. 3.

[23]Günter Grass, *Deutscher Lastenausgleich. Wider das dumpfe Einheitsgebot. Reden und Gespräche* (Frankfurt am Main: Luchterhand, 1990), 8, 11.

[24]Wolf Jobst Siedler, "Berlin kommt um den Wiederaufbau des Schlosses nicht herum," *Die Zeit* (10) (5 March 1993). See on the same page, Ulrich Greiner's answer: "Weshalb Berlin um den Wiederaufbau des Schlosses herumkommt." See also previous articles and readers' letters, i.e., Manfred Sack, "Das Berliner Schloßgespenst," *Die Zeit* (52) (18 December 1992) and letters to the editor, *Die Zeit* (3) (15 January 1993).

[25]A few lone voices put *Ost-* and *Deutschlandpolitik* into question. See, for example, Seebacher-Brandt, *Die Linke und die Einheit*. See also Gesine Schwan, "Vom schwierigen Handeln in der Grauzone," *Die Zeit* (18) (24 April 1992).

[26]These polls were conducted by the Zentralinstitut für Jugendforschung, *Quo vadis Deutschland* (Berlin: Herbert-Quandt-Stiftung, May 1990). Quoted by Werner

Weidenfeld and Karl-Rudolf Korte, *Die Deutschen. Profil einer Nation* (Stuttgart: Klett-Cotta, 1991), 188.

[27]Elisabeth Noelle-Neumann, "Aufarbeitung der Vergangenheit der Stasi. Selbstgespräch und Wir-Gefühl in den neuen Bundesländern," *Frankfurter Allgemeine Zeitung,* 6 August 1992.

[28]Poll conducted by the Institut für Demoskopie, Allensbach, and quoted by Marc Fisher, "For Germans, a New Lesson About Walls," *International Herald Tribune,* 28 June 1993.

[29]Quoted in "Distanz, Enttäuschung, Hass," *Der Spiegel* (34) (17 August 1992).

[30]The historian Christian Meier underlines, however, that the Federal Republic was not a postnational construct precisely because it was on the verge of becoming a nation. Meier, *Die Nation die keine sein will,* 36.

[31]A certain public distrust in Germany of European integration or German foreign policy in the Balkans is accounted for by many different explanations.

[32]Arnulf Baring, *Deutschland: Was Nun?* (Berlin: Siedler, 1991); Hans-Peter Schwarz, *Die Zentralmacht Europas: Deutschlands Rütkkher auf die Weltbühne* (Berlin: Siedler, 1994); and Rainer Zitelmann et al., *Westbildung: Chancen und Risiken sür Deutschland* (Frankfurt am Main: Verlag Ullstein, 1993).

[33]See Jürgen Habermas, "Die zweite Lebenslüge der Bundesrepublik: Wir sind wieder 'normal' geworden," *Die Zeit* (51) (11 December 1992).

[34]A notion widely accepted by the political establishment while it is being increasingly put into question by historians.

[35]Meier, *Die Nation, die keine sein will,* 12, 29. See also the controversy opposing Robert Leicht, "Ohne Patriotismus geht es nicht," *Die Zeit* (5) (9 January 1993); Dieter Buhl, "Keine Angst vor dem P. Wort," *Die Zeit* (7) (12 February 1993); and Thomas Schmid, "Ein Vaterland der Bürger," *Die Zeit* (10) (5 March 1993) to Gunter Hofmann, "Patriotismus—nein danke!," *Die Zeit* (6) (5 February 1993).

Stephan Eisel

Political Dynamics in Germany

I MAGINE YOURSELF AT HOME ON CHRISTMAS DAY, celebrating with your family, when suddenly you hear a knock at the door. The visitors turn out to be relatives, people with whom you exchange Christmas cards, but otherwise you have not had much contact with them in the last few years. They ask if they can come in; they have lost their home and need a place to stay.

You are only too glad to help, and happy to see them. You bring out your best bottle of wine. Of course they are welcome to stay for a few days; there is plenty of room. But later, after two or three weeks, you start to grow a little uneasy: Your relatives seem to like it at your house, and they are making themselves at home. The visitors have turned into housemates, who expect not only a share of your sympathy but also of your belongings.

From the visitors' point of view, however, the host who initially was so generous and hospitable is now becoming a kind of authoritarian master of the house. At first, it does not matter what is served, but the longer meals have to be shared, the more important the question becomes of what there is to eat, and who chooses the menu. Anyone wanting to grasp the psychological situation in Germany after unification would do well to keep this image in mind.

CONTINUITY AND CHANGE

Affluent West Germany feels that its peaceful existence has been considerably disrupted and that it must constantly confront new

---

Stephan Eisel is Director of the Political Academy of the Konrad-Adenauer-Foundation, Germany.

167

demands and expectations. East Germany, milked dry for decades, tends to compare its situation not so much with conditions under the communist regime but with the far better conditions in the West. In addition, the emotions of many in both the East and the West are dominated by conflicting desires to reach out to one another and to seal themselves off. Here a renaissance of the German Democratic Republic (GDR) identity promoted by interested groups has its counterpart in Western nostalgia for the clear-cut conditions that existed before the Wall came down. In this ambivalent mood, the anxious feeling of uncertainty in the face of rapid change often dominates over the sense of satisfaction at the collapse of communism and optimism about the opportunities that this has opened up.

These new shifts in balance between the desire for continuity and change are currently determining the political climate in reunified Germany. Central political questions are characterized increasingly by disagreement over what *ought* to remain the same and what ought to be changed: Does German reunification mean a transformation of the whole society, or rather an extension of tried-and-true policies to new areas? Does it mean change first and foremost, or does it mean adjustment? How has unification affected political institutions, the political atmosphere, and the political balance of power? How have the political parties reacted? Where are they capable of change? Where do they embody continuity? Are citizens still prepared to accept them in their traditional forms? Will Germany retain its inner orientation toward the West and its foreign policy ties to its Western allies?

These questions have the urgency of the new and unforeseen. Germans perceive unification less as a return to normality, the end of an exceptional state of affairs, than as a *departure* from normality. Only slowly are people realizing that what they took to be an exceptional situation is actually the new norm, and that the new unity will be the lasting foundation of their society. For this reason, genuine discussion about the shape Germany's future domestic and foreign policies should take has begun only recently, in a delayed reaction.

Within Germany, the forty-year division of the country had long since come to seem the norm. Although the high percentage of West Germans declaring their support for the constitutional aim of reunification remained constant (70 percent), the population had in fact begun to accept partition as a given. One-third of West Germans regarded the GDR as "a foreign country," and during the 1980s only half considered Germans in the GDR to be "fellow countrymen." When Willy Brandt—whose career as a politician was closely tied to the German question, not least through his years as mayor of Berlin—declared in 1988 that "the hope of reunification" had become "the living lie of the Second German Republic," he expressed a widely held view.

CHANGES WITHIN AND WITHOUT

The question of a divided Germany was an issue of freedom rather than of national feelings. The peaceful East German revolution is said to have taken its starting point here. The chant "*Wir sind das Volk*" ("We are *the* people") came before "*Wir sind ein Volk*" ("We are *one* people"). The unnatural border running through Germany, fortified by the Wall, barbed wire, and armed guards with orders to shoot, had created a sense of isolation. And the intimidating effect of half a million Soviet troops stationed on GDR territory was enough to finally bring down the communist regime.

The urge to escape the clutches of the government remained strong in 1989, despite the considerable relaxation of travel restrictions achieved in the 1980s by the Kohl government. Whereas in 1982 only about fifty thousand citizens of the GDR below retirement age were permitted to travel to the West, the number had risen to 240,000 in 1986, 620,000 in 1987, and more than one million in 1988. During this period, the communist regime determined which citizens would be allowed to travel; permission to leave the country was not a basic right but a favor dispensed after careful calculation. For example, all members of a family were not permitted to leave the country at the same time, in order to ensure the travelers' return.

When the Wall came down and free travel and permanent settlement in the West became possible, an unprecedented number of people voted with their feet: As late as August 1989, the regime had allowed only 683 people to move permanently to the West; and the opening of the Hungarian border led to the departure of fifty-five thousand East Germans in September and twenty-one thousand in

October. When the Wall came down, the numbers increased dramatically: 157,813 in November; 54,000 in December; 73,729 in January 1990; 63,893 in February, and 46, 241 in March—it should be noted that these figures reflect emigrants, not vacationers planning to return.

This mass migration, of the young and highly educated, created such intense internal political pressure that the free elections to be held in the GDR in May 1990 were moved up to March, and their unexpectedly clear mandate for the mainstream democratic parties, the Christian Democrat "Alliance for Germany," proved beyond all doubt that communist rule had ended for good. The results of this election also made it possible to proceed swiftly with currency union, without which it would have been difficult or impossible to stem the tide of emigration. By December 1989, East Germans were already marching at demonstrations with banners that read, "*Kommt die DM, bleiben wir, kommt sie nicht, geh'n wir zu ihr!*" ("If the deutsche mark does not come to us, then we will go to it!")

People in the West followed the collapse of the communist regime as if they were at the movies, watching a historical documentary. Even in the climactic months in the autumn of 1989, when the now famous demonstrations were taking place every Monday in the East, there were no mass demonstrations or rallies in the West. Westerners experienced the precipitous developments in the East through the filter of the media, and many have already repressed the dramatic nature of these events. The question so frequently heard today—"Did it all have to happen so fast?"—is prompted by emotions that totally neglect the momentum of the real situation only a few years ago. Television brings epochal events into our living rooms, and with constant repetition, they become humdrum and banal. Furthermore, the East German feeling of being "shut in" had no counterpart in a Western sense of being "shut out." Although the Communist Party's policy of sealing off East Germany drove its own citizens to rebellion, it proved effective in the West. Even today, the flow of visitors from West to East remains far smaller than from East to West.

The disintegration of the Soviet Union and Yugoslavia and the breakup of Czechoslovakia took place virtually simultaneously with the unification of Germany. Although the Germans certainly benefited from the breakdown of communism, they did not initiate the events that destabilized what appeared to be a firmly entrenched system in Central and Eastern Europe. Without Solidarnosc, without the opposition movement led by Václav Havel in Czechoslovakia or the opening of the Hungarian border in August 1989, Honecker would surely not have been toppled so quickly. For the Germans, unification thus involved changes both inside and outside their "home," which they had been able to design with full freedom only between 1918 and 1933. It is as if, while they were preoccupied with remodeling indoors, the landscape outside was undergoing an equally thorough transformation, particularly to the East. Suddenly their formerly distant relatives are sharing the house with them, and the windows of the newly furnished living room no longer look out on the familiar landscape. The security of the old status quo has vanished.

GETTING A GRIP ON CHANGE

The reality of German unity is still difficult for many to grasp, precisely because it seemed an utterly illusory goal for so long. And the sense of unreality is reinforced by the fact that West Germany's political scene has altered: the old tension between the desire for political stability and the need for reform is seeking a new equilibrium.

After Germany's dramatically new course was set in the postwar period, the decade of the 1960s saw the growth of structural stability in the old Federal Republic. Political opposition to these structures began with the student protest movement and carried over to the reformist euphoria of the Social Democratic Party-Free Democratic Party (SPD-FDP) coalition governments of the early 1970s. Dynamism and change had become political goals in their own right. The mood of the public focused on breaking up rigid structures, creating forward motion in a society that had grown all too static.

Chancellor Willy Brandt's philosophy of reform that emerged from this was fueled by a general impetus for social change, but in the last analysis was based on faith in the efficacy of government to solve problems. It progressed very little beyond the stage of mere rhetoric and was followed by the "caretaker" government of Helmut Schmidt. It is difficult to recall any significant impulses or initiatives from his time in office. Maintaining a deteriorating status quo became the goal of his chancellorship: crisis management instead of creative policies.

This provided the background for the Christian Democrats' program under Helmut Kohl's leadership in the early 1980s, which concentrated on overcoming the economic crisis and reshaping society. Successful achievement of the latter aim in particular has brought about profound changes in Germany's social and political landscape. Before 1982, such ideas as government paid and guaranteed leave for parents (*Erziehungsgeld und Erziehungsurlaub*), privatization of radio and television, the introduction of cable television, lead-free gasoline, and recycling programs were at best little more than political slogans; now they characterize everyday reality.

Through such changes in many areas, West German society became a society on the move. With continuing economic growth in a secure and familiar setting, these reform goals satisfied the general desire for a better, freer, more responsible and humane society, and an improved quality of life.

While in theory unification remained their greatest wish for change, it was considered totally unlikely to happen. When this wish was fulfilled, however, voters' priorities suddenly shifted. The achievement of German unification seemed to transform so much, to alter the appearance of so many familiar things, that citizens began turning to their politicians with the appeal, "Give us something stable to hold on to!" The practical need and political desire for change are running up against the voters' need for stability and security. This will remain the case for some time. Unification set processes in motion that have not yet slowed to any significant degree.

A NEW RELATIONSHIP: FROM NEIGHBORS TO PARTNERS

Unification has brought together two very different societies with very different structures. Overall, the population of the Federal Republic of Germany (FRG) has increased approximately 25 percent, from about sixty-three million to seventy-nine million inhabitants. The territory of the Federal Republic increased by 24 percent.

If we take the three-fourths to one-fourth ratio of the two population groups as a basis, differences become evident between East and West in such areas as generational structure, marital status, and religious orientation (see *Table 1*).[1]

TABLE 1. West-East Ratio in Reunified Germany (in percentages)

	West	East
Population		
Total population		
(79.6 million)[2]	75.7 %	24.3 %
Estimated population in 2040		
(73.4 million)	84.3	16.7
Generational Structure[3]		
Over sixty-five years of age		
(11.8 million)	79.4	21.6
Over eighty years of age		
(3.0 million)	82.0	18.0
Under fifteen years of age		
(12.9 million)	75.7	24.3
Marital Status		
Single[4]		
(30.2 million)	79.9	20.1
Married		
(38.5 million)	79.1	20.9
Widowed		
(7.6 million)	70.4	29.6
Divorced		
(3.6 million)	72.6	27.4
Religion[5]		
Catholic		
(27.6 million)	96.7	3.3
Protestant		
(29.1 million)	86.1	13.9

Only slightly more than 50 percent of the people in the new *Länder* are members of a religious denomination (46 percent of the total population are Protestant, 7 percent are Catholic), while in the West over 80 percent of the population has a religious affiliation (divided evenly between Protestant and Catholic). Eighty-six percent of school pupils and students in institutions of higher learning say they have no religious affiliation; in the West it is only 16 percent. The often heard statement that Germany has become a more Protestant country through unification is not accurate. In truth, it has become more secular: in the West only about 54 percent describe themselves as "religious"; in the East, where the Reformation began, it is barely 33 percent. In the West, 20 percent of the population responds to the question of how often they go to church with "never"; in the East it is 46 percent. Ninety-two percent of the children born in the West are baptized, as compared to 36 percent in the East.

It is not only with regard to objective data, however, that East and West Germany show profound differences; many differences in attitude exist as well. Various polls taken in 1990 show that in the new *Länder* significantly greater importance is attached to values such as hard work, security, ambition, job performance, prosperity, and property than in the West. It will be interesting to see whether this evens out, and how long it will take.

Among the areas where developments in East and West Germany have differed widely is the percentage of foreigners. Two years before unification, foreigners comprised only 0.3 percent of the population of the GDR (2.8 percent if one includes Soviet military personnel), whereas in the West the figure was 6.8 percent. The social status of foreigners in the East and the West also differed. In the East, most foreigners belonged to privileged groups, such as the military personnel of the Warsaw Pact countries and their families and the small number of university students from developing countries. In the West, the majority of foreigners were, and still are, "guest workers" in average blue-collar jobs.

Meanwhile, the percentage of foreigners in Germany as a whole has risen to 7.3 percent: approximately 5.8 million in the West, only 110,000 in the East. The largest contingent is 1.8 million Turks, followed by about 1 million from the former Yugoslavia, 500,000 Italians, 350,000 Greeks, and 290,000 Poles. Almost half have resided in Germany for fifteen years or more. By and large they have been successfully integrated into German society. Approximately 11 percent of the children born in Germany have foreign parents, another 5 percent have one German and one foreign parent. Approximately 140,000 people a year become German citizens, a significant rise since the immigration laws were liberalized in 1990. Approximately 1.8 million Germans have dual citizenship (a status that an international treaty recommends should not be granted), most of them the offspring of binational marriages.[6]

The subject of foreigners has become politically controversial in recent years, largely because Germany's prosperity made the country a magnet for immigrants. Immigration was made easier by very liberal regulations on political asylum, especially because the mere request for asylum was coupled with a right to remain in the country. The opening of the borders to the East played an important role in this context. One hundred and ninety-three thousand people sought asylum in 1990; 256,000 in 1991; and 400,000 in 1992. In addition, immigrants of ethnic German origin were arriving from Poland, Rumania, and the former Soviet Union at the rate of two to three hundred thousand per year.

The most important motive for immigration to Germany—which receives more than 60 percent of the applications for political asylum in the European Community—is certainly the hope of increased prosperity. But Germany has been particularly affected by the wave of refugees fleeing from the war in the former Yugoslavia; it has taken in eight times as many refugees from that area as all other countries combined.

In order to stem the tide of immigration from economic motives, the political parties agreed after long discussions in the spring of 1993 on a constitutional amendment that limits abuse of the asylum laws. The decision was highly controversial and required a correction of their policy by the Social Democrats, as a two-thirds majority is needed to amend the constitution.

This compromise, preceded by years of discussion, was overshadowed by a wave of violence against foreigners beginning in 1990.[7] A small percentage of these crimes was carried out by organized political extremists: only about one-quarter of the suspected perpetrators are estimated to belong to extreme right-wing groups.[8] Various studies have shown that almost three-quarters of the suspected perpetrators of such crimes are between fifteen and twenty years old; only 8 percent are older than twenty-five. Studies in the new *Länder* have even documented that between one-half (in Berlin) and two-thirds (in Saxony) are between the ages of fourteen and eighteen. Without doubt, such violence presents a particularly grave problem for German society.

AN ECONOMY UNDERGOING STRUCTURAL CHANGE

The differences between East and West Germany are particularly marked in the economic sector. This has a significant effect on politics because the extent of the economic catastrophe in the GDR was underestimated by the West and probably by the ruling class in the GDR as well. The propaganda of earlier years—that the GDR was the leading industrial country in Eastern Europe—has taken its toll.

After the opening of the Wall in 1989, Hans Modrow, the last Communist premier of the GDR, estimated the country's total wealth at around DM 1,500 billion. Lothar de Mazière, the Christian Democrat who succeeded Modrow after free elections and later worked to promote unification, corrected the estimate downwards to DM 800 billion. After unification on October 3, 1990, Carsten Rohwedder, a successful executive from the steel industry, took over leadership of the Treuhand, the agency created to privatize the state-owned industries of the GDR. At that time the Treuhand estimated the total value of the more than nine thousand state-owned enterprises with over forty thousand production sites at DM 500 billion.

Shortly before he was assassinated by left-wing terrorists in the spring of 1991, Rohwedder predicted that assets and liabilities would roughly cancel each other out. In the autumn of 1992, his successor, Birgit Breuel, presented a closing balance with a deficit of at least DM 420 billion. Of this sum, approximately 250 billion represented losses incurred through privatization of state industries, 28 billion came from the national debt of the GDR, and about 110 billion was attributed to the cost of the currency union. An additional 30 billion must be added from the still unpaid costs of public housing construction in the GDR.

The political mood in Germany has altered as awareness of the actual extent of this deficit has grown. It has become increasingly clear that paying off the burden inherited with unification involves sacrifices from everyone. The West Germans, the vast majority of whom were born or grew up during the era of the Wall, are learning about the rest of their country only slowly. And the words of the East German writer Christoph Hein spoken in November 1989 still apply to many citizens of the former GDR: "We have been living in a country that we are only now getting to know."[9]

Despite the staggering figures, it is impossible to express the total inherited burden in purely monetary terms. The infrastructure was badly underdeveloped; roads and railway lines were in a state of disrepair, such that trains could often travel no faster than a few miles per hour. Untreated toxic wastes were dumped into rivers, large industrial complexes were built without air filters or water purification systems, and radioactive wastes were stored without special precautions. Every atomic power station in the GDR had to be shut down for safety reasons after unification. Forty percent of the multi-family dwellings in the GDR needed major repairs; 11 percent were uninhabitable by the standards of the old Federal Republic. Between 1989 and 1993 the number of telephone outlets had to be doubled (at a cost of DM 60 billion), since previously only slightly more than 25 percent of all households had been equipped with a telephone (compared to 98 percent in the West).

In light of all this, it is not surprising that levels of economic productivity in the old and new *Länder* differ so greatly. In 1991, productivity in East Germany averaged DM 12,000 per capita, in West Germany DM 41,000 per capita. Productivity in the manufacturing and service sectors in particular was significantly higher in the West.

The social consequences of economic restructuring that entailed a rapid reduction of jobs in the overrepresented primary and secondary sectors have affected many in the new *Länder*. To make matters worse, it takes longer to create new jobs than to eliminate old ones. The resulting unemployment, easily translated into a sense of hopelessness, is the greatest political problem in the new *Länder*.

The need to restructure the economy is not limited to the eastern part of Germany, however. West Germany has encountered considerable problems in remaining economically competitive, particularly in the growth industries of the future (biotechnology and information technology). The causes of these problems lie in the rigid structures of an affluent society and have little to do with unification,[10] but the economic crisis in the East has increased general awareness of Western problems. In this context it should be noted that in the new *Länder* the investment rate (the ratio of investment to gross domestic product, [GDP]) was 42 percent in 1991, rose to 46 percent in 1992, and is expected to be over 53 percent in 1993— these are unprecedented figures in German economic history.

BUILDING UP THE EAST COMES BEFORE EXPANSION IN THE WEST

Closing the gap between the East and the West is the pressing issue of the present. For example, almost 40 percent of households in the West have a monthly income of more than DM 4,000, while the corresponding figure in the East is 10 percent. Monthly incomes of under DM 2,000 are reported by 17 percent of households in the West and by 44 percent in the East. In 1989, the average wage earner in the GDR received only 35 percent of his West German counterpart's wage; by 1993 net pay in the East had risen to 69 percent of that in the West. Complete wage parity will take some years to achieve. Despite evidence of an improved economic situation in the East, polls have revealed a troubling contradiction: on one hand, almost half the population of the East affirm that they can afford to buy more since reunification—only 15 percent say their prosperity has declined; on the other hand, approval of a market economy has dropped dramatically—from 77 percent in the spring of 1990 to 44 percent in the summer of 1992.

In the autumn of 1992, Helmut Kohl proposed a Solidarity Pact. Kohl appealed to the West to replace the goal of economic growth with that of economic consolidation and to give the rebuilding of the East precedence over expanding the economy in the West. The Solidarity Pact, approved by a consensus of all mainstream parties, foresees a large scale redistribution of wealth. The Bundesbank has calculated that the net contribution of West German taxpayers will amount to DM 107 billion for 1991, DM 115 billion for 1992, DM 129 billion for 1993, DM 139 billion for 1994, and DM 155 billion for 1995. This reflects more money being transferred every year than the total Marshall plan distributed to all receivers. With sums of this size being transferred, the Kohl government has initiated cuts and consolidation measures above and beyond the Solidarity Pact, in order to keep the national debt within acceptable limits.

DECENTRALIZATION AS A FORCE FOR UNITY

Passage of the Solidarity Pact, requiring a consensus of the political parties in the *Bundestag* and the approval of the *Länder*, put to test the federal structure of the German government. As *Table 2* indicates, however, the federal structure, made up of the eleven old

Länder and the five new *Länder,* contains significant imbalances with regard to size and economic well-being.

TABLE 2. West-East Ratio in Unified Germany

Land	Population (in millions)	Governing Party/ Coalition	Budget Deficit (in percentages)	Population (per square km)
North Rhine-Westphalia	17.3	SPD	8.7%	502
Bavaria	11.4	CSU	4.1	159
Baden-Württemberg	9.8	CDU/SPD	7.3	269
Lower Saxony	7.4	SPD	8.7	154
Hesse	5.7	SPD/Greens	7.7	268
Rhineland-Palatinate	3.8	SPD/FDP	7.2	186
Berlin	3.4	CDU/SPD	16.0	3,860
Schleswig-Holstein	2.6	SPD	9.3	165
Hamburg	1.6	SPD/ Independents	13.3	2,153
Saarland	1.1	SPD	15.2	414
Bremen	0.7	SPD/FDP/ Greens	16.8	1,667
Saxony	4.8	CDU	15.9	267
Saxony-Anhalt	2.9	SPD/Greens[11]	14.8	145
Brandenburg	2.6	SPD/FDP/ Greens	26.5	91
Thuringia	2.6	CDU/SPD	18.0	165
Mecklenburg-Vorp.	1.9	CDU/SPD	19.3	82

These numbers suggest that the smaller *Länder,* old and new, are probably too small to be economically viable. Only Berlin and Brandenburg are currently holding negotiations about merging. A United Europe will make the restructuring of the German *Länder* all but inevitable.

Failure to deal with such matters in a timely fashion is likely only to swell the problems of the future as indicated by recent redistricting experiences in the new *Länder.* In the unification negotiations, the historical divisions that had existed prior to 1945 were taken as the standard. That made the debate all the more heated when, in 1993, administrative redistricting proved necessary.

The federal structure, with its decentralization of power and the participation of all mainstream parties at the *Land* and community levels, has proved to be a strong unifying force in both the East and the West. The *Länder*, singly and in combination in the *Bundesrat*, tend to stress their independence from the federal government. Amendments have been made to the constitution, giving the *Länder* a stronger voice in decisions pertaining to European integration, and almost every *Land* now sends its own representatives to Brussels.

THE PAST AS A TEST IN THE EAST AND THE WEST

Among the political parties, the Social Democrats got off to the slowest start in unified Germany. A significant contributing factor was the group's acceptance of the division of Germany: it was cited again and again as grounds for Germany to pursue its own path of neutrality between Eastern and Western alliances. One can hardly claim that the Christian Democratic Union/Christian Social Union (CDU/CSU) unwaveringly pursued unification as a concrete political goal, but they persisted in keeping the option of unity open as a question of freedom and democracy. Helmut Kohl's record on this point is particularly convincing: Even during Honecker's state visit in 1987 Kohl expressed his disapproval of the communist regime in East Germany in a widely quoted after-dinner speech.

By contrast, the SPD followed a strategy of effecting "change through rapprochement" (Egon Bahr) in the years from 1984 to 1987, going so far as to participate in joint working groups and to issue joint papers with the Socialist Unity Party (SED). Only a short time before the collapse of the GDR, the SPD was still urging recognition of GDR citizenship. During the *Bundestag* election campaign in late 1990, the SPD leader Oskar Lafontaine's evident skepticism regarding unification stuck in the minds of voters in the new *Länder*. The first *Bundestag* elections in unified Germany resulted in a clear victory for Helmut Kohl and his coalition.

The great majority of delegates from the new *Länder* are newcomers to politics. A large number are engineers, physicians, and clergymen—professions with virtually no previous representation in West German politics. Those who had been in public life before 1989 or held political office under Communist rule had lost all political credibility. The debate over the past has become particularly acrimonious in the East, where activists from the opposition movement against the old GDR government continue their sharp questioning of former members of the Communist state establishment.

One such example is Arnold Vaatz (CDU), Minister of the Environment in the state government of Saxony, who has kept Manfred Stolpe (SPD), the premier of Brandenburg, under considerable pressure to explain earlier statements. Vaatz makes it well known that while he was serving a prison sentence as a critic of the regime in the mid-1970s, Stolpe received permission to travel to Geneva to a meeting of the Protestant World Federation in 1976 as a representative of the East German churches. There Stolpe delivered a speech in which he said:

> Freedom of movement in the GDR has been clearly established and is regulated by law. It has been fully achieved within the country despite considerable housing problems in the major cities. Very few restrictions apply to travel to neighboring socialist countries; in some cases no visa is required. According to the law, travel to capitalist countries must be approved. Such approval is granted at the discretion of the authorities. It is granted as a rule for business trips, to citizens above the retirement age, and in cases of family emergency. General permission to travel for all citizens is not possible at the present time. It would immediately trigger an objective defense mechanism, to which a large number of people, blinded by the false lure of prosperity, might well succumb—causing considerable harm to society and thus all its members.[12]

Despite such statements and his former contacts with the State Security Service (*Stasi*), Stolpe remains in office and continues to receive high approval ratings in the polls. Many citizens of the former GDR can identify with his ambivalent role in GDR times. Other leading politicians of the transition era, Ibrahim Böhme, party chairman of the East German SPD prior to unification, and Lothar de Mazière (CDU), the last premier of the GDR, for example, did not survive revelations of their activities in the GDR. Connections to the *Stasi* played a major role in both cases. This secret agency employed more than eighty thousand people and had the additional services of some five hundred thousand "unofficial" informants.

The question of involvement with the Communist system, particularly the *Stasi*, has continued to determine more than just the political debate. It has also played a crucial role in the merging of the police forces and the armies. The unified army refused to accept East German officers above the rank of colonel. East German generals and admirals were discharged, as were a total of 67 percent of officers and 58 percent of career soldiers.[13] The officers who found employment in the army of the Federal Republic were demoted by at least one rank, and it will be at least eight years before the first former East German soldier can be promoted to the rank of general.

THE ROLE OF POLITICAL PARTIES IN INTEGRATING THE TWO GERMANYS

The dictatorship of 1933, followed by Communist rule until 1989, eradicated any preexisting democratic structures in East Germany. Citizens voting in the parliamentary elections of 1989 had to be at least seventy-nine years old to have voted in the last free election in 1932. This is reflected in the very low membership rates achieved by the SPD, the CDU, and the FDP. The only party with a solid base in East Germany is the Party of Democratic Socialism (PDS), the successor of the SED. It has 146,000 members, only two thousand of whom live in the West. How these former Communist Party members should be treated is one of the most controversial questions in contemporary German politics. The CDU, acting on the initiative of its state organizations in the East, has refused to accept former Communists as members, but this policy is repeatedly debated within the party. The SPD and the FDP have accepted former SED members from the start.

Approximately ninety-eight thousand of the 714,000 members of the CDU[14] live in the East, as do approximately fifty thousand of the total FDP membership of 110,000. Both the CDU and the FDP merged with former "block parties," allegedly independent parties allowed to exist in the GDR but co-opted by the Communists in 1948.[15] The SPD encountered no natural partner among the existing parties in the East, as the old SPD had merged in 1946 with the prewar Communist Party of Germany (KPD) to form the ruling SED. When, in the summer of 1989, an opposition group in the GDR revived the SPD, calling itself the SDP, West German Social Democrats gave them the cold shoulder. Today only about twenty-five thousand of the SPD's 902,000 members are to be found in the new *Länder*.

Approximately 2,700 people belong to the "Alliance '90," which failed in its aim to collect the various opposition groups under one banner. The opposition group "New Forum" dominated the transition period, but as its leadership (Bärbel Bohley) remained independent and mistrustful of organized politics, its large membership distributed itself among the other parties.

In general, all parties are experiencing a membership imbalance, each being overrepresented in one part of the country and underrepresented in the other (see *Table 3*). This situation is unlikely to change in the near future.[16]

TABLE 3. West-East Ratio in Reunified Germany (in percentages)

	West	East
Politics		
Eligible voters		
(60.4 million)	79.8%	20.2%
Party Membership		
CDU/CSU		
(895,000)	89.1	10.9
SPD		
(902,000)	97.3	2.7
FDP		
(110,000)	54.6	45.4
Alliance '90/Greens		
(38,000)	90.3	9.7
PDS		
(146,000)	0.5	99.5
Republicans		
(20,000)[17]	75.0	25.0

1994: A YEAR OF DECISION

Trends in the political landscape of reunified Germany were set in the "super"-election year 1994, when nineteen separate elections took place for local offices, the *Länder* parliaments, the *Bundestag*, and the European Parliament.

Two dates were of particular significance in that election year: On May 23, the Christian Democrat Roman Herzog was elected Federal President, beating the SPD-nominated North Rhine-Westphalian Prime Minister Johannes Rau (by ninety-one votes). Psychologically it was very important that the CDU/CSU-FDP coalition stood together despite SPD attempts to persuade the liberals to vote for their candidate. The second significant date was June 12.

The election for the European Parliament, held on that day, functioned as a trial run for the national election. The result was very encouraging for the government, especially since all opinion polls had predicted a Social Democratic victory: the CDU/CSU won 38.8 percent (an increase of 1.1 percent), the SPD won 34 percent (a decrease of 5.1 percent), and the Greens won 11 percent (an increase of 1.7 percent).

A dramatic prediction of the fates of the smaller parties in October's national election could also be found in June's election results: The right-wing radical Republican Party failed to make the 5 percent hurdle, winning only 3.9 percent. They lost half of their votes and had to leave the European Parliament. This was mainly a consequence of being isolated by all the other parties. Subsequently, the Republican Party did not play any role in the national election and more or less disappeared from the political stage.

The communist PDS won a surprising 4.7 percent, just missing the 5 percent hurdle. In the West, the PDS got only 0.6 percent; in East Germany they had 18.7 percent. Most of those votes came from the old SED membership (2.4 million), many of whom lost their privileges through unification. Others voted for the PDS because they felt overwhelmed by the ongoing changes and were tempted by simple ideological answers. In the regional and local parliaments of the new *Länder* the Communists got 20–25 percent of the votes, thus forcing the CDU and the SPD to form grand coalitions. From these results of the election for the European Parliament and the regional elections, then, the dominant topic of the national election campaign developed: How will the SPD deal with the PDS?

The question became urgent when the Social Democrats in Sachsen-Anhalt decided to form a minority government with the Greens and accepted the support of the PDS. But many people totally opposed the political successors of the GDR dictatorship getting influence in the democratic process. SPD party leader Rudolf Scharping again and again found himself confronted with the question of whether he would accept PDS votes when running for the chancellorship. Ultimately this question was a main reason why the SPD lost the election.

The second most important campaign question rose from the poor showing by the FDP in both the European Election (4.1

percent) and most of the *Länder* elections. Almost everywhere they missed the 5 percent hurdle. While it was obvious that the Social Democrats only could win together with the Greens *and* the PDS, everybody also knew that Kohl would need the FDP to get into the *Bundestag* in order to get reelected as chancellor.

The liberals concentrated their campaign on the slogan "Each vote for us is a vote for Kohl." They hoped for a split voting, whereby every voter casts two votes: one for the constituency/candidate and the other (and more important) for a party. This tactic proved successful. Many Christian Democrats voted for the local Christian Democratic candidate and gave the second vote, which decides how many seats a party gets, to the liberals. (See *Table 4*.)

TABLE 4. The Results of the Election for the *Bundestag*, October 16, 1994

	Party vote[1]	Vote for Constituency[2]	Seats
CDU/CSU	41.5 (-2.3)	45.0	294
SPD	36.4 (+2.9)	38.3	252
Greens	7.3 (+2.2)	6.5	49
FDP	6.9 (-4.1)	3.3	47
PDS	4.4 (+2.0)	4.1	30
Republicans	1.9 (-0.3)	1.7	–

[1]The party vote decides the percentage of seats a party gets and therefore is the most important (despite being called the "second vote").

[2]The constituency vote decides *who* gets the seats (half of the parliament consists of directly elected MPs, the other half are elected from party lists).

The CDU/CSU/FDP coalition gained a narrow majority of ten seats and Helmut Kohl won his fourth national election. The result was so close because the PDS won four direct seats in East Berlin and therefore was not effected by the 5 percent hurdle.[18]

The result of the federal election raised several major questions for Germany's political future: Will the election success strengthen the liberals or will it endanger the stability of the Kohl government? Will the Greens, strengthened through the federal election, continue to be a natural coalition partner for the SPD? Or will they, despite all political differences, become a possible partner for the Christian Democrats—if the liberals were to disappear from the political stage? What are the political consequences of the grand coalitions between the CDU and the SPD that already exist in four *Länder*?

And last but not least a question that is increasingly discussed inside and outside the Christian Democratic Party: What follows after Kohl? The Chancellor himself provoked this question shortly before the election when he said this was his last campaign. To date, all potential answers to this question have been unsatisfying; new pressure might be put on Kohl to run again. Although Kohl is often criticized on certain issues, he inspires a basic trust, repeatedly reflected in election results. Kohl's reputation in foreign affairs, so important in times of unrest abroad, is indisputable and virtually unchallenged.

There is a changing of the guard going on in the CDU, mainly initiated by Kohl himself. He knows that it has become more difficult from election to election to beat the general trend of "It's time for change." Social Affairs Minister Norbert Blüm is the only cabinet member of Kohl's team from 1982 still in office.

Number two after Kohl, and supported by him, is Wolfgang Schäuble, the majority speaker. There are, however, reservations about him because of his polarizing way of debating. In the next rank, one would find Defense Minister Volker Rühe, who has not too much support in the party, Transport Minister Mathias Wissmann, whose popularity is growing, and "Future Minister" (Research and Education) Jürgen Rüttgers. Those three belong to a generation between Kohl and Schäuble, on one hand, and a new generation of younger leaders in the *Landtage* (Wulff, Böhr, Reul, Müller, Oettinger, Koch) on the other.

The SPD entered the election of 1994 with new leadership. The former SPD chairman and candidate for chancellor Björn Engholm resigned from these offices and as premier of Schleswig-Holstein when it was discovered that some of his statements to a parliamentary investigating committee had been only half-truths. This plunged the party into a crisis in the spring of 1993. An open struggle broke out between different wings of the party over the question of his successor. Premier Schröder of Lower Saxony, who favors a coalition with the Greens, was pitted against the somewhat more moderate Rudolf Scharping, head of the government of Rhineland-Palatinate, who would like to revive the old coalition with the FDP. The two factions, deadlocked within the national committee, decided to poll the membership.

The unexpectedly high participation rate (over 50 percent of SPD members) and the campaign preceding the vote (which bore some resemblance to an American presidential primary) gained the party a great deal of positive coverage and attention. It revived the discussion about more inclusive and participatory procedures and increased the pressure on other parties to strengthen the rights of their members. The ambiguous nature of such a procedure has hardly been discussed, although the outcome certainly demonstrated it: Rudolf Scharping emerged as the victor with 40 percent of the vote, largely because the left wing was split between Schröder and a third candidate.

Scharping's authority within the party was greatly strengthened by the direct vote of the members. But while the left wing of the SPD has accepted his election, it has not truly accepted his program for the party. This was made obvious by Kohl's dominance over his challenger. The SPD changed its strategy and integrated Scharping into a "troika" of three, including Schröder and Saarland's premier, Oskar Lafontaine.

In the summer of 1995 there were ongoing, open rivalries between Scharping and Schröder, which led the party to a historical low in opinion polls, causing a disastrous result in the election for a new legislature for the state of Berlin.

The Social Democrats were so nervous that on the morning of his scheduled reelection as party chairman at the party convention in Mannheim in November 1995 Scharping was surprisingly challenged and defeated by Lafontaine. This was the first time in German postwar party history that such a coup—which included a spontaneous change of the statute—happened at a party convention.

The new SPD leader has a talent to motivate his party followers, but at the same time he will lead the party to the left. He openly discusses cooperation between the SPD, the Greens, and the PDS. It remains unclear whether Lafontaine will run against Kohl, who defeated him in 1990. Some observers expect that he will promote

Schröder as Kohl's challenger, since Scharping is now out of the race.

The Greens stabilized their political support by becoming more and more "established." They combined with the GDR opposition group "Alliance '90" early enough to improve their image as a party to be taken seriously. Furthermore, as coalition partners in *Länder* governments, the Greens have disavowed the "spontaneous" ideas of their founders and showed themselves capable of governing, and most of the leftist extremists (often with a Maoist orientation) have left the party.

The FDP has to overcome its structural problems. Both Hans Dietrich Genscher, for years the front-running vote-getter, and Otto Count Lambsdorff, a key spokesman for the economic concerns of FDP voters, have retired from active party leadership. New Party Chairman and Foreign Minister Klaus Kinkel had already experienced setbacks. The discussions about another party leader never stopped. Early in the summer of 1995 Kinkel decided not to run for reelection. He remains Foreign Minister and the Party Chairman is now Wolfgang Gerhardt, who was the architect of the successful CDU/FDP coalition in Hessen.

All these developments, and the results of the 1994 elections, indicate an increasingly dynamic political landscape in Germany. The stage of the political system is stable, but the performance on it may become less predictable. The long-term trend has shown a steady rise in the number of independent or swing voters. Members of this group may also abstain from voting as a conscious protest. Swing voters tend to be self-confident people who want to be convinced in each new campaign. This means that the parties must accept "heretical" questions put to them from the outside. Questions that are not asked in the mainstream parties will not simply go away; if ignored, they will be taken up by others and become symbols of protest.

The recent increase in nonparty (swing) and protest votes indicates, at bottom, a growing reluctance to be part of the political struggle and a romantic longing for harmony that has shaped the history of political thought and political culture in Germany. It is a preference for the Platonic ideal of oneness over Aristotle's plea for diversity, for Rousseau's enthusiasm for harmony over John Locke's principle of "agree to disagree."

Against this idea of harmony and perfection, the diverse reality must appear to be rather incomplete. Germany's main challenge for the future is to become immune to this ideological approach, to discover Kant instead of following Fichte and Hegel, and to accept "*Verantwortungsethik*" instead of "*Gesinnungsethik*" (Max Weber). This is as true for future internal development as it is for foreign policy.

In his already legendary negotiations with Gorbachev, Helmut Kohl made continued membership in NATO an indispensable condition of German unity. With this indication of the future direction of the country, fully in harmony with Adenauer's motto "freedom before unity," he prevented the loss of orientation in foreign affairs. The Europe of Western values is Germany's raison d'état. After the collapse of the Iron Curtain, the EC is beginning to become a European society. The option of "the East," which often played a virulent role in German history, has lost the attraction of proximity. Germany now is surrounded by Western neighbors.

Being an equal member of the Western community brings with it the responsibilities as well as the rights that link Germany with its neighbors and will stabilize the Western orientation at home. Unification will be the path to normality for Germany.

Translated by
Deborah Lucas Schneider

ENDNOTES

[1] These numbers are based on the figures issued by the Federal Office of Statistics between 1990 and 1993.

[2] It is interesting that the birthrate fell by 40 percent in East Germany since 1990, while in West Germany it remained relatively stable. In 1991, in the West there was an increase in the birthrate by 820,000, in the East a decrease by 200,000.

[3] The percentage of the population over sixty years of age has changed from 15 percent in 1950 to 20 percent in 1991, and will become an estimated 34 percent by 2040.

[4] The birthrate for illegitimate children has remained constant for years in the old *Länder* at about 12 percent, while in the new *Länder* it is about 40 percent.

[5] These figures include German citizens only. Of the approximately 28,400 Jews living in Germany, only about two hundred live in the new *Länder,* primarily in East Berlin. Almost all of the fifty thousand German Muslims live in the West.

[6]The trend in this area is reflected by a 10 percent increase in the birthrate among foreign residents in Germany and a 4 percent decrease among German citizens.

[7]The police investigated approximately 2,400 violent crimes against foreigners in 1991, about 6,300 in 1992, and about 2,000 in the first six months of 1993.

[8]Some of the chief agitators in the new *Länder* were active in communist youth organizations in the GDR era.

[9]Christoph Hein, "Die fünfte Grundrechenart (Aufsätze und Reden)" (Frankfurt/Main: 1990), 209.

[10]See the article by Kurt J. Lauk in this issue of *Dædalus*.

[11]Minority government SPD/Greens supported by the communist PDS.

[12]Quoted in Streitfall, *Zweites Deutsches Fernsehen,* 7 May 1992.

[13]The army of the GDR consisted of about fifty thousand career soldiers and volunteers and thirty-nine thousand draftees.

[14]To this should be added the 181,700 members of the CSU, its sister party in Bavaria. On the whole, the significance of the CSU has decreased in united Germany, as it is not represented in the new *Länder* and remains limited to Bavaria. The idea of expanding to the new *Länder* led to dissension within the CSU, but de facto the discussion has been ended by the failure of the DSU to gain a foothold there. (The DSU was an opposition party founded during the transition period with about nine thousand members, almost all of them in the East.)

[15]The CDU merged with the Eastern CDU, which had 140,000 members during the communist era, and with the German Farmers' Party, which had 115,000 members. The FDP merged with the LDPD (Liberal-Democratic Party with 104,000 members) and the NDPD (National-Democratic Party with 110,000 members).

[16]The FDP appears as the sole exception, as a result of declining membership in the West.

[17]This figure is based on the party's own estimates; its reliability is difficult to gauge.

[18]If a party wins at least three direct seats, all of its votes are counted, despite the 5 percent hurdle.

Jürgen Kocka

Crisis of Unification: How Germany Changes

G ERMANY HAS CHANGED MORE IN THE LAST four years than it has in the last four decades. How are Germans coping with the opportunities and challenges created by the breakdown of communism and national unification? Will the new Germany be mainly a continuation of the old Federal Republic? Or will it be a different country? In which respects? How does the German case compare with other experiences in the postcommunist world? How should it be evaluated in the light of historical experience?

THE EXIT FROM COMMUNISM: THE GERMAN PATTERN

The East German revolution has been part of a cycle of interrelated revolutions that dramatically changed Eastern and Central Europe in 1989 and 1990. In basic respects, it resembled the revolutions in Poland, Czechoslovakia, Hungary, Bulgaria, and Romania. Like the German Democratic Republic (GDR), these countries had been the objects of Soviet domination since the end of World War II, and liberation from Soviet rule was a central element of all the revolutions in 1989–1990. There were many underlying, contributing, and facilitating factors, but none was as important as the sudden weakening of Soviet control and the unwillingness of the Soviet government to send troops in support of befriended governments that were challenged by their subjects. With the exception of Romania, the revolutions were nonviolent. They were not prepared in advance. They were not led by clearly defined elite groups striving

Jürgen Kocka is Professor of Modern History at Freie Universität Berlin.

for power. They were not guided by nor did they bring about new sets of ideas. Rather they were inspired by democratic, liberal, and social-democratic ideas that have become central in Western political thought since the eighteenth century: the norms and ideals of modern civil society. Given the nonviolent, "reformist" character of those revolutions, their immediate structural impact was limited. The change in the political system was significant; but social structures, economic relations, culture, and collective mentalities have only begun to change.[1]

The postcommunist situation is characterized by elements of breakdown, destruction, and vacuum, in which older traditions regain some weight and new structures emerge rather slowly. Three tasks everywhere seem to be on the agenda: the transition to democracy, the building of an open society, and the introduction of a market economy. As the German sociologist Claus Offe has pointed out, an overlapping of these three major initiatives has been rare in history. It explains why "the exit from communism" has been so difficult. Postcommunist societies are heavily dependent on what Western countries offer or deny them. In every case, transition has been slower than expected and only partly successful. The optimism of 1989 is gone. One is increasingly made to realize how difficult it is to transfer the Western model to a part of the world without the economic, social, and cultural conditions that model seems to presuppose. Doubts about the universal applicability of the Western model grow, both in the East and the West.[2]

In these respects, the East German gains and challenges—which have become the gains and challenges of unified Germany—are of a more general nature: part of the fate of "the East."[3] Germany is not only a well integrated part of the West, but she has also absorbed part of the East and has to deal with some of its problems.

East Germany's geopolitical situation and advanced industrialization helped the ruling Communist Party elite to integrate large parts of the population and to avoid reforms. Compared with Poland and Hungary, change came late in East Germany; when it came, it came fast, like an implosion. It was heavily based on mass-mobilization. The (Protestant) Church played a larger role in changing East Germany than it did in changing other countries. But what made the experience of the GDR really unique was the national situation. The GDR was one of two German states: there was no congruity between state and nation. The GDR had to cope with the existence of a strong noncommunist state of the same nationality, the Federal Republic of Germany (FRG), which never fully accepted the nation's division. It is this particular national situation that distinguished the transition in East Germany from similar transitions in other countries in 1989–1990.[4]

Since 1953, the internal opposition against the regime in East Germany had been remarkably weak. The Polish Solidarnosz, Hungarian reform communism, and the Czech Charta 77 had no equivalent in East Germany. Intellectual dissidents were rare. Part of the explanation is to be found in the fact that there was another German state, which always accepted actual and potential dissidents from East Germany, thereby weakening the GDR's internal opposition. While in other communist countries dissidents could use national arguments and refer to national traditions when they wanted to criticize dictatorial rule and Soviet domination, arguments of this kind were taboo for East German intellectuals as long as they did not want or dare to question the existence of an independent GDR altogether (which was virtually impossible inside the country). In 1989–1990, the dissident elite turned out to be small in number and of little weight; they could not act as a counterelite, and they disappeared quickly from positions of power.

It should be stressed that the breakthrough phase of the East German revolution—from late September to November 1989—was an endogenous development, neither engineered nor triggered by the West Germans. But in an indirect way, the Federal Republic played an important role in the East German revolution: the mass exodus of East Germans to the West decisively fueled the internal demands for change, the mass demonstrations, and their powerful challenge to the communist establishment. "Exit" produced "voice" in this case, to use the well-known terms of the political economist Albert Hirschman. This mass exodus would not have been possible without the influence of the West German media in the GDR and the citizenship law of the Federal Republic, which served as a standing invitation to all ethnic Germans, including those in the GDR. The East German revolution in its second phase—between the opening of the Wall in November 1989 and the first free elections to the East German *Volkskammer* in March 1990—took a national turn. The demand for reform of the GDR, which would become democratic but stay independent, was gradually eclipsed by the quest for national unity. Large majorities of the population supported this national turn, articulating East German dissatisfaction, their distrust in the changeability of the GDR, and, above all, their hope of quickly improving their lot by joining the more wealthy, more liberal, more attractive FRG. This national turn would not have been possible without the existence of another German state, its principal support for unification, and the promises of its governing elite (which were not kept). From December 1989 onwards, the influence of the West German government quickly increased, became direct and open. The East German revolution became a movement for national unification that had no parallel in any other country. The East German exit from communism led into a process of self-dissolution; the East German state finally acceded to the Federal Republic and ceased to exist.[5]

The decisive changes related to unification have been generated within the GDR. This holds with respect to the revolutionary mass movements in the autumn and winter, which brought down the Socialist Unity Party (SED) government, forced the opening of the Berlin Wall, and initiated basic reforms; the ensuing drive towards unification; and the self-dissolution of the GDR.[6] But in this process of unification, within the emerging national framework, the tremendous inequality of the two German societies quickly made itself felt. Already in the winter of 1989–1990 the center of gravity started to move from the East to the West, from Leipzig, Berlin, and other East German cities to Bonn, from the grass roots to the centers of government, from a spontaneously organized movement to the established parties and administrations. Certainly, initiatives from below have continued, albeit in different, less spectacular forms. They have found new bases in the communities, regions, and *Länder* of the East in recent years. But those who had improvised mass actions, had founded groups and parties, and had raised from anonymity to unstable leadership positions in the first phase of the revolution, quickly lost out.

In the following months and years, the revolution became something like an orderly "revolution from outside and above," increasingly controlled by the dominant West and engineered by professional politicians and administrators.[7] Basic constitutional change continued throughout 1990. The process of restructuring the economy, social relations, cultural institutions, the educational system, and other spheres of life speeded up and deepened in 1990 and has continued in the following years. The transition from communism became part of a process of incorporating the East into the West by transferring institutions, resources, elites, and ideas from the West to the East.

No other postcommunist countries have had this experience. Change and recovery in East Germany are based on resources that her Eastern neighbors can only dream of. In East Germany, the transition is faster and more thorough than anywhere else. At the same time, it is less autonomous, less self-controlled, and leads to new contradictions.

INCORPORATING THE EAST INTO THE WEST: ACHIEVEMENTS, LIMITS, AND *PROBLÉMATIQUES*

The Basic Decision

In 1990, an extended debate took place about which constitutional form unification should take. Should it be enacted according to ARTICLE 146 of the West German Basic Law, which provided that in case of unification a new constitution should be framed and voted upon by the people? Or should unification be brought about along the lines offered by ARTICLE 23, which made possible the accession of the GDR to the Federal Republic, whose constitution would remain unchanged and apply to Germany as a whole?

ARTICLE 146 would have made necessary an extended process of consulting and bargaining that would have offered the opportunity to bring elements from both the West and the East together into a new and better solution. It would not only liberate the Easterners from their socialist constitution, but also, hopefully, overcome some of the weaknesses of the West German political order. This is how advocates of ARTICLE 146—mostly on the Left or left of the center—justified their demand. They also thought that such an extended public debate on the constitutional core of unification would present the necessary platform on which the Germans could find out why and how they wanted to get together. It would help the new Germany and its emerging constitutional order to get popular support and legitimation, for the sake of democratic stability.

This strategy would have taken much time, which, as those favoring ARTICLE 23 felt, was not available given the unstable international situation. A basic change inside the Soviet Union, which was not altogether unlikely, could easily close the "window of opportunity" for German unification. The very unstable situation within the GDR also seemed to require a quick decision. The Basic Law had proven its strength; it enjoyed broad acceptance among West and East Germans. Why dispose of it and increase the uncertainties of an already risky unification? Advocates of ARTICLE 23 doubted that much improvement of the Basic Law could be found in the East German constitution. To find international acceptance for German unification was a difficult task that would only become more difficult if the actors on the international scene had to deal with a new Germany whose constitutional order and basic profile would only slowly emerge in a long and painful debate. The international obligations of the Federal Republic were not to be questioned. Advocates of ARTICLE 23 thought that it offered a simple and appropriate way to bring about unification without jeopardizing the basic continuity between the old Federal Republic and the newly emerging Germany.[8]

German unification was enacted on the basis of ARTICLE 23. Apart from some minor exceptions, temporary arrangements, and limited amendments to be negotiated later, the constitutional order of West Germany was extended to the East. This debate and its outcome had paradigmatic character. Not only with respect to constitutional law, but in nearly all other respects as well, unification was drafted as a process of transferring the internal order of West Germany to East Germany, with only minimal changes. Unified Germany was not meant to be something new. It was meant to be an enlarged Federal Republic of Germany.[9] Has the strategy worked, so far?

Political System

The official name—the Federal Republic of Germany—has not been changed, nor has the national hymn, although alternatives were proposed and discussed in 1990. The West German flag became the flag of united Germany. In general, the constitutional and legal system proved to be flexible enough to be extended to the new *Länder*. The reconstruction of the administrative and judicial system according to the West German model is under way.[10] But there are exceptions and countertendencies.

In the constitutional debates, East German participants—frequently supported by West German speakers representing parties from the Left—tend to emphasize the need for more plebiscitary elements (i.e., referendum) and for a broader formulation of some basic rights especially with respect to social conditions (i.e., the right to work), ecological protection, and gender equality. These preferences may result in part from the East German lack of experience with a representative multiparty system, from memory of the successful mass movements during the autumn and winter of 1989–1990, and from the widespread tendency in the East to expect much from "the state" and less from the market. Such preferences have not had much impact on the national level. Although a Constitutional Committee, consisting of members of the *Bundestag* and representatives of the *Länder*, has been set up as recommended by the Treaty of Unification, its conclusions as to amending the Basic Law have remained extremely cautious. But those preferences have influenced the framing of the new constitutions of the East German *Länder*.[11] They increasingly influence the general debate.

Political Parties

The West German parties have quickly spread to the East by absorbing some of the SED-dependent parties existing throughout the years in the GDR (in the case of the Christian Democratic Union [CDU] and the Free Democratic Party [FDP]), by fusing with parties newly created in the GDR during the revolution (the Social Democratic Party [SPD] and the Greens), and by trying to establish a new local and regional base. Apart from the Party of Democratic Socialism (PDS), the successor party of the SED (11 percent of the vote in the East and 2 percent in the West in the *Bundestag* elections of December 1990), there has been no significant change in the West German party system as it extended to the East.[12] Roughly the same can be said with respect to the unions and other large associations. This bird's eye view does not, however, allow one to discover the limits of the transfer of such institutions. Party membership is desperately low in the new *Länder*. It is difficult to find enough activists (candidates) for local elections. The decades of dictatorship and the abrupt changes of 1989–1990 seem to have produced a vacuum. East German church membership lags far behind West German. People are reluctant to enter new stable commitments beyond the private sphere.

West German institutions have spread to the East but they have barely taken root in the population. Traditional loyalties have broken down; new ones are not yet established. The social composition and the priorities of the East and West branches of one party frequently differ. Parties, unions, and associations are internally torn by the task of bridging differences and contradictions between their Eastern and Western members. Still, thus far they have managed to avoid being split along regional lines. As of yet, regional parties and movements have not emerged, at least not successfully (apart from the PDS). The system is creaking but not breaking.[13]

Economic Change

In July of 1990, the economic order of the West was abruptly introduced to the East. Custom borders and mobility barriers were removed, and, before it existed as one state, Germany was a single market with a common legal framework and a common currency. This was a political decision against which some economists cautioned. But in the last years, the economic structure of the GDR has been quickly molded according to the West German model.

Privatization has proceeded faster there than anywhere else in the postcommunist countries. The Treuhand-Anstalt, a public, government-controlled, but highly autonomous and controversial corporation, founded in 1990, was charged with taking over and privatizing the state-owned and collectivized enterprises of the GDR. Of a total of roughly sixteen thousand units, the Treuhand, by July 1993, had sold about 78 percent and liquidated 17 percent. Seven hundred and forty units remain under Treuhand control to be sold as soon as possible. When transferred to private investors, entrepreneurs, and managers, most of whom come from West Germany and abroad, the units were usually restructured, rationalized, and reduced, frequently with the help of public money.[14]

Measured by the distribution of the economically active population among industrial sectors, the economy of the GDR in 1989 was far behind Western countries. By 1992, the West-East difference had nearly disappeared.

Before celebrating this dramatic change as a clear indicator of economic modernization, one has to take into account that it was accompanied by an equally dramatic decrease in overall employment. In 1989, 920,000 were employed in East German agriculture; by 1992 this figure had gone down to 280,000 (a 70 percent reduction). Manufacturing industries employed 3.17 million persons in 1989, but only 1.29 million in 1992 (roughly a 60 percent reduction). Employment in mining and energy production decreased by 39 percent from 1989 to 1992. By contrast, the reduction in the services (including state) amounted to only 22 percent (from 4.35 million to 3.41 million), and employment in the construction trades even grew by 10 percent (from 563,000 to 620,000).

In short, the number of jobs available in East Germany decreased by 34 percent between 1989 and 1992, from 9.3 to 6.2 million. Had it not been for the public works programs (now scheduled for elimination), the reduction would have amounted to 38 percent. Three million jobs were lost within the first three years following unification. And the process of erosion seems to be continuing in 1993. The official unemployment figures—in July 1993, 1.67 million or 15.3 percent in the East, 2.33 million or 7.5 percent in the West—do not fully show the dramatic nature of the breakdown. It is not at all clear when the trend will be reversed, and part of the erosion will probably be permanent.[15]

East German industries were overstaffed, with a relatively low degree of productivity, and, thus, were not able to compete with the West. Because Western firms frequently disposed of nonutilized capacities, they could quickly increase their production. Despite vigorous attempts at rationalization and effective improvement of the traffic, transport, and communication system with the help of public investment, the competitiveness of many East German firms was countered by rising labor costs—due to an upsurge in costs of living and the dynamic wage policy of the unions. Other factors, including the breakdown of markets in the East, legal obstacles in the period of transition, inefficiencies of the administration, and the worldwide recession, played a role as well.[16]

Research and Universities

In nonmarket sectors, policy decisions had similar, though less brutal effects. Take research and higher learning as an example. The

GDR had adopted the Soviet system, which provided for a clear institutional separation between universities, oriented towards the training of students (although not exclusively), and the institutes of the Academy of Sciences, exclusively responsible for research. In West Germany, research and teaching are integrated under the roof of the universities whenever possible, particularly in the social sciences and the humanities. After unification, the huge research institutes of the East German Academy of Sciences, which employed more than twice as many people as the universities, were evaluated by expert commissions in which Western scholars and officials played the major role. The criteria of evaluation were academic quality and efficiency, measured by international standards as well as compatibility with the basic principles of the West German system of research and higher learning. Among those principles, the autonomy, unity, and decentralized structure of research and teaching ranked high. More often than not, the "international standard" was defined by the situation in the old Federal Republic and in other Western countries.

Evaluation was a complicated process, which, in the end, was regarded as relatively fair on both sides. It resulted in the dissolution of most academy institutes, in the founding of many new extrauniversity research institutions, and in a vigorous but difficult attempt to reintegrate some members of the academic staff of the dissolved institutes into the university system. Less than 50 percent—some estimate only 30 percent—of the former personnel of the academy institutes are now employed in newly founded institutes and in the universities.[17]

The GDR universities were tremendously "overstaffed" as compared to West German universities (which is a particularly problematic yardstick since the West German system of higher education is in bad shape and suffers, among other things, from a disadvantageous staff-student ratio). The departments of the GDR universities had been structured to meet the needs of the old regime—particularly in the humanities and the social sciences—and the imperatives of the Comecon, particularly in the economic and technical disciplines. In the humanities and social sciences, the degree of specialization was very high, the system of rewards little developed, mobility and communication restricted, and access to international literature frequently difficult to obtain. There had been scholars and achievements of high quality, but far fewer than in the West. Political instrumentalization had played a detrimental role, particularly in the humanities and social sciences.

The East German university system has been deeply restructured in the last three years under the control of the *Länder* governments and with effective participation of Western scholars and administrators according to the West German model. Three processes should be distinguished: *1)* The system was reduced in size. *2)* University law and organization, the structure of the departments, and the patterns of specialization were deeply altered, and positions and tasks were redefined. As a consequence, existing qualifications were depreciated and new ones were demanded. On the professorial level, the old personnel had to apply and compete with other applicants, in many cases from the West. *3)* Screening processes took place (in "commissions of honor" inside the universities), which led to the exclusion of persons found guilty of having discredited themselves by moral and political standards.

The necessary shrinking due to financial limits and pressures as well as the widespread redefinition of qualifications due to the change of system accounted for many more layoffs and personnel exchanges than did political screening. In Saxony, the universities employed thirty-nine thousand persons (among them fifteen thousand scientists) in 1989. In the future, they will employ only 11,200 persons, among them 7,800 scientists. One can estimate that only a small minority—perhaps 10 percent—of those employed in 1989 were dismissed on political and moral grounds.

The influx of Westerners has remained limited, considering the whole system of research and higher learning. About 10 percent of all positions in the universities and research institutions—mostly the leading positions—have been filled by West Germans and, in a small number of cases, by persons from abroad. In fields like history and sociology, the percentage of Westerners is much higher. Of the twenty-nine professors of sociology in East German universities today, only four come from the East. A similar ratio can probably be found among history professors. But there is less change on the level of the nontenured personnel and in such disciplines as mathematics, the natural sciences, medicine, and the technical fields.[18]

Social Inequalities and Mental Distances

Once the basic political decision had been made to execute unification by transferring the West German order to the East as quickly and completely as possible, the rest followed with a certain necessity: market forces, on the one hand, and policy decisions, on the other, restructured the East German system according to the West German model. A tremendous destruction took place. The present situation is difficult, but it can be hoped and expected that the reduced and deeply restructured system of work in the East will eventually be able to compete and grow again.[19]

It is quite evident that the restructuring and incorporation of East Germany is heavily dependent upon West Germany. Without the know-how and personnel from the West, this process of revolutionary change could not have been undertaken. Without money from the West, it would not have been socially bearable.[20]

Because of the massive financial transfer from West to East, the crisis of restructuring has not led to mass poverty in the East. In fact, a majority of the East Germans seem to be and to feel better off today than before the revolution. The unions negotiated huge pay hikes, applying the bargaining rules and tactics of the West. Those who have work can afford more than they used to, and they have access to a whole variety of goods that most of them only dreamed of under the old regime, including the opportunity to travel. Those who lived on pensions were particularly poor and underprivileged in the GDR; most of them now enjoy improved living conditions. Academics who have managed to stay employed have to work more, but do so under better conditions. Life has become freer, the scope of choices has broadened, and new opportunities continue to arise. There also has begun to emerge a new layer of self-employed persons, both in the trades and in the professions.

Not everyone, however, is enjoying an improved standard of living. Many who held power and privilege because of their proximity to the party apparatus and the state have been déclassé, although some have apparently managed to be well placed again, particularly in the world of commerce and services. Women, the large majority of whom had been part of the labor force in the GDR, combining family and job, are now clearly overrepresented among the unemployed. Those who raise children and work outside the home deplore the breakdown of day-nurseries and the disappearance of other public facilities. Careers for women have become less accessible. In addition, new groups have appeared: the homeless, drug addicts, and the long-term unemployed.[21]

Inequality is growing, between income groups, between men and women, between those who have work and those who do not, between nouveaux riches and déclassés, between those who manage to hold on to their property and those who must move out. The reinstating of a system of private property after so many years leads to new inequalities and injustices. More than half of the population has experienced some change of vocation, and a change in mobility—upward, downward, or laterally.

Does all this mean that life in the East has become more similar to life in the West? Yes and no. The East German situation remains clearly distinguished, in at least three respects.

First, this is a period of revolutionary change in the East, requiring rapid adjustment. Routines have broken down, trust has been shattered, new orientations are needed, anxiety is widespread, and self-assuredness is scarce. Crisis and rapid transition define the lives of many in the East, but not so in the West. Though collective protests have so far remained weak and scattered, the East German crisis is deep. The East German birthrate has fallen by 60 percent, the marriage rate by 65 percent, and the divorce rate by 81 percent between 1989 and 1992. Declines of this quantity are extremely rare in history. Only the Great Wars offer similar examples. Nothing comparable is happening in West Germany. It is not unreasonable to attribute this demographic breakdown to the crisis caused by transition in East Germany. Early in 1990, the fast pace of unification was justified by the Bonn government by pointing to the East-West mass migration, which would not be halted except by economic and monetary unity. Yet, even with such unity, East-West migration continues. Between 1973 and 1989 the East German population hovered around 16.5 and 17 million. By 1992, it had fallen below 16 million, and the loss of population continues.[22]

Second, a mixture of repression and paternalism, specific to politics and life in the GDR, left East Germans little accustomed to quick change, uncertainty, competition, and the risky utilization of new opportunities.

Third, the difference between East and West continues to be pronounced and visible with respect to income, life-style, status, power, and quality of life. In contrast to popular expectations and convincing promises in the first years, it is increasingly clear that equalization of living conditions will take decades. The resulting feelings of inequality, frustration, and inferiority on the part of the East Germans maintain a psychological distance. Tension and mutual reservation, resentment, and outright rejection play an increasing role.[23] There is, of course, some mixing. A thin layer of West Germans live and work in the East, usually in leading positions. East Germans move to the West to work and be trained. Still, different newspapers are read in the East than in the West, and the best-seller lists differ. West German and East German historians tend to publish in different journals. Even in united Berlin, the circles of intensive communication and collegiality, friendship, and marriage continue to be divided between East and West.

On the level of social and personal relations, of customs and everyday life, integration and incorporation of the East are clearly limited. In these respects, one can still speak of two different societies, and awareness of this split seems to grow. Some East German intellectuals have begun to consider whether the separate development of an East German society—different and relatively independent from the West—could become a desirable possibility in the long run: two societies within one state.[24]

This may sound unrealistic, but it is not coincidental that such ideas are voiced as it becomes increasingly clear that the Westernization of the East will take much longer and require more effort than originally expected. Perhaps the aims should be redefined.[25]

Political Culture

Public opinion surveys have discovered typical differences between East German and West German attitudes. Easterners seem to expect more from "the state" in terms of securing economic growth, stabilizing prices, and guaranteeing employment. They hold old-fashioned virtues such as obedience, orderliness, modesty, cleanliness, and duty in higher esteem. Work represents a more central value to Germans in the East than in the West. East Germans tend less to hedonistic, postmaterialistic, and individualistic values than do West Germans—although the difference is less significant among the younger respondents. East Germans are less likely to identify with political parties and party democracy, and are more sympathetic towards plebiscitary or grass-roots democracy. To some observers, Easterners appear more "German" than Westerners, in that they are more deeply rooted in older German traditions.[26]

Until 1990, East Germans and West Germans were exposed to different interpretations of recent German history. They also differ in formative experiences. Survey-based research has discovered that the national-socialist period, World War II, the German persecution of the Jews, and the immediate postwar developments largely contributed to the historical self-understanding of a multigenerational majority of West Germans. A highly critical view of the Nazi period serves as a negative foil and reference point in contrast to which the political culture of the Federal Republic has frequently been defined. East Germans also lean away from a positive view of the Nazi dictatorship, but the period is less central to their historical self-understanding. The type of "antifascism" that was taught and propagated in the GDR has helped to remove the Nazi experience from the historical self-definition of many East Germans. They seem to have a less abashed view of German national history and are more intent on reconciling their own GDR past.[27]

Such data does not indicate a widening gap between East and West, but the existence of deep cultural and political differences. They can be viewed either as consequences of different patterns of socialization throughout the last decades or as reactions to present problems posing themselves differently in the two parts of Germany. Under the institutional roof of a common constitution and a largely unified party system, there still seem to exist the elements of two different political cultures.

THE PARTS AND THE WHOLE: CONCLUSIONS AND OUTLOOK

In Germany, prior to unification, nation and state were not congruent. The East German exit from communism took the form of self-dissolution and unification with the West German state. In these most fundamental ways, East Germany differed from all the other countries of East and East Central Europe that were moving away from communism in 1989–1990. Transition proceeds faster and reaches deeper in East Germany than anywhere else, and the long-term prospects seem brighter. At the same time, the East Germans have to bear more destruction and uprooting than do their Eastern and Southeastern neighbors. Transition has taken the form of a "revolution from outside and above," again making the East Germans objects of change.

Underlying the transition is the decision to accomplish unification by incorporating the East into the West and by extending the basic order of the Federal Republic to the Eastern part of the country. According to this master plan of 1990, unification meant changing the East but not the West. Unified Germany was not intended to be a new invention nor a compromise between West and East, but an enlarged version of the old Federal Republic.

The transfer of the West German order to the Eastern *Länder* has worked relatively well on the constitutional, legal, and institutional level. However, it has met stiff resistance and has not progressed far on the level of social relations, political culture, and everyday life. On other levels (i.e., the economy), the transfer of the West German order has led to destruction and crisis, as the demographic breakdown shows. Despite efforts to incorporate and integrate the East, a separate GDR identity seems to have been revived, defensively and obstinately documenting the present limits of Westernization.

How will all this affect the system at large? As the role of government in social and economic processes becomes strengthened, the relationship between *Bund* and *Länder* will be readjusted.

Recovering from unification cannot be solely the responsibility of those in the East. Rather, it demands extraordinary efforts on the part of the whole population. The burden is already beginning to be felt: taxes and fees are raised and the public debt is growing. Unification will put to the test parliamentary institutions and political parties. Will it be possible to reach a consensus on the necessary redistribution? Will it be possible to convince West German voters that it is in their interest to share with the citizens in the East? While unification remains a positive experience for a clear majority of East Germans, in West Germany the skeptics have started to outnumber the supporters.[28]

The crisis in the East brings the weaknesses of the whole to the surface. Take, for example, the right-wing extremist attacks in Hoyerswerda and Rostock. They started in places characterized by high unemployment, disintegration, and dissatisfaction as well as by a weak police force and an evident lack of public authority. But they have triggered waves of extremist attacks on a nationwide scale.

With respect to their basic profiles, the GDR and the old Federal Republic were mutually dependent. For the GDR, the Federal Republic was a permanent challenge and a source of indirect destabilization. For the Federal Republic, the GDR served as a negative foil and as a source of collective stabilization. Both German states were creations of the Cold War. Their internal structures and external affiliations were deeply influenced by the system of international relations. Now Germany is compelled to find a new place in a changing international environment. This will deeply affect the mood of the country, its self-understanding, and its political substance. Unified Germany will not and cannot be merely an enlarged version of the old Federal Republic. Change, it seems, will extend much farther than the architects of unification intended.

ENDNOTES

[1]Cf. Judy Batt, "The End of Communist Rule in East Central Europe: A four-country comparison," *Government and Opposition* 26 (1991): 368–90. Jürgen Kocka, "Revolution and Nation—1989/90 in Historical Perspective," in Bernd Hüppauf, ed., *United Germany in Europe. Towards 1990 and Beyond: European Studies Journal,* Special Edition (Fall 1993).

[2]Cf. Claus Offe, "Capitalism by Democratic Design? Democratic Theory facing the Triple Transition in East Central Europe," *Social Research* 58 (1991): 865–92; Claus Offe, "Die Integration nachkommunistischer Gesellschaften: die ehemalige DDR im Vergleich zu ihren osteuorpäischen Nachbarn" (forthcoming); Kenneth Jowitt, *The New World Disorder. The Leninist Extinction* (Berkeley, Calif.: University of California Press, 1992).

[3]The patterns of change within the Soviet Union and its successor countries were and are different. Because of other differences, Yugoslavia is excluded from the present considerations as well.

[4]A good account is Konrad Jarausch, *The Rush to German Unity* (New York: Oxford University Press, 1993).

[5]Pending the consent of the international powers, this direction was clear after 18 March 1990, when a large majority of the East Germans voted for parties supporting such a course. Formally, the GDR ceased to exist on 3 October 1990. Albert O. Hirschman, "Abwanderung, Widerspruch und das Schicksal der Deutschen Demokratischen Republik," *Leviathan* 20 (1993): 330–58.

[6]The best account and analysis of the mass movements is Hartmut Zwahr, *Ende einer Selbstzerstörung. Leipzig und die Revolution in der DDR* (Göttingen: Vandenhoek & Ruprecht, 1993).

[7] I take the term "revolution from outside and above" (*"Revolution von außen und oben"*) from the East German economic historian Jürgen Kuczynski who used it to characterize the basic reforms in Prussia from 1807–1813 which had been triggered by the Napoleonic challenge and which were largely executed by the civil service.

[8] Cf. Bernd Guggenberger and Tine Stein, eds., *Die Verfassungsdiskussion im Jahr der deutschen Einheit. Analysen-Hintergründe-Materialien* (München: Hanser, 1991).

[9] A central source is Wolfgang Schäuble, *Der Vertrag. Wie ich über die deutsche Einheit verhandelte* (Stuttgart: Deutsche Verlags-Anstalt, 1991).

[10] The local self-administration, for example, has been restructured. Qualified personnel is scarce. The problems tend to surmount the capabilities of the agencies. Cf. Martin Osterland and Roderich Wehser, "Kommunale Demokratie als Herausforderung. Verwaltungsreorganisation in der Ex-DDR aus der Innenperspektive," *Kritische Justiz* 24 (1991): 318–32.

[11] Cf. Peter Häberle, "Die Verfassungsbewegung in den fünf neuen Bundesländern," *Jahrbuch des Öffentlichen Rechts der Gegenwart* 41 (1993): 70–307.

[12] I leave the Deutsche Social Union (DSU) aside, a splinter party on the moderate Right. On the first *Bundestag* elections in united Germany (December 1990), see Ursula Feist, "Zur politischen Akkulturation der Vereinigten Deutschen," *Aus Politik und Zeitgeschichte. Beilage zur Wochenzeitung Das Parlament,* B 11–12, 8 March 1991, 21–32.

[13] Articles on the major parties after unification are in Ibid., B 5, 24 January 1992. A good case study is Stephen Silvia, "Left Behind: The Social Democratic Party in Eastern Germany," *West European Politics* 16 (2) (April 1993): 24–48. Heinrich Tiemann et al., "Gewerkschaften und Sozialdemokratie in den neuen Bundesländern," *Deutschland-Archiv* 26 (1993): 40–51. Of the East German population in 1991, 6 percent belong to the Roman Catholic Church, 27 percent to the Protestant Church. The West German figures are 42 percent and 45 percent respectively. "Committees for justice" were launched in the summer of 1992, trying to work on a multipartisan basis and serve as a platform for formulating East German interests. It did not amount to much.

[14] *Treuhand Information* (19) (29 July 1993): 7–10. On this peculiar institution, in general, see Jürgen Turck, "Treuhand-Anstalt," in Werner Weidenfeld and Karl-Rudolf Korte, eds., *Handwörterbuch zur deutschen Einheit* (Frankfurt: Campus, 1992), 667–73.

[15] The figures are taken and tabulated from an unpublished paper by Jürgen Müller, "Strukturelle Auswirkungen der Privatisierung," Deutsches Institut für Wirtschaftsforschung, preliminary version June 1993, tables II.1 and III.1; and from Rainer Geißler, *Die Sozialstruktur Deutschlands. Ein Studienbuch zur gesellschaftlichen Entwicklung im geteilten und vereinten Deutschland* (Opladen: 1992), 118.

[16] Cf. W. R. Smyser, *The Economy of United Germany. Colossus at the Crossroads* (New York: St. Martin's Press, 1992).

[17]Cf. several articles in *Aus Politik und Zeitgeschichte. Beilage zur Wochenzeitung Das Parlament,* B 51, 11 December 1992, especially by Wilhelm Krull and Dieter Simon. Figures from "Wissenschaft in Deutschland," *WZB-Mitteilungen* (Wissenschaftszentrum Berlin für Sozialforschung) 58 (December 1992): 38–42.

[18]Ibid., 41; Hansgünther Meyer, "Konkordanz und Antinomie der Hochschulerneuerung in Deutschland nach der Wiedervereinigung" (lecture manuscript, 20 April 1993, unpublished), 8, table 7. M. Rainer Lepsius, "Zum Aufbau der Soziologie in Ostdeutschland," *Kölner Zeitschrift für Soziologie und Sozialpsychologie* 45 (1993): 305–37; Gerhard A. Ritter, "Der Neuaufbau der Geschichtswissenschaft an der Humboldt-Universität zu Berlin—ein Erfahrungsbericht," *Geschichte in Wissenschaft und Unterricht* 44 (1993): 226 –38.

[19]Signs of recovery are clearly visible. For one example cf. Bernhard A. Sabel, "Science Reunification in Germany: A Crash Program," *Science* 260 (1993): 1753–758; also see the report by Patricia Kahn in Ibid., 1744–746. On the rise of a new stratum of self-employed persons both in industry and the professions, cf. Rudolf Woderich, "Neue Selbständigkeit in Ostdeutschland," *Public. Wissenschaftliche Mitteilungen aus dem Berliner Institut für Sozialwissenschaftliche Studien* 11 (1993): 57–67.

[20]About DM 150 billion are annually transferred from the West to the East.

[21]Cf. Christine Bialas and Wilfried Ettl, "Wirtschaftliche Lage, soziale Differenzierung und Probleme der Interessenorganisation in den neuen Bundesländern," *Soziale Welt* 44 (1993): 52–74; Geißler, *Die Sozialstruktur Deutschlands,* chaps. 5–7.

[22]Cf. Wolfgang Zapf and Steffen Mau, "Eine demographische Revolution in Ostdeutschland?," *ISI. Informationsdienst Soziale Indikatoren* 10 (July 1993): 1–5; Siegfried Grundmann, "Thesen und Hypothesen zur Entwicklung der ostdeutschen Binnen- und Außenwanderung," *Public. Wissenschaftliche Mitteilungen aus dem Berliner Institut für Sozialwissenschaftliche Studien* 9 (1992): 89–100.

[23]Cf. the articles by the Greiffenhagens and by Hans-Joachim Maaz and Ursula Meckel in Werner Weidenfeld, ed., *Deutschland. Eine Nation—doppelte Geschichte* (Cologne: Verlag Wissenschaft und Politik, 1993).

[24]Cf. the debate in *Public* 9 and 10 (1992–1993), especially the articles by Thomas Koch, Rudolf Woderich, and Rolf Reißig.

[25]Cf. the interview with two important East German intellectuals and political speakers: Jens Reich (Neues Forum) and Friedrich Schorlemmer (SPD), "Wer ist das Volk. Die deutschen Integrationsformeln greifen zu kurz," *Blätter für deutsche und internationale Politik,* February 1993, 158–70.

[26]From articles by Martin and Sylvia Greiffenhagen, Helmut Klages and Thomas Gensicke, Jörg Ueltzhöffer and Bodo Berthold Flaig, Hans-J. Misselwitz and Wilhelm Bürkling in Weidenfeld, ed., *Deutschland;* "Ökonomische Kultur in Ostdeutschland," *WZB-Mitteilungen* 58 (December 1992): 27–30; *Allensbacher Jahrbuch der Demoskopie 1984–1992* 9 (1993): 718–19 (on parties and grassroots democracy); Thomas Gensicke, "Lebenskonzepte im Osten Deutschland," *Public* 9 (1992): 101–122.

[27]Cf. the articles by Felix Ph. Lutz, Bernd Faulenbach, and Bodo von Borries in Weidenfeld, ed., *Deutschland,* 157–208.

[28]The change came in the middle of 1992. *Allensbacher Jahrbuch,* 452–53.

Ludger Kühnhardt

Multi-German Germany

O N AUGUST 2, 1802, A LETTER WAS SENT from Chateau Coppet, a small castle on the shores of Lake Geneva to Charles de Villers, a French officer, journalist, and scientist then living in Germany. Signed by Anne-Louise-Germaine de Staël-Holstein, née Necker, better known as Madame de Staël, the letter confirmed from a distance Villers' impressions of the state of contemporary Germany:

> *"Je crois avec vous, que l'esprit humain, qui semble voyager d'un pays à l'autre, est en ce moment en Allemagne. J'étudie l'allemand avec soin, sûr que c'est là seulement que je trouverais des pensées nouvelles et des sentiments profonds."*

In 1803, 1804, and again in 1807, Madame de Staël undertook extensive travels through Germany. Inspired by the desire to find "world-mindedness" between the rivers Rhine and Oder, she shared her observations with the world in 1810 when her famous essay *"De l'Allemagne"* appeared.

This was much more than an essayist's portrayal of a neighboring country and its people. Hers was the discovery of classical German culture through the eyes of someone from the outside world. It was simultaneously a mirror held up to postrevolutionary French society to make that society feel its own inadequacies before the new glory of German classicism. In letters Madame de Staël wrote during her first journey through Germany, she reported a certain depression and boredom on the other side of the Rhine, and spoke of insipidity and poverty. She missed the *"savoir vivre"* and cosmo-

---

Ludger Kühnhardt is Professor of Political Science at Albert-Ludwigs-Universität Freiburg.

211

politan air of her home country. However, after a prolonged stay in Weimar, where she came to know Goethe and Schiller, conversed with Wieland, and frequented the court of the duke Karl-August, she began to change her mind. *"De l'Allemagne"* became an enthusiastic eulogy about the new cultural center of Europe—as seen from her perspective. It documented the lives of a strong, vivacious, and thriving people, an effusive description of Germany's intellectual and spiritual powers in the decade of German classicism. In 1803, Madame de Staël was still reprimanding the Germans for their insensitivity; she complained about the *"brutalité allemande."* By 1810, there was no longer any mention of an absent *"esprit de société"* but only of an inborn disposition to deep feelings, intelligent thoughts, and utmost civility. For Madame de Staël, Germany had become *"la nation métaphysique par excellence."*

Were Madame de Staël to travel through Germany again at the end of the twentieth century, she would have to look long and hard to find that "world-mindedness." Where did this strange creature that played such a conspicuous part in Hegel's philosophy go? Is the worldly spirit, shared by so many Germans, on a prolonged holiday? Why has it left a country that considered itself the "happiest in the world" after the fall of the Berlin Wall on November 9, 1989, and has since fallen into that all-too-well-known gloom and depression? Why has that world-mindedness vanished? Should it not feel at home in a Germany that, on October 3, 1990, saw, after forty years of artificial separation, the two parts of the country joined into one national political entity, achieving this with the consent of all neighboring nations? Whoever attempts to look closely at Germany three years after reunification cannot but wonder. The mood is sour, worse than many of the various and well-reasoned analyses of actual conditions are able to justify. With great shock and exhibiting new symptoms of old fears, the media around the world report xenophobic aggression against resident foreigners in Germany. It is skinheads who are depicted. Where are the poets of Goethe's time? Instead of enthusiasm for a peacefully regained freedom for all German citizens, whimpering is the near universal cry. The party is clearly over, and on the Federal holiday commemorating German unity on October 3, 1993, the president of the Commission of the European Community, Jacques Delors, a Frenchman, had to encourage Germans to be more cheerful, more optimistic about the future. Germany has not been dealt such a bad hand; the apocalyptic concerns being voiced in this country are unjustified.

Germany must come to terms with its successes, accept its joys, and understand its newfound sorrows. It has to reconcile itself to the changed reality of a single people, inwardly only semirelated, living very different lives in the East and the West. The current mood of melancholy and frustration, which seeks scapegoats among politicians no less than among foreigners, is only superficially the consequence of the unavoidable transition crisis of a postcommunist Eastern society that is trying to integrate itself into a postmaterialist, yet fundamentally materialistic Western society. The West, it seems, has won the Cold War, but it has become the cause of the constant revolutionary quaking that some detect beneath European ground. Many believe that with its stability turned into stagnation, its complacency and occasional self-satisfaction, the West has become the real obstruction to Germany's unification process. The substantial state contributions transferred from the West to the East do not give much satisfaction on either side. They seem to reach all too deeply into the pockets of affluent German citizens, who protest, as do more ordinary West German citizens, seized by fear of an economic downturn. Many seek comfort and direction from the new Pied Pipers of national populism. The readiness to recognize the need to make adjustments in the welfare state is not one that is very welcome anywhere in the industrialized world in the last decade of the twentieth century. This, of course, is also true in West Germany. There, however, the displeasure coincides with an absence of new goals. Since Germany has achieved its unification, realized its lofty ideal, it appears to be in danger of losing its sense of direction. The paradigm of German democracy is becoming less well-defined, the turns to be taken are less carefully and clearly analyzed. The whole effort is laborious and painful.

All nations that today live above the tectonic plates of recent large European quakes are acutely conscious that this is one of the "turning points of history," to use Karl Dietrich Bracher's apt expression. While the Eastern part of Europe is required to endure existential changes, the Western regions can no longer close their eyes to the consequences of their own development. Opposing camps in the earlier East-West conflict chained the antagonists to each other; with the dissolution of the conflict, the chains remain, though in very altered form. In this sense, Germany has become the new mirror of European development, the focal point of the crisis of change in the East and the crisis of adjustment in the West. While the European revolution continues, the Germans seek reconciliation; while the continent suffers from the realization that its unity has not been achieved despite all the rhetorical predictions of 1989, the Germans suffer from having been united too quickly, too closely, too intensely. While the overwhelming majority of Germans certainly have no wish to bring back the Wall and the unnaturalness of that division, even to mention longing for the return of the past is to sound a strange note. Yet, it is a comment on the discussions now taking place in Germany that such talk is heard in private.

In 1990, everything seemed so simple. The territory of the German Federal Republic, enlarged by 108,333 square kilometers, was expanded to 356,957 square kilometers. The population, increased by 16.1 million, numbered 79,670 million. The former German Democratic Republic (GDR) was divided into five Federal states under the technocratic sounding term "new *Länder,*" and East and West Berlin were collapsed into one new *Bundesland.* The unification process was given new impetus by the decision of the *Bundestag,* the newly comprehensive German parliament, to make Berlin the capital of Germany. In this exemplary fashion, the future was supposed to join together what had always belonged together. The framework of the well-tested West German constitution, the Basic Law, remained intact; so also did membership in the Western communities of integration and alliance, the European Community and NATO. There was much talk about a new normality—normalization—but few were able to define very clearly what this meant. The debate about normality soon changed into seemingly endless, metaphysically colored reflections about German identity and Germany's exceptional situation in the era after Hitler and the Holocaust.

Critics began to note that the new normality could easily lead to a new form of moralistic abnormality. Consciousness of Germany's "exceptionalism" was again rediscovered. Old and new volcanoes of nationalism started to erupt. While most of the credit that had gone to the old Federal Republic was attributed to its having irrevocably integrated West Germans into the Western community of culture and values, the question was suddenly in the air again.

Were those connections irrevocable? Should everything remain unexamined, given that the country was now larger, more fully sovereign, and had moved geographically into the very center of Central Europe? Friends of Germany in the West, and friends of the West in Germany, began to ask whether and how the country could be kept on its Western course. However distorted these concerns may have been, however reflective of deep feelings of relief in the German soul, however exaggerated by the media, they were again to the fore.

The frustration and disorientation, expressed in serious eruptions of violence and aggression, promised no good, dredging up old memories—unfair though they might be—and creating panic in some quarters. Politicians sought to reassure the public, to insist on Germany's dependability and stability. However, for quite a few Germans, politics had long ceased to be an effective system for representing popular opinion. They doubted that politicians could themselves cope with the crises of transition. For them, politics had become *the* problem.

* * *

Unification was accomplished through a political contract negotiated by Chancellor Helmut Kohl, who achieved the apex of his political career at that moment. The political community of reunited Germany, however, remained unstable. The social contract had to be refashioned, taking into account the changed nature of German society itself, with its altered political constellations. The old social contract is under close scrutiny, and many believe it to be in danger. It certainly needs to be revised. Some point at the politicians as the scapegoats for the crises of transition, but German society must look at itself. What is it that holds Germans together today? This has become the central question and is likely to remain so for many years. Politicians play only a secondary role in all this: the very fabric of society has been shaken, making many feel insecure. While social ties have been weakened in all parts of the Western world, and in all postcommunist states the crises of transition and dissolution are particularly conspicuous, it is only in Germany that the two come together.

The long-term consequences of these social adjustments and changes cannot fail to have their effect on Germany's political structures. Uncertainty about Germany's inner strength and cohesion has already had immediate and explosive consequences for its image, for its reputation as one of the leading European powers. How much does Germany trust itself? How much can the rest of the world trust Germany? What can it expect or hope for? Are its fears justified? An exhausted country, barely able to give precise, assuring, and reliable answers, is in no position to organize Europe. Intellectually malnourished and politically undefined, Germany is unable to fulfill its role in a post-Genscher Europe. Indeed, a confused Germany only serves to confuse an already rattled Europe.

The Germans are expected to redefine and clarify their interests, state their priorities, and depend on something other than outward rhetoric. In 1989, they were thought to be the happiest people in the world. They have enjoyed no reprieve that would allow them to heal their wounds, to cope with the problems of an East German citizenry entangled in the dictatorship of the old GDR. There has been no time to dry tears over the loss of workplaces in enterprises in the East, no longer nationally or internationally competitive. Nor has there been time to adjust the entire German social welfare state to the fact of scarce public funds. Germany's political structure is today being observed with keen interest; its role in Europe and the world is under close scrutiny. Europe expects stability from the country in its geographic center. The ability to act, to articulate values, to establish priorities must arise from within and cannot be wished on Germans from the outside. This is why Germany's social fiber and political development is of interest to many who live outside its borders.

Germany is in a transition crisis. No textbooks exist to explain how a centrally planned economy is to be converted into a market economy, especially one in which the attribute "social" is to be retained. Privatization and the restructuring of the economy, and of public life more generally, has taken place, at times largely as a process of learning by doing. Mistakes have been made. While there have been notable successes, many choose to dwell on the failures. Such a critical stance may be a virtue in the process of self-examination. It certainly explains the tales of woe spread by the media. Thousands of state enterprises have been privatized in East Germany since 1990; hundreds of thousands of new and secure workplaces have been created. Thousands of kilometers of rail have been laid down, and streets have been modernized. Telephone connections between East and West have been markedly improved. The Federal government cites transfer payments from the Fund of German Unity in the amount of DM 160 billion until 1994, but Germans are psychologically and culturally not brought together by such transfer payments, no matter how impressive they look. The climate has become rougher, in the West no less than in the East.

Strikes and threats of strikes are again making the headlines, providing noises not much heard in the old Federal Republic. The ironic phrase, *"ex oriente lux, ex occidente luxus,"* expresses a decision that is substantially less offensive than what is said in private. New public debates are today being conducted, with many demanding the need for new taxes and others arguing for the renegotiation of the Solidarity Pact, claiming that it has created new injustices. While in the Eastern states whole areas are threatened with deindustrialization, West Germans ask whether unification will indeed achieve its objectives. Did West Germans work productively for decades so that East Germans could drive on highways as good as their own? Was this what they sacrificed for? West Germans worry about losing their vaunted life-style comforts; East Germans find themselves thrown helplessly into torrential competitive waters. The unification of these mind-sets will not occur quickly.

West Germans have long since forgotten that their economy has enjoyed a net profit from the opening of the East. Few are prepared to accept that the economic recession and the unavoidable crisis of adjustment of the social state that existed before 1989 were in fact slowed down by unification. The "East/West division" and its postunification survival derive from a perspective that is much too superficial. For centuries, the true demarcation line in Germany was not East/West, but of peoples and regions: those in the Northwest and West, Catholic and influenced by Roman-Latin legacies, enjoyed a long tradition of open interaction with Western Europe; those in the Northeast and East, strongly Protestant, had infrastructures shaped by large property owners and were oriented toward the Slavic part of Europe. Whatever may still be relevant regarding these historic ligatures, the new economic dividing lines must have cultural and political influence on the powers that will compete in united Germany. Before unification, a lively debate took place in West Germany regarding the geographic advantages enjoyed by those who lived in the South over those who inhabited the North. Today, all economic indicators point to the fact that the South of the former GDR—Thuringia and Saxony—are experiencing a more speedy economic and technological renewal than the Northern areas of Germany. If these areas, with their old industrial centers, do not soon catch up with the South and the West as gravitational fields, new North/South divisions may overlay, and at times replace the Cold War East/West split.

Even after the "second death" of Karl Marx, certain of his insights remain relevant: being does determine consciousness. But what form of being determines the consciousness of a united Germany? So far, appeals to public virtue have largely dissipated, like smoke in air. Former Chancellor Helmut Schmidt characterized West German society as a "society of greed," unwilling to share its wealth, to show solidarity. In the East, the accumulating effects of materialism are quickly observed; it is today very far removed from anything that can be interpreted as postmaterialist forms of expression. But who can hold this against them when one considers that until recently East Germans had to wait five or more years to buy a new car of a quality not worth mentioning and were unable to travel to places many wished to go to? East Germans were obliged to live the gray existence of everyday socialism while hearing people in the West always insist that things in the GDR were not really all that bad and that conditions were bound to improve with time. That the East Germans wish to be Germans of affluence is scarcely surprising. Who can blame them for it? In fact, certain West Germans do. In these circumstances, what Germany is missing overall, in a peculiar sort of way, is a national discussion about the future orientation of the country, the future way of life of German society.

* * *

Germany is in danger of turning on its own axis, of consuming itself. Yet, questions about the future cannot be answered until the Germans come to terms with the past. How is the GDR to be categorized historically? What remains of it now that it has ceased to exist politically? During the decades of division, both German states were normative, not normal, products of World War II, German capitulation, and the decision made by the victorious powers. They were dependent states, adopting and pursuing the antagonistic values and objectives of their patrimonial allies. While West Germany was in a position to mesh its philosophy of life and its principles of statehood with that of Western civilization—many thought it to be the West's most diligent student—the GDR remained more an ideal than a viable entity. With communism as its legitimizing ideology, those states, whose *raison d'état* was nurtured by the promise of a utopia without social classes, were expected one day to disappear, but not in the way that they did. The GDR disappeared for the same reason that the other artificial states of Central and Eastern Europe went. They were supposed to embody the inevitable triumph of communism as a system providing material abundance. They failed on that score and on others, in the end losing the protection of their sole patron, the Soviet Union.

The historical investigation of the double history of Germany has only just begun. Germany has not just experienced a single and parallel "double history." It leaves the twentieth century with the experience of a double dictatorship. Both—the GDR and the Federal Republic— considered themselves the morally superior response to the tragedy of German twentieth-century history. The antifascist myth of the origins of the GDR never acknowledged or legitimized what it had itself become, a second German dictatorship. The East Germans, unable to escape their German identity by eliminating the concept of the "German nation" from their constitution, will one day have to confront the fact that the extinct GDR may be compared with the National Socialist dictatorship. The singularity of the Nazi horrors, for which the first German dictatorship is unquestionably accountable, will not absolve historical scholars from asking what habitual common elements existed between the two forms of totalitarian rule that established themselves on German soil in this century.

Coming to terms with the past and meeting the future will always lead to the same eternal question: What does it mean to be a German? While some in Germany imagine that they can answer this question by distancing and separating themselves, sometimes even feeling superior in a chauvinistic manner from non-German foreigners, others doubt whether the profile of "being German" can still be recognized in a reality of cultural diversity where more than four million foreigners are living permanently in Germany. Within the concept of multiculturalism, a "German identity" may only have as much meaning as can be given to cultural diversity in a situation where a common language and the recognition of a common legal system are accepted. In the old Federal Republic, constitutional patriotism surfaced as a substitute for national identity. The limits of this concept are now apparent. It is obvious today that "being German" means being part of a large and diverse family, with different cultural traditions and modes of thought, forms of architecture and ways of life, religious affiliations and communal ties. In its deepest foundations, German federalism, as it is recognized worldwide, reflects that multi-German reality. There are almost too many definitions of what makes a German or what a German is supposed to stand for. Behind the debate about a multicultural German future—which seems to center on the problem of how to facilitate the acquisition of citizenship—lies the much deeper question regarding the cohesion of a multi-German society. What holds them together, these Germans of so many origins and religions? This has become the really probing question that a reunited Germany is obliged to cope with. The discussion about foreigners and the eruptions of xenophobia are simply reactions to an unanswered basic definition of what it means to be German.

The cohesive power of inherited traditions has eroded in all "modern" societies, and, thus, is not a phenomenon specific to the Germans. It would only become important if, by resorting to a national myth, it became a quick and superficial recipe for integration. The tendency is not decisive. From all directions, Germans are today being urged to articulate their interests for the future, and not only in foreign politics, and to do so clearly and precisely. Certainly this is needed, but it is not a concept useful for structuring a future. Enthusiastic speculations about "civil society," for example, have remained largely theoretical so far. In both parts of Germany, the tendency toward individualism continues, combined with a diminished readiness to accept social ties and responsibilities. This, again, is not a uniquely German process; under German conditions, however, the mixture of insecurity and the longing for togetherness create a fertile climate for national-populist simplifications. One need not travel too far back in order to move again from a call for freedom to a longing for equality. Fears of an economic downturn, particularly among lower economic groups in the West, but also in the overprotected East, where memories of full employment and other social security benefits persist, make this a dangerous time. Far-Right populist groups are exploiting these dissatisfactions with a political establishment tending towards oligarchy for their own ends. Still, the German Republicans, for example, are probably less neo-National-Socialists than they are Social-Nationalists, if such a sophistic distinction is indeed permissible.

In Germany, it is true also that new vitality and creativity almost always return from the perimeters of the society. At the moment, however, what is noticed is a crumbling at the political periphery; there are few innovative impulses from the cultural and social fringes of society. The generation associated with the student revolts of 1968 has long since slid away from the social edge to the safe solidity of the saturated middle. The problems of their inheritance are apparent in a quite different realm, in the effects they (the parents of the late 1960s) had on their children and on their students. "1968" was as much the end of a development as the beginning of new tendencies. Mechanisms set free, allowing handed-down norms and traditions to be questioned and undermined in all Western societies, have had unintended consequences. Emancipation and participation replaced discipline, authority, and responsibility as the principal virtues of late bourgeois society. The result has been new freedoms, but also an absence of a sense of obligation; new opportunities in life have been opened, but old and valued relationships have been destroyed. In Germany, debates about the consequences of these developments converge with a search for new forms of relationships among East Germans, who were misused by an authoritarian state, who are now looking for new paths. Frustrated and irritated youth in both German societies are rapidly approaching the abyss where blind rage and an absence of social values turn them to violence. May one of the lessons from the violence against foreigners in Germany be that plural relativistic values can easily degenerate into self-destruction?

Where are new social ties to come from in united Germany? Is it not a mistake to question the spiritual powers of the church in a country whose peaceful revolution was to an important extent carried by Protestant ministers? From the beginning, such men played an important role in Germany. Madame de Staël, indeed, concluded her own investigations of late eighteenth and early nineteenth-century Germany with extensive consideration of the role of the Christian denominations in Germany. Protestantism, she thought, was the specific expression of a medieval German character. Its energies go inward, to the *"conviction intérieure,"* and draw their strength less from deed than from word, the word of scripture, discovered and interpreted more in Germany than almost anywhere else. Some choose to see Germans as a nonreligious, though theological people. For Madame de Staël, Martin Luther was the quintessential German man, driven by an inspiring fanaticism and courage, easily frozen into stubbornness and immobility, but dominated by a passion for the truth. German Catholicism, Madame de Staël wrote, was the religion of minorities compelled to adapt themselves to Protestant Germany. She saw them as more tolerant than Catholics in many other parts of Europe—more tolerant but also softer, perhaps less well-defined. In any case, German Catholics remained largely on the defensive during long stretches since the Reformation. Not until recent times—during the years of the Federal Republic—were they able to constitute a numerical majority. Given the basically Catholic orientation and philosophy of the Christian Democrats, many were tempted to characterize the link from Adenauer to Kohl as the link of Catholic Germany. Certainly, the convictions of West European Catholic leaders after the War—Konrad Adenauer, Robert Schumann, and Alcide de Gasperi—were immensely influential with respect to European politics.

What has remained of all this? Since unification, the German Protestants have again become the majority of German Christians. Luther's country appears to be returning to its traditions. Still, this may be a premature assessment. In reality, the churches of East Germany have become steadily emptier since the end of the revolution; as empty as they have been for a long time in West Germany. Only about 66 percent of all Germans belong to one of the two Christian churches or are even baptized. In East Germany, the number of people without a religious affiliation is estimated at 50 percent. The consequences of handed-down atheistic indoctrination during the years of the socialist regime merge today with the effects of Western secularization, which may be best described as a weakening of all confessional and church ties. The churches in Germany—

the Roman-Catholic as well as the Evangelical—remain highly institutionalized and socially important. At the same time, they have themselves become, to a large extent, one expression of the pluralism of the society. Their ranks are not a mirror image of the ethical and political spectrum of society, and their authority in providing moral direction to the society as a whole has suffered significantly. Neither the Church nor the various religious affiliations—let alone God—are the links that hold the Germans together.

Every contemporary analysis of religious phenomena in Germany must take into account two factors that are new, that are worth considering. First, there is a rebirth of Jewish communities. Two generations after the Holocaust, some forty thousand Jews have chosen Germany as their homeland. This is not a large number, not nearly enough when one considers the importance of Jewish culture in Germany, of all the traditions destroyed by the Nazis. Still, new Jewish communities have become established in various German cities, and a considerable number of Jews who emigrated from Russia have settled in Germany. Berlin seems to be closer for them than Jerusalem. Second, there are now more than a million Muslims in Germany. The majority belong to the large contingent of Turkish guest workers and their families who have brought multicultural character to the life of so many metropolitan cities.

Muslim communities are today a solid presence in German society, but the use of the Turks as scapegoats to explain the difficulties of reunification—in the minds of some Germans at least—have raised doubts about how accepted they really are. The suggestion of a possible dual citizenship to improve the legal rights of Turks living in Germany, together with the debates on the narrow ethnic definition of the legal status of Germans, defines the nature of today's battles. Should citizenship be expanded? It is for the Germans to decide, and not the foreigners. Germans, extremely heterogeneous, and frequently unsure about the proper conduct towards each other, let alone foreigners, are uncertain. Are they more afraid of the others or of themselves? The discussion about a multicultural society in Germany is principally about self-acceptance by Germans.

But where do we find Germany's driving intellectual powers? Where can the *"esprit humain"* be found, which Madame de Staël so extravagantly lauded at the start of the nineteenth century? The spirit of "world-mindedness" must have found a new refuge; it is certainly not inside German universities, which for a very long time figured as the paradigm of German cultural life. Wilhelm von Humboldt's enthusiastic spirit of reform has been replaced by educational bureaucracies that manage academic life less well than their once-criticized predecessors. Mass applications and diminished quality, an absence of competition and vision, not least concerning the concept of the university, have taken hold in Germany. The recent German Nobel laureates are all working in private institutions and enterprises. German higher educational institutions go on debating essentially trivial matters, hoping to conceal their inner atrophy. Structurally, these institutions resemble the bureaucratic socialist bodies of the recent past: responsibilities have become anonymous; democratic committees lack higher aspirations and have little impact. In the absence of quality control, of real competition, there is no choice in selecting students. The doubtful assurances by the state regarding the continued financing of tenured faculty are not believed in. The German university system has become the Achilles' heel of German society, whose primary resource needs to be education and knowledge. Instead of urgently initiating necessary structural reforms, the West German university system was exported to East Germany with great promise. It is one of the most conspicuous failures of the German unification process.

Personality and character cannot be produced in the way that cars and machines are made. But even those naturally endowed, entrusted to be the spiritual and the moral examples to the nation— the intellectuals—are speechless and colorless. Many among the East Germans are licking the wounds incurred by uncovering the truth about their opportunistic proximity to the old regime of the GDR. Many among the West Germans seem to excuse what they once said and wrote; their efforts to maintain the same distance from the Honecker regime as from specific Western societies are recognized to have been a delusion. While in certain other postcommunist countries intellectuals have become the new moral leaders, in Germany there is no adequate treatment of the demise of the GDR, the dismantling of the Wall, the reunification of the country. In a country where the lives of millions were deeply affected, the ink has dried up for those who once paraded themselves as keen observers, even creators of the *Zeitgeist*. Whimpering replaces the sense of greatness and drama at a time of continuous change in both Germany and the whole of Europe. The true promoters of the "spirit of the age" in Germany today are the electronic media. The talk show has established itself as *the* discussion forum in public life. Evening after evening, displays of the inadequacies of the unification process are celebrated. The powerful figures of the media frequently employ an excited, highly-pitched language grotesquely imitative of the reality it is supposed to represent. Here — and this again is not a phenomenon unique to Germany—the fires of opinion are fueled, and public courts of inquisition are set up, especially against politicians who have become unpopular. Can it, in the end, be the media—particularly television—that holds German society together? Do these television moguls determine what Germans think, decide who they ought to be, what is good for them? "Infotainment"—a benighted mixture of entertainment and political reporting—takes over every topic of quasi-public interest. In the process, the forum of politics is shifted onto television. The more the parliamentary processes of politics—and especially their actors—are criticized, the more the questions "who controls those who are prominent in the media?" and "who are politically powerful?" have to be raised. Currently, such issues scarcely figure in open political discussions.

This is all occurring in a climate where the tone of politics is becoming increasingly rough, more unforgiving. West German democracy achieved its strength through the power of its consensus-forming mechanisms. Coalition talks, compromises on a common denominator, seeking to please as many as possible, and the distribution system guaranteed by the welfare state assured an atmosphere of civilized well-being. This stability—in a certain sense—has turned into stagnation. The Germans criticize themselves by imagining that they can place the blame wholly on the politicians. How can tried-and-true consensus politics flourish unscathed in a society where consensus is no longer believed in? Germans are confronting years of more conflictual weather than many of them have ever experienced.

The reasons in the East and the West may be different, but nothing will arrest the tempest. In this situation, German democracy will again have to prove itself. Debates about the first nationwide election of the new German head-of-state have already provided a taste of what is to come. Through unification, the country has returned from the artificial to the real. The environment of the premier structural and institutional frameworks—the constitutional state and the social market economy, membership in the European Community and North-Atlantic Alliance—provide hopeful insurance. The contents of the framework, however, are no longer subject to traditional procedures and tried stereotypes.

New debates regarding distribution are taking place under the pretext of the necessity of tax increases, in the context of the Solidarity Pact. Serious concerns are being voiced about the ability to govern in the future, caused by growing dissatisfaction with compromises largely reduced to formulas by coalition politics, but also by new opposition parties. The "people's parties"—one of the more valuable guarantors of stability in the democracy of West Germany so far—are experiencing the threat of losing support from larger groups of people than ever before. Exhaustion takes its toll in the midst of success, as do new experiences of the limits of politics as such, particularly under conditions of profound social change.

While German society has begun to sort itself out, to redirect itself, to redefine itself, painfully and at times unwillingly, early signs of a process of renewal of political life in the whole of united Germany are only barely visible. Predictions go against the grain of any sober analysis of the present situation. Still, it is obvious that this multi-German society may soon be confronted with multiparty parliaments and not always stable coalitions. Former Chancellor Helmut Schmidt has recommended the introduction of a majority voting right. Like other voices on this issue, his remains largely unheard in a state where established coalition parties still govern. This may soon change.

Germany is today facing great opportunities and new dangers. Its most pronounced break with nineteenth- and twentieth-century German history may well lie in the possibility of the country continuing its support of integration into the supranational structures of the European Community. The greatest difficulty for the Germans, now living in their second, however Europeanized, nation-state, is to keep the right balance between efforts of national and European integration, not to stretch the bow too tightly in either direction. Today, optimists are those who think that the future is uncertain.

Were Madame de Staël to return to Germany today, she would be shocked by the absence of enthusiasm, the confusion and uncertainty of public discussion about values and goals, interests and ideals. The Germans must resolve their own problems. Their encounter with the future began with the removal of the Wall. Germany, and all those who view the country from the outside, ought to draw comfort from the past, from the democratic decades of West Germany and the peaceful revolution in the GDR, from the economic miracle in the West and, in spite of all the difficulties that exist, the first economic and social signs of renewal in the East. The constitutional consensus and friendly ties with all neighbors passed the test of reunification. One basic fact has surely changed since Madame de Staël's visit to Germany: the joys and sorrows of today are only in small measure specifically German. The transition phase in Germany reflects the revolutionary developments taking place throughout Europe. One may very well intensify and accelerate the other. History has become open again. In Europe, unification remains an inspiring goal, however far removed from reality. In Germany, unification has occurred; it is impossible to escape its consequences. Whether the *"esprit humain"* will be able to find a new, firm, and lasting place in a freedom-loving and peaceful harbor here or there is quite another matter.

Translated by
Lieselotte Anderson

"People are born as revolutionaries," the German liberal Bamberger wrote during his Parisian exile in 1862, as he attempted to explain the enigma of Bismarck's personality. "The accident of life decides whether one becomes a Red or a White revolutionary." Many years later Bismarck said that Bamberger was one of the few authors who had understood him.

What is a revolutionary? If the answer to this question were not ambiguous, few revolutionaries could succeed; the aims of revolutionaries seem self-evident only to posterity. This is sometimes due to deliberate deception. More frequently, it reflects a psychological failure: the inability of the "establishment" to come to grips with a fundamental challenge. The refusal to believe in irreconcilable antagonism is the reverse side of a state of mind to which basic transformations have become inconceivable. Hence, revolutionaries are often given the benefit of every doubt. Even when they lay down a fundamental theoretical challenge, they are thought to be overstating their case for bargaining purposes; they are believed to remain subject to the "normal" preferences for compromise. A long period of stability creates the illusion that change must necessarily take the form of a modification of the existing framework and cannot involve its overthrow. Revolutionaries always start from a position of inferior physical strength; their victories are primarily triumphs of conception or of will.

Henry A. Kissinger

From "The White Revolutionary: Reflections on Bismarck"
Dædalus 97 (3) (Summer 1968)

Mary Fulbrook

Aspects of Society and Identity in the New Germany

W HEN THE GERMAN DEMOCRATIC REPUBLIC (GDR) collapsed in 1989–1990, West Germany's success story—a story of economic prosperity and democratic stability—appeared to have been vindicated. The accession on October 3, 1990 of the newly recreated East German *Länder* to an enlarged Federal Republic of Germany, under the existing West German constitution, was predicated on the hope that soon the East would, essentially, become like the West.

Yet, the years since 1990 have shown these early hopes and assumptions to have been mistaken. Despite the circumstances of its birth, the new Germany is not going to be simply an enlarged, dyspeptic version of the former Federal Republic, suffering a little bout of indigestion in the wake of swallowing its smaller, poorer neighbor. Although more is changing, and will continue to change, in the Eastern *Länder* than in the West, something new is emerging for all Germans. The leadership of the new Germany is floundering, searching for an appropriate international and European role; the populations of East and West Germany are registering degrees of divergence and dissimilarity, trying to define new identities in the face of complex social changes. While it is too early to predict what will emerge, it is possible to identify some of the current transformations in social and national identity in the new Germany.

A SENSE OF *HEIMAT?* LANDSCAPES AND BOUNDARIES

In ways difficult to define, but immensely important, identity is often rooted in a sense of place. The German preoccupation with

Mary Fulbrook is Director of the Centre for European Studies at University College London.

229

Heimat—an essentially untranslatable word referring to one's home-land with which one closely identifies—is traditionally very strong. Dialect, accent, custom, modes of behavior, landscape, and bound-aries are all important.

There has been a major impact on West Germans, with reverber-ations that will not go away soon. Put most starkly, the Iron Curtain has moved from West to East: from being the Western boundary of the Soviet Empire, designed to keep the Eastern Euro-pean population in, to being the Eastern boundary of "Western Europe," increasingly designed to keep unwanted migrants out. The most important visible result for West Germans of the changed boundaries of Germany has been the rapid increase in the number of people moving from East to West: the asylum seekers and economic migrants from the newly opened countries of Eastern Europe and elsewhere. The impression of being "swamped" by "floods" of foreigners has created widespread unease. The loss of faith in the established political parties is palpable even among many "respectable" Germans who would not normally sympathize with overt acts of violent xenophobia, but who nevertheless feel that a "problem" exists that no major political party is prepared to grapple with.[1] In the years following the fall of the Berlin Wall, the comment was often made, only half in jest, that "it would have been better if, instead of pulling the Wall down, they had made it a little taller."

It is not so much the visible boundaries as the invisible ones—those defining citizenship and immigration, who is welcome and who must be kept out—that West Germans are now being required to rethink. And, as the debates over citizenship and immigration during the last year have revealed, a majority of Germans continue to think primarily in terms of a culturally homogenous, monoethnic community, the "purity" of which must be protected. In the cozy decades of material well-being and closed borders to the East, the old conceptions of "who is German" could rest dormant, unexamined; this is no longer the case.

For East Germans, nearly everything has changed. They gained long coveted West German citizenship without needing to go into exile to the West; but all around them their homeland has not remained the same. Some changes are clearly highly desirable, at least in their initial political import. The long line of the former inner-German border, with its wire, tank tracks, and mine fields, will soon revert to grass and undergrowth punctuated by deserted watchtowers and the ruins of heavily fortified crossing points. Where the Berlin Wall once stood there are now property developers and wastelands, occupied by the stalls of peddlers selling off the insignia and memorabilia of the old regime.

The whole landscape of East Germany itself is being radically transformed. Roads are being resurfaced, buildings renovated, streets and squares renamed; statues and memorials are being pulled down, tourist attractions spruced up, and new telephone boxes installed on street corners. Gone are the old banners (*"Alles zum Wohle des Volkes!"*); in their place are advertisements for cigarettes and savings banks. But not everything is undergoing renovation and renewal: far from the "blossoming landscapes" promised by Chancellor Kohl, recurrent features of the East German landscape are deserted factories, rusting industrial dinosaurs lying idle and empty as they await their fate in the privatization lottery.

Changes are partially creeping, partially planned, partially contested; while deserted industrial plants may be taken over by rust and weeds, cultural high spots—the classical center of Goethe's Weimar and the Wartburg castle where Luther translated the New Testament—are being invested with a double significance: they are at once symbols of the continuity of the German *Kulturnation,* the acceptable cultural unity of Germans, and, at the same time, they will aid the ailing East German economy by attracting quantities of Western tourists. While this represents some continuity with East German policies of the 1980s, it is now undertaken with Western capital and consumerist expertise. The preservation and representation of the past in museums and archives—the bases for the construction of a public memory—have been the focus of heated attention, while massive debates surround plans for city-center renovation in that symbol of the horrors of World War II, Dresden, and in the designated political capital of the new Germany, Berlin.

In the former GDR, everything now looks different, or nearly everything. Although the lines on the map remain much the same, some of them have been reconnected and blank areas filled in; the names, symbols, and colors of the environment have changed.

This is disorientating, particularly for the old, who are unnerved by the new card-operated telephones, the changes in the names of streets and squares, the revolutions in the transport networks, and the expansion of horizons. For many East Germans, who in principle welcome the modernization of facilities and services, there may yet remain a tinge of ambivalence, linked with a more generalized sense of colonization by the affluent Big Brother from the West. Although it is very difficult to define precisely, a sense of identity—personal, social, and national—is very closely tied in with the landscape in which one lives and moves. The outward and visible changes in the appearance of East Germany are the external correlate of the dramatic reshaping of the contours, rules, and symbols of the less tangible social landscape in which citizens of the new Germany have to learn to live.

THE HISTORICAL FORMATION OF *WESSIS* AND *OSSIS*

As West and East Germans started to renew their acquaintance with one another after the fall of the Wall, the claim to be *"ein Volk"* was rapidly replaced by denigratory jokes about the newly perceived differences between *Wessis* and *Ossis*. Can the historian, anthropologist, or sociologist tell us about the historical processes shaping different patterns of motivation and reaction, different perceptions and personality types, and the sociopolitical production of different psychologies? How have different groups responded to the new interactions and challenges of the "united" Germany of the present?

The political structures of the two Germanys were radically different. Despite the fact that both East and West Germany were developing industrial societies, with associated tendencies (more marked in the West than the East) to urbanization, the expansion of new technologies and the growth of the service sector, and the political conditions of socialization, work, leisure, and social involvement were, nevertheless, so very different that quite different practices and perceptions were found in the two states.[2]

The East German leadership devoted strenuous efforts to seeking to create a new national identity for East Germans. In the early decades, this was predicated on the claim to being the "better Germany," having made the more complete break with the Nazi past, representing a stage on the allegedly inevitable path of historical progress towards a utopian future. Later, after *Ostpolitik*, more attention was paid to the here and now: the stressing of a distinctive GDR identity, the amelioration of social conditions, the resurrection of links with long German traditions, and the reappropriation of heroes from the past.

These efforts were, in the presence of a visibly more affluent and liberal society on the other side of the Wall, never entirely successful. Yet, the pressures of living in constrained political and material circumstances left their stamp on the social characters of the population.

The key factor in the East was the issue of political conformity. From this everything else essentially flowed. Talent in combination with political conformity—better still, active engagement—was the key to personal advance. Refusal to conform—worse, visible nonconformity—effectively meant renouncing any serious career aspirations and running the risk of a lifetime of surveillance and insecurity, imprisonment or exile.

A minority were committed to the proclaimed goals of the ruling Socialist Unity Party (SED). This was a "mass" as well as a "cadre" party, one in five of the adult population being a member of it in the early 1980s. The majority of grass-roots members—not functionaries or activists—of the SED and of the affiliated "bloc" parties and mass organizations were often members for personal reasons of conformity and career advancement rather than genuine conviction. Many who made this choice at the time, and who by virtue of their positions effectively sustained the regime, are now finding themselves personally penalized in often quite disproportionate ways.[3]

A majority of the population could be classified as those who engaged in a combination of "*Anpassung und meckern*": conformity and grumbling. Allotment gardens, weekend cottages, and nightly watching of Western television provided just enough relaxation and escapism, in what Günter Gaus has classically dubbed the "niche society," to make life tolerable. The majority of the East German population suffered decades of deprivation in an often dispirited conformity, quite realistically judging that, in the presence of the Wall and Soviet tanks, there was in fact no plausible alternative.

Sullen acquiescence was punctuated occasionally by more active expressions of popular discontent. The extent of popular unrest in the GDR is only now beginning to become apparent with the opening of the archives. There were far more unofficial work stoppages, industrial disputes, daubing of subversive slogans, and distribution of forbidden leaflets than ever previously appreciated. Discontent and opposition were usually based in criticisms of, or in protests against, particular local conditions: changes in wage levels or working conditions, arbitrary dismissals, or poor food from the canteen. Occasionally—as in the late summer of 1968, when Warsaw Pact tanks rolled into Czechoslovakia to suppress the Prague Spring—protests were more directly political in nature. But for the most part, while it was very clear what political protests were directed *against*, it was less clear what any positive popular program might be. A certain ideological confusion (aided by the regime's own conflation of Western democracy and fascism) allowed appeals to both Adenauer and Hitler, democracy and Nazism, in support of opposition to the communist regime of the GDR. The fact that an uprising on the scale and visibility of June 17, 1953 did not reappear until the mass demonstrations of the autumn of 1989 is a testimony more to the cohesion of elites and the rapid repression and isolation of popular discontent than to any real lessening in the extent of the latter.[4]

Finally, there were those—a small minority—who refused to conform. Many prominent intellectual dissidents in the GDR were "Third Way" Marxists, democratic socialists or humanistic communists, who opposed the neo-Stalinist, bureaucratic perversion of socialist ideals. They failed to gain mass followings, for one reason or another (not least the rather austere character of some of their programs). From the late 1970s, grass-roots pressure groups began to develop under the partially protective wing of the Protestant Churches, following the historic church-state agreement of 1978. These groups played an important role in the "gentle revolution" of 1989; it was these people who were the most bitterly disappointed by what they saw as the ultimate betrayal of their hopes for a better GDR.

The official attempts at creating a "GDR national identity," whether through international sporting successes or pride in historical traditions and legacies (the resurrection of Martin Luther and Frederick the Great), had manifestly never completely succeeded. The lures of material plenty in the West, enjoyed vicariously through television over decades, were sufficient to cause a stampede of the masses once the Wall was breached. "*Wir sind das Volk,*" the slogan of the courageous few who dared to demonstrate for reform and dialogue within the GDR in the early days, was rapidly replaced with "*Wir sind ein Volk*" when Western standards of living appeared within the grasp of the masses.

Who then were the West Germans from whom the Eastern brothers and sisters had been separated for so long and with whom they now proclaimed a common identity? The West Germans had also traveled a long road since they had started rebuilding from the ruins and rubble of 1945. A few brief remarks must suffice here to suggest some salient points of contrast. First, the Federal Republic of Germany prior to unification was both economically successful and politically stable. The "economic miracle" of the 1950s served to anchor the new democracy in a manner never granted to its ill-fated grandparent, the Weimar Republic. The relative leniency, indeed inefficacy, of the half-hearted policies of mass denazification in West Germany, combined with the Cold War concentration on the enemy without, communism, and a focus on the future ("*Wir bauen auf!*"), allowed for a rapid absorption and reintegration into the mainstream of those who might have presented a source of political disaffection and revisionism. Although the attempts of West Germany to overcome its past were always problematic, by the 1980s a new generation was beginning to heed the cry, prevalent in some quarters, that it was time to "normalize" the past and enjoy the more privileged status of those fortunate enough to have been born afterwards. With a widespread rise in standards of living, and the existence of an easily ignored underclass of *Gastarbeiter* (guest workers) to carry the burden of poverty, many West Germans felt it was possible, if not to be proud to be German, then at least to be proud of the German economy. For left-liberal critics of the *Bundesrepublik*, this could be denigrated as "deutsch-mark nationalism"; for them, however, a discredited German nationalism could arguably be replaced by a "patriotism of the constitution," a pride in the Basic Law (*Grundgesetz*), which seemed to have performed remarkably well in securing democracy in Germany.

West Germans, by the later 1980s—despite characteristic angst and agonizing, whether over the death of the forests or the quest for national identity—were in general a relatively satisfied population, enjoying a degree of material prosperity, financial stability, industrial harmony, and social security that was the envy of many

European neighbors. There were, of course, unresolved problems and unsettling trends—growing unemployment and slowing rates of economic growth, an aging population, a rise in industrial disputes, increasing voter disaffection and volatility, the continued, if sporadic, actions of left-wing terrorists (particularly the Red Army Faction, RAF), and the development of new right-wing movements and parties in the 1980s. But for all the individual criticisms and campaigns, for all the political scandals, for all the vituperation and intellectual sniping so prevalent in German public debate, there was a broad, albeit unspoken, consensus that basically things were moving in the right direction: that conflicts could be resolved within the standard parameters of the political system, that economic troubles would eventually give way to renewed growth, that the essentially inexorable road to European integration would ultimately resolve Germany's identity crises once and for all in a postnational era.

And then came the "national" unification of two disparate societies. The future now looks very different.

SOCIAL CHANGE IN EASTERN GERMANY: AN AMBIVALENT EXPERIENCE

The acquisition of formal freedom and a democratic political system is clearly to be welcomed. It was this, after all, for which citizens of the former GDR voted—along with West German living standards—in their only free elections in March 1990. But there are associated social upheavals. There has been an as yet incomplete process of transformation of elites. Obviously, members of the prominent political elite groups lost their former positions rather rapidly. So have large numbers of people who had made compromises with the former regime and led modestly successful lives pursuing professional careers. Here I shall concentrate not on the formal or structural political changes and exchange of political elites, but on selected aspects of social life.

The *Stasi* witch-hunt, whipped up by the media—and certainly a fascinating topic in a postdictatorial society—has led to a widespread climate of resentment tinged with suspicion and self-justification. Revelations about the extent of *Stasi* infiltration and informing, and the sheer vastness of the *Stasi* archives, ensure that this will long remain a contentious issue among those East Germans who held positions of prominence in a wide range of professions. Generally, East Germans between forty and sixty years old, who had climbed an often arduous ladder in the GDR to hold positions of responsibility, are finding that they are now effectively consigned to the professional scrap heap. Alongside the bitterness of wasted years are accusations of harm done to others under the previous regime. To understand the intricacies of the *"Täter/Opfer"* (oppressor and victim) claims and complaints will require a far more differentiated and extensive interpretation of the functioning of the East German dictatorship than is presently informing either official policy or popular debate.

Many more East German workers are experiencing uncertainties and unemployment for less personal reasons. The politically motivated decisions to have a one-to-one exchange rate, to raise Eastern wage levels towards Western standards even before there were comparable productivity levels, and to complicate the legal tangles of privatization by privileging restitution over compensation have combined to exacerbate the economic problems of a postcommand economy which has lost its Comecon markets and is newly exposed to the chill winds of Western competition. The real unemployment rate is quite devastating for people who had been accustomed to a degree of security (at the price of freedom) under the old regime. The mood in East Germany is, of course, very mixed: for those with work, and with wider horizons and more exciting prospects, a sense of optimism is well-founded. But others are finding out the hard way that not all of the former regime's propaganda about the difference between real and formal freedoms under capitalism was false. This ambivalence is evident, whichever social group one chooses to focus on. Let us take the example of women.

For the vast majority of East German women, unification has meant a major change in life-style and prospects. The much vaunted "emancipation" of women under actually existing socialism meant effectively the carrying of a "double burden." It was a woman's duty, as well as right, to work: over 50 percent of the GDR work force was female, and female participation in the paid labor force was supported by generous maternity benefits combined with an extensive network of state child-care provision, from crèches through kindergartens to after-school facilities. The correlate for many women, in a society where the division of labor in the household remained largely traditional, and where there was a relatively high incidence of divorce and single-parent families, was an extremely long and demanding day. Nevertheless, for women with the appropriate talents and commitment, the GDR offered genuine opportunities; in virtually all walks of life, with the notable and major exception of the higher echelons of politics (where, of course, all real power was concentrated), women were represented rather more equally in the GDR than in West Germany.[5] It became more or less taken for granted that women would not only work (which was a legal obligation), but would have education, training, and career aspirations largely comparable to those of men, in a way that never became the norm in the West.

Many East German women who had become accustomed to working are now faced with all the psychological and social consequences of the loss of affordable child-care facilities and the experience of unemployment for the first time in their lives.[6] Moreover, the introduction of Western work practices into East Germany appears to have had wider effects on the employment of women, irrespective of whether they are mothers of young children. In a situation of rising unemployment, more women than men have lost jobs. Women have also been reemployed at a lower rate than men. Sectors of the economy that traditionally employ female labor (such as the tertiary service sector) have not been growing as fast as predicted. Moreover, women are generally less likely than men to commute very long distances or to seek work in the West. In January 1992, women represented 61.6 percent of the total unemployed in Eastern Germany, and the real percentage is likely to rise—although in the course of time, many women will ultimately be lost to the statistics as they choose to remain in the home.[7]

Interestingly, increasing numbers of East German women are reacting to the new uncertainties on a range of fronts—unemployment, loss of child-care facilities, the abortion debate—by simply renouncing family life: the birthrate fell by half in the two years after unification, while, with the loss of free contraception in all states except Brandenburg, the number of sterilizations increased dramatically.[8] East German women appear to be losing not only their "double burden," but also the possibility of enhanced choice and independence that unification might have brought. It seems that Western assumptions and practices are taking precedence over forty years of combining career and family—but in a situation where women were previously organized from above and have little experience of independent political organization and mobilization.[9] This appears to be very much a case of "one step forward, two steps back": loss of economic independence without either a Western standard of living or patterns of political activism.

THE RISING GENERATION: YOUTH, EDUCATION, AND SOCIALIZATION

It is predominantly young people, those who had not advanced high enough to be seriously tainted politically, and who show talent and willingness, who can now seize the opportunities available to them in united Germany—within the context of rising unemployment and severe competition for jobs. There was a certain paradox about the mutual perceptions of young people, East and West, before 1989. Unable to penetrate beyond the Iron Curtain, young East Germans retained a lively interest in the forbidden fruits of the other side. They watched Western television with interest, followed the Western youth music scene, led the way in the pursuit of Western fashions. But the interest was not mutual. Many young West Germans, for whom the Iron Curtain was entirely permeable if they had the desire to travel as tourists to the East, in practice evinced ever less any sense of common identity with or interest in the East, any sense of belonging to two parts of a divided country.[10]

There continues to be such asymmetry since unification. Although there are clearly underlying trends affecting young people in Western Germany—particularly relating to the impact of economic recession and rising unemployment—the education and training systems have remained essentially the same. The West German vocational and apprenticeship systems continue to be renowned for their thoroughness, the overcrowding at West German universities continues to be bewailed as ever-worsening. But in East Germany, for young people everything has changed. For many young East Germans, the world has been opened up. The fall of the Wall has presented tremendous opportunities. The chance to travel, to explore countries that had previously been blank areas on the map of the "capitalist-imperialist" West, to study and debate freely, and to follow a career on the basis of talent rather than political conformity should not be underestimated.

But the picture is not all so rosy. Freedom in theory is tempered by constraints in reality, and even by the loss of many social and economic supports that were present in the old regime, whatever its political shortcomings.

The education system has undergone massive upheavals and transformation. Teachers have been purged, syllabuses revised, expectations and performance criteria radically altered. Universities in the five new *Länder* have been radically restructured, faculties of Marxism-Leninism abolished, other (politically sensitive, regime-supportive) departments pruned, overhauled, effectively dismantled, and reconstructed with "politically acceptable" individuals, very often Western imports. Established East German academics, to retain their positions, have to prove their political cleanliness as well as their academic achievements and potential. This is often an impossible combination, since quantitative productivity was strongly correlated with political conformity under the old system, and academic originality, innovation, and openness to empirical evidence—the criteria of the West—were in many fields associated with constrained career advancement and the restriction of opportunities to publish or participate in international debates.[11] This situation has provided a rich hunting-ground for frustrated talents from the West, seeing dramatically improved opportunities for rapid promotion in a part of Germany to which many West Germans are not tempted to remove themselves.

For those young enough to be coming to maturity in the new, still rather uncertain circumstances, it is not too difficult to adjust; for those who had developed under the old system, more rethinking and reorientation is required. For people in whom it had been instilled from birth that conformity to official views (whatever one's private opinion) was the main prerequisite for personal advancement, a certain relativism has set in. If history is no longer the history of class struggles, each stage leading inexorably on to the next higher stage of world-historical progress, then how are we to interpret the past? If what we were told (or were not told) about the Hitler-Stalin pact of 1939 was wrong, if what we have been led to believe about the liberation of the innocent German victims of fascism by the glorious peace-loving Red Army was misleading, then how do we know that any of the (often mutually conflicting) Western accounts of the Third Reich are any more true? Young East Germans often resign themselves to the view that they simply have to learn new orthodoxies and doctrines, and find out what it is that they now ought to be repeating to their teachers in order to succeed.

The degree of intellectual anomie experienced by the loss of authority—or of authoritarianism—in the educational field is associated with a broader problem of the newfound freedom, the loss of state organization of leisure. Not that the SED state ever entirely succeeded in fitting a perfect straitjacket to its young people, but there was at least a framework within which to conform or against which to rebel. This has been replaced, for many young East Germans, by something approaching a vacuum.

The use of free time by youth in the GDR was always a problematic issue for the authorities. From the earliest years after the War, the Communists had been faced with reeducating young people who had been subjected to over a decade of Hitler's propaganda and organizations, such as the Hitler Youth. Young people were the locus of both fear and hope for the Communists: apprehension about their likely attitudes if left too much to themselves or under the uncontrolled influence of adults; recognition that young people would provide the cadres, the leadership, the socialist personalities of the future. SED youth policies were marked by a combination of a desire, on the one hand, to treat youth with tolerance and understanding, and a determination, on the other, that they should be sufficiently controlled and influenced as never to wish or be able to deviate from the party line.

In the 1950s, there was a degree of justified concern about how to gain even a foothold among the young people of East Germany. As reports that have now become available in the East German archives reveal, in many areas patterns of social activity continued that seemed impervious to Communist penetration. A variety of strategies—including not only improvements in the attractiveness of Free German Youth (FDJ) offerings, but also vicious attacks on the Christian *Junge Gemeinde* organization and the attempted displacement of confirmation in church by the secular ceremony of the *Jugendweihe* (introduced in 1954)—were deployed to rectify this state of affairs.

By the 1960s, the organization and institutional support of the SED youth organizations were clearly far better developed, and the more informal associational life of parishes was in some decline. But youth disaffection and unwillingness to be completely coerced into formal state-organized activities remained a perpetual, if fluctuating, problem for the regime throughout the 1970s and 1980s.[12] A majority conformed sufficiently to evade any disadvantaging of their school career or future prospects: a minority at each end of the spectrum was prepared either to participate more actively, to take on a position as a functionary and seek to get ahead, or to take a principled stand, refuse to join in, and be sidelined into a marginal position in "actually existing socialism," irrespective of talent and achievement. Youth disaffection in the GDR has been captured in numerous images, which have by now gained a wider audience, ranging from the literary representation in the novel by Ulrich Plenzdorf, *Die neuen Leiden des jungen W.*,[13] to the emergence of the variant colors of the "alternative" youth scene of the 1980s, including—to name a very disparate list of often totally opposing groups—rock fans, punks, skinheads, dissident poets, environmentalist and peace activists, drug addicts and alcoholics, and a mass of generally disaffected, dispirited, but essentially apathetic others. In short, the SED never succeeded entirely in its aim of capturing and converting the whole of youth, of bringing people up with a sincere conviction in the rectitude of SED goals and an energetic commitment to personal participation in the active building of socialist society.

And yet, there were structures. There were places to go. There were organizations, meetings, ceremonies, rituals—however formal and meaningless, however enforced and empty. There were uniforms and banners, parades and honors, functions and friendships. There were parameters of social life, however one might snipe and sneer, rebel or resist. These have now gone.

In the often dismal towns and villages of the former GDR, groups of young people are at loose ends. The wave of "*DDR-Nostalgie*," a nostalgia for a rose-tinted view of the good old days, is rooted partly in a sense of anomie—of normlessness, however much one might previously have railed against the externally imposed norms. In the dark streets of town centers where plaster crumbles off the facades of decrepit old buildings, or in the desolate wastes of the vast concrete housing estates of actually existing socialism, young people may have freedom, but it is the freedom to wander the streets, to stare forlornly into run-down ice-cream cafes or super-markets, offering a range of goods beyond their pockets. While the vast majority of young people would abhor acts of racism and violence, it is in this soil that, among an ever more active minority, neo-Nazism has been able to put down distinctive roots.

From the perspective of the West, the fear of change is arguably more important than the reality. Fear of unemployment, of having to bear a greater burden of the costs of unification, of the "floods" of foreigners and the loss of the comfortable securities of old all give rise to the pervasive sense of drift, of loss of faith in established political parties, of loss of belief in European integration as the panacea for all ills, particularly now that there are so many new problems in Germany's own backyard. Although with the passage of time things may settle down—particularly if there is a major economic upswing in Germany, which few economists are optimistic enough to forecast for the near future—we may well now be seeing "two German nations in one German state." Or even, given the broader context of increased international migration, two German nations in one multicultural state. It is to the vexed issue of the German nation and the nature of German nationalism that we must finally turn.

THE NATIONALIST FRINGES AND THE QUESTION OF GERMAN IDENTITY

Undoubtedly the first reactions from abroad to the unification of Germany were ones of some apprehension. For all that scholars could say about historical transformations in what the general public tended to conceive as a "German national character," British politicians such as former Prime Minister Thatcher and the late Lord Ridley still viewed the Germans as inherently, to borrow a phrase from the American songwriter and mathematician Tom Lehrer, "war-like and mean." Most worrying from the point of view of foreign observers was the sudden rise in incidents of racist violence. While the current political elite might be basically peace-loving and democratic, was not the newly strident popular xeno-phobia in Germany reminiscent of the early 1930s? Might not another Hitler be brought to power on the back of an apparently popular right-wing extremism in the volatile circumstances of the new Germany? Was this a throwback to a long dormant past, or an entirely new phenomenon, a consequence of the dislocations of overhasty unification? In short, should one be seriously alarmed, or merely observe with disquiet while waiting for things to settle down?

The threat of the radical Right in contemporary Germany should not be downplayed. From Hoyerswerda to Rostock in the East, from Mölln to Solingen in the West, there have been violent attacks on hostels housing asylum seekers and on foreign residents of Germany. Before the Rostock riots of late August, there had been eight hundred attacks of an extreme right-wing nature in 1992; by late October, this figure had risen to 1,800.[14] While those actively involved in the rioting and arson attacks were predominantly young people—around 70 percent of the offenders were under twenty years old, only 2.7 percent were over thirty—a worrying feature was the apparent support given to rioters by middle-aged onlookers. Equally a cause for concern was the apparent inefficacy of police responses, particularly in the Rostock-Lichtenhagen incident, when police forces were prematurely withdrawn, leaving a number of Vietnamese residents stranded in a burning hostel. Anti-Semitic incidents have also been on the increase. Jewish cemeteries have been desecrated, memorials defaced, and a block at Sachsenhausen concentration camp was set on fire. In late November 1992, an old man was kicked to death on the misapprehension that he was Jewish, while many others have been more fearful for their safety in the new Germany than they have been for decades.

These incidents of racist violence and extremist attacks on those designated "outsiders," for whatever reason, are highly disturbing. But they do not represent a return to the 1930s, and to overstate the historical parallels is to misunderstand the present. Nor, however, are they entirely new phenomena: there is a background to the rise in right-wing extremism in both East and West Germany prior to 1989.

There has been what was somewhat tendentiously termed a "foreigner problem" in West Germany at least since the mid-1970s. The *Gastarbeiter* had been welcomed in to supply cheap migrant labor in a period of continued economic expansion in the 1960s (after the supply of refugee labor from the East dried up with the building of the Wall). *Gastarbeiter* cost nothing to train, were largely nonunionized, easily exploited, and contributed to state pension funds while they would themselves (it was thought) have long since returned to their countries of origin by the time they reached a pensionable age. Following the oil crisis of 1973, a halt was called to the recruitment of foreign labor, and by the later 1970s and early 1980s governments of all political persuasions (Social Democratic Party/Free Democratic Party [SPD/FDP], until 1982, Christian Democratic Union/Christian Social Union/Free Democratic Party [CDU/CSU/FDP], thereafter) were exploring ways of trying to encourage *Gastarbeiter*—no longer such welcome guests—to return home, even though many had been living in the Federal Republic for many years, and their children had been born and brought up in Germany. By 1982, as many as 62 percent—nearly two-thirds—of the West German population agreed that there were too many foreigners in Germany; 50 percent thought that they should be sent back to their countries of origin.[15]

Given the restrictive and essentially ethnic (or "blood-right") basis of West Germany's citizenship law,[16] only half-hearted attempts were made at either assimilation or the propagation of notions of a multicultural society. Until the winter of 1992, and conveniently ignoring a century of mass population migration from Central and Eastern Europe, Chancellor Kohl continued to assert that "Germany is not a country of immigration." The CDU fraction leader and longtime unofficial crown prince, Wolfgang Schäuble, was quoted in March 1993 as saying, "We gain our identity, not from commitment to an idea, but from belonging to a particular *Volk*."[17] Despite the officially ordained philosemitism of West Germany, with its (entirely laudable) desire to make reparations to Jewish victims of the Holocaust, the more general issue of relations between ethnic Germans and "others," particularly foreign labor, was less directly addressed.

In this general context, there was also a more specific set of political phenomena in the 1980s: increasing voter volatility, increasing disaffection with the major political parties (which seemed to be set in a rut of scandals, corruption, and inability to deal with the economy), and a notable move to the Right. Partly the latter was related to the *Tendenzwende*: the more conservative, self-assertive mood of the mid-1980s, with the claim that the time for taboos on national pride was over, evidenced in such phenomena as the 1985 Bitburg debacle or the *Historikerstreit* of 1986–1987. The general drift to the Right both provided the context for and developed in some response to the formation of two new right-wing parties: the *Republikaner*, led by a former *Waffen-SS* member, Franz Schönhuber, in 1983; and the *Deutsche Volksunion* (DVU, German People's Union), led by the editor of the right-wing *Deutsche National Zeitung*, Gerhard Frey, in 1987. The *Land* elections of 1989 in Berlin and Hesse and the Euro-election of 1989 revealed the extent of support for such initiatives: around 7.5 percent of the population was prepared to vote for the *Republikaner* in Berlin and in the Euro-elections. These parties trod a delicate line to stay just within constitutional bounds; beyond them were a variety of more militant neo-Nazi groupings, such as the *Wehr-Sport-Gruppe Hoffmann*, which spent their time practicing paramilitary skills rather than competing for electoral support.

In the very different political context of the GDR, such organized right-wing extremism was clearly impossible. But there were different problems. Although West Germany had not developed a successful strategy for the harmonious integration of the work force from abroad, the East German government had never even seriously confronted the problem. Despite official protestations of socialist internationalism, only around 1 percent of the East German population was foreign—mainly students from Vietnam, Cuba, Mozambique, North Korea, and Poland—and this small percentage was kept tightly segregated from the indigenous population, restricted to the confines of special hostels rather than living in the community. So, the East Germans had never really experienced living in a multicultural, multiethnic society (apart from the local enclaves of indigenous ethnic minority Slav groups, such as the Sorbs in the southeastern corner of the GDR). Nor, given the lack of any state-ordained philosemitism comparable to that of West Germany since the early 1950s, had East Germans seriously confronted the issue of Nazi racist policies as such: official recognition of the existence of popular anti-Semitism and East German responsibility for the Holocaust was extremely belated. Moreover, the GDR was the self-proclaimed "antifascist state." To express rebellion against the state, people might naturally choose the symbols to which the state was most hostile. To flaunt a swastika in the GDR in the 1980s was less to hark back to Hitler than to demonstrate against Honecker. Right-wing skinheads and hooligans were a home-grown product of the GDR, not a flashback to the Third Reich; and they were an increasing problem in the 1980s, long before anyone dreamed that the Wall might fall.

In the volatile circumstances since unification, these elements have come together and have been transformed. Problems have changed and have been redefined; new horizons have been opened up. The number of asylum seekers increased ten-fold between 1983 and 1991 (and doubled from 1989 to 1991); with the opening of borders and recent political and economic upheavals in Eastern Europe, asylum seekers have taken advantage of Germany's uniquely liberal asylum laws. Foreigners provide a convenient scapegoat in the context of domestic ills; fear of losing one's job, housing pressures, and economic insecurity are taken out on the identifiable "other." Disaffected *Ossis*, sensing they are being denigrated as second-class citizens in a still divided fatherland, assert their "racial superiority" over Gypsies, Romanians, and other "inferior" groups in ways startlingly reminiscent of the Nazis. In Hoyerswerda in 1991, people feeling powerless in the face of rising unemployment and social chaos exerted a sense of empowerment by driving asylum seekers away from their territory. Similar attempts to "restore order," often justified by arguing that the immigrant populations allegedly had tendencies to criminality and were responsible for theft and vandalism, rubbish-dumping, and other hazards to public health, have been evident in other incidents.

The attempts to gain electoral support and party membership by the "respectable," organized right-wing extremist parties, the DVU and *Republikaner,* have not been making much additional headway since unification. Their votes have remained essentially stable: 10.9 percent for the *Republikaner* in Baden-Württemberg in April 1992, 6.3 percent for the DVU in Schleswig-Holstein in the same month, 8.3 percent for the *Republikaner* in Hesse in March 1993. At the same time, the less organized extremist scene has exploded across Germany. The *Bundesverfassungsschutz* (Office for the Protection of the Constitution) estimated that there were nearly 41,000 right-wing extremists of one flavor or another active in Germany in 1991, including around 4,200 neo-Nazi skinheads.[18] Most worrying, perhaps, is the general disaffection of the German population with the current political scene; as the news magazine *Der Spiegel* pointed out, the "largest party" in Germany in the spring of 1993 was the "party of nonvoters": an unusual development in a country that had traditionally enjoyed high electoral turnouts.[19]

On some views, recent responses of the German government have been at best tardy and half-hearted: seeking to restrict the numbers of asylum seekers by introducing the notion of "safe third countries" has taken precedence over the speeding up of processing applications for asylum or any major relaxation of citizenship entitlement (such as allowing dual citizenship to long-term residents). The governing coalition, with the consent of the opposition, essentially conceded the definition of the problem to the far Right: there are too many asylum seekers, hence the "solution" is to restrict entry. Less public attention was focused on the issue of citizenship entitlement, with the associated implicit assumptions of what is "essentially German," and hence exceedingly difficult for foreigners to attain. Even those children of *Gastarbeiter* who have been born and bred in Germany are essentially forced to renounce any alternative heritage and assimilate to German norms. German elites are clearly still having some difficulty swallowing any idea of the transformation of their newly united ethnic nation into a multicultural society of citizens. This tends to undermine the depth of the recently proclaimed West German commitment to being a "postnational nation."

But for all these developments, Germany in the early 1990s is not the Germany of the early 1930s. For one thing, large numbers of Germans are prepared to condemn racism and violence, to demonstrate in candle-lit parades against hostility to foreigners. But most importantly, whatever their difficulties over individual policies, such as the right to asylum, German political elites are committed to upholding democracy, not to undermining it. There is no parliamentary majority for obstructing democratic processes. There is no revisionist army waiting in the wings. Unemployment may be rising, the economy may be entering recession, there may be all manner of social difficulties in the new Germany, but there is a will at the center to stem the tide, to ensure that the historical clock is not turned back. Weimar democracy was not felled purely from below, from the growth of a mass movement under the banner of the original Nazi party (NSDAP); it was also destroyed from above, by the effective abdication of the old elites who felt that they could no longer control the situation or seek to uphold a system to which they felt no ideological commitment. This is not the case in the Germany of today.

OVERCOMING THE PAST, DEFINING THE PRESENT: WHITHER GERMANY?

The new Germany faces many challenges. Not least are the issues of overcoming the recent past: understanding the nature of repression, accommodation, and resistance in the East German dictatorship; dealing sensitively with the reinterpretations of individuals' biographies and careers, deeds and misdeeds, as they enter a new political context and era. The often misguided debates over prominent cases of former *Stasi* informants—those who, wittingly or unwittingly, supped with the devil in the former GDR, whether for personal gain or for political purposes—have served only to highlight the difficulties of attempts to come to terms, not only with the earlier Nazi past but also with the more recent divided past. The disputes over the former role of the prominent writer Christa Wolf, or of Manfred Stolpe (now Prime Minister of the Land Brandenburg) as attempted mediator between church and state via the *Stasi*, illustrate the complexities of the roles of intellectuals, church people, dissidents, and politicians in the former GDR. Similar debates revolve around the lives of less prominent people—husbands, wives, neighbors, and friends—who in the light of recent revelations can no longer be trusted. The abortive efforts to bring the top leadership to justice have deflected attention from the more general questions of responsibility, civil courage, and political compromise within a repressive regime. The social psychology of a postdictatorial society, with post hoc maneuverings among the roles of would-be victim and perpetrator, fellow-traveler and innocent, has many problematic facets.

There is also much to be learned about more general experiences and patterns of orientation of ordinary people in different generations and social groups, as they developed in the past and as they are having to rethink their activities in what is still, three years after formal unification, a divided nation. The conflicts between *Wessis* and *Ossis* will not go away soon. If anything, the economic and social watershed between East and West, with attendant frictions and uncertainties, will in the short run only exacerbate the stereotypes. Intellectuals and political leaders will have to rethink old certainties in the context of new challenges in a changed European and world context. Having achieved the closest it has ever come to being a nation-state, the new Germany may have to redefine its concept of national identity and free itself from the centuries-old concept of the ethnically homogenous, if regionally differentiated, German *Kulturnation*. Real "unity" may mean abandoning the quest for homogeneity. But the new Germany is neither an extension of the old West, nor a simple repeat of the long-distant past. The future is open.

ENDNOTES

[1]Cf. *Der Spiegel* 47 (9) (1 March 1993). In answer to the question, "Which party do you think is able to get the problem of asylum seekers under control?," 34 percent felt that *no* party was competent in this area; as many as 11 percent considered that the right-wing Republican party *was* competent in this field, although only 5 percent would vote for the Republicans in a general election (still just enough to gain national representation under the German electoral law).

[2]I have explored these differences at greater length in Mary Fulbrook, *The Divided Nation: A History of Germany 1918–1990* (London: Fontana, 1991; New York: Oxford University Press, 1992).

[3]It seems as if the West Germans are — inappropriately— seeking to learn the lessons of inadequate denazification after the War, by punishing the *Mitläufer* of what was in fact a far less murderous regime more harshly than they themselves were punished after 1945.

[4]For further details, see Mary Fulbrook, "Popular discontent and political activism in the GDR," *Contemporary European History* (forthcoming, April 1994).

[5]For further details, see Fulbrook, *The Divided Nation*, chap. 9.

[6]An experience which may not even be reflected in the statistics: If a mother who no longer has any, or affordable, child-care facilities is effectively forced to stay home to look after her children herself, she is deemed to be "no longer available for work" and therefore not officially "unemployed."

[7]Rachel Alsop, "The Experience of Women in Eastern Germany," in Jonathan Osmond, ed., *German Reunification* (Harlow: Longman, 1992), 187.

[8]Ibid., 194 –95.

[9]East German women were essentially organized from above in the state-run Democratic Women's League, the DFD. The social and structural supports for women

in the GDR were essentially granted to them by the state, partly for ideological reasons and partly because of the need for the full exploitation of female labor in a period of labor shortage. Hence the conditions for female training, education, and participation in the paid labor force (and hence economic independence) were not gained by female mobilization and pressure from below. To the extent that there was any independent women's movement in the GDR, it consisted more in a rather amorphous, essentially intellectual and literary debate, exploring distinctive aspects of women's experience through imaginative literature and "protocol" writing.

[10]See, for example, Gerhard Herdegen, "Demoskopische Anmerkungen zum Geschichtsbewußtsein der Deutschen (West) im Kontext der deutschen Frage," in Werner Weidenfeld, ed., *Geschichtsbewußtsein der Deutschen* (Köln: Verlag Wissenschaft und Politik, 1987). David P. Conradt, *The German Polity,* 3rd ed. (London: Longman, 1986), 49, points out that while in the 1950s reunification ranked as the, or one of the, most important problems for West Germans, by 1983 less than 5 percent thought this. The decline was more marked among young people than old. See also the opinion poll surveys carried out by the Allensbach Institut für Demoskopie. The large numbers of East Germans taking the often risky opportunity to apply for exit visas to the West highlight the continued salience of the "German problem" for those living on the wrong side of the Wall.

[11]On the "restructuring" of history and the social sciences, see, for example, Jürgen Kocka, *Die Auswirkungen der deutschen Einigung auf die Geschichts- und Sozialwissenschaften, Gesprächskreis Geschichte,* Heft 1, Forschungsinstitut der Friedrich-Ebert-Stiftung, 1992; Günter Krause, "The economic sciences in the reunification process," *German History* 10 (3) (October 1992): 405–11; Kurt Pätzold, "What new start? The end of historical study in the GDR," *German History* 10 (3) (October 1992): 392– 404; see also Gerhard Ritter's reply to this in *German History* 11 (3) (October 1993).

[12]For very interesting details (based on East German sociological surveys) on the rise in conformity among East German youth in the mid-1970s, and then its fragmentation and decline in the 1980s, already *prior* to the autumn of 1989, see Karen Henderson, "The Search for Ideological Conformity: Sociological Research on Youth in Honecker's GDR," *German History* 10 (3) (October 1992): 318 –34.

[13]Ulrich Plenzdorf, *Die neuen Leiden des jungen W.* (Berlin: Henschelverlag Kunst u. Gesellschaft, 1974).

[14]Press release from the Embassy of the Federal Republic of Germany, 18 December 1992.

[15]Nora Räthsel, "Germany: one race, one nation?," *Race and Class* 32 (3) (1991): 31– 48.

[16]Given the unwillingness of the newly created Federal Republic in 1949 to recognize the changed frontiers of Eastern Europe or concede legitimacy to what continued to be dismissed as the "Soviet Zone of Occupation," ARTICLE 116 of the Basic Law bestows automatic rights of citizenship on those who are, or are descendants of, citizens of the Germany of 1937—which in turn was based on the 1913 *Reichs- und Staatsangehörigkeitsgesetz* defining citizenship in terms of "race" rather than territorial residence.

[17]Quoted in *Der Spiegel* 47 (11) (15 March 1993): 53.

[18]Bundesminister des Innern, *Verfasssungsschutzbericht* (Bonn: Bundesminister des Innern, August 1992), 72.

[19]*Der Spiegel* 47 (9) (1 March 1993): 24 –29. Some political scientists interpret high turnouts as evidence of authoritarian rather than democratic attitudes; nevertheless, the fact remains that expressed voter disaffection is rising.

Barthold C. Witte

Two Catastrophes, Two Causes, and How the Germans Dealt with Them

ERMAN UNIFICATION AND THE END of the East-West conflict, with its visible and foreseeable results for the Germans, their neighbors, and the world, have reopened chapters of European history that some believe had been forever closed. With the breakup of the multinational states of the Soviet Union and Yugoslavia, an ominous resurrection of war-causing tensions is evident. According to Francis Fukuyama,[1] the end of history as we know it came with the death of communism. But in Central and Eastern Europe a new authoritarianism has risen. Many believed that the nation-state was no longer serving the interests of Europe as a political form of organization and as a spiritual raison d'être. Meanwhile, however, a wave of nationalism is rolling across the continent, and it remains to be seen whether it will take hold only in the East.

For the Germans, two deep historical chasms are reopening: one is "German hegemony over Europe"; the other is "dictatorship over Germany." These two chasms may have devastating effects for Europe as well as for the world at large.

One of the peculiarities of German history that is barely comprehensible to an outside observer is the surprising but obvious fact that these chasms have been attractive to the Germans for a long time. A Wagnerian explanation would be to remember the "Twilight of the Gods," the gruesome but beautiful finale of the story of the Nibelungen Ring symbolizing the end of civilization. One could also remember Hölderlin's Empedocles, the philosopher who seeks

---

Barthold C. Witte is Editor of the German quarterly "liberal" and a former Under Secretary of State for Cultural Affairs in the German Foreign Office, Bonn.

253

and finds death in Aetna's crater; or Thomas Mann's alter ego, the aging author Gustav von Aschenbach, who met his death in Venice because "he did not want sobriety: the rapture was too dear to him."[2] These fictional accounts illustrate a central aspect of the German mental tradition. Indeed, historical events—recall the Ghibelline emperors and their nobles, the Catholics and Protestants during the Thirty Years' War, and, in this century, the German Reich—more than literature call to memory times when the German irrational longing for the absolute or for the highest degree of power led to a fall into the chasm, the addiction to death.

There is, of course, no straight line leading from Emperor Friedrich Barbarossa over Luther and Bismarck to Hitler. The Prussian nobleman Otto von Bismarck, founder and manager of the short-lived Hohenzollern Empire, the "Second Reich," was neither a totalitarian dictator nor one who pursued an unbridled *Machtpolitik*. One can understand, however, how Germany came under Hitler's dictatorship, his bid for world power, and the catastrophe of World War II if one remembers the first, albeit relatively mild, German and European catastrophe, namely World War I. This is all the more necessary since economists and Marxist historians have focused the research for the origins of Hitler's regime on economic conditions. It is true that the inflation of the early 1920s, following the defeat in World War I, and the Great Depression of the early 1930s were among the factors that brought Hitler to power. But why did a racist dictatorship emerge only in Germany while other similarly affected European countries, such as France and Britain, retained democracy and the rule of the law? Even fascism in Southern Europe, not to speak of the authoritarian governments in other parts of the continent, did not establish a fully totalitarian rule. Why did only the Germans reply to the challenge of the Leninist "dictatorship of the proletariat" by taking to their own dictatorship? There are no simple answers to these questions. But obviously the German nation-state created by Bismarck must have developed some peculiarities that laid the groundwork for what began in 1933.

In a historical perspective, an analysis of the outbreak and outcome of World War I brings at least some of these peculiarities into the open. At the end of the war, the victorious Allies assigned guilt solely to the defeated German Reich. The German leaders were forced to acknowledge this guilt by signing the Versailles peace treaty. That was a mistake of historical proportion. The policy of the Berlin government before and during 1914 did not aim at stabilizing peace in Europe but instead led to a situation in which war, especially after the incident of Sarajevo, remained the only available option. The other Great Powers had their share of responsibility, but it was no accident that the war had been fought around Germany. Ironically, in the end it was not the German Reich that broke into pieces but the Hapsburg Empire, while the Czarist Empire, not Berlin, fell during the Bolshevik Revolution. Germany remained basically intact, though territorially amputated and militarily reduced. And yet the war was fought over Germany, over its *Griff nach der Weltmacht* (bid for world power), as Fritz Fischer has so pointedly called its policy.[3]

Weltmacht was not meant to be a world power similar to the British hegemony over the world during the era of Queen Victoria. Rather, the Germans hoped, as they put it at the time, for "a place in the sun" with full equality with London, St. Petersburg, and Paris. The most visible sign of this was the construction of the German battleship fleet, built up against the strongest power, England. As a result, the European balance of power, as it had been determined after the fall of Napoleon I and reconstructed several times since, began to totter. What Bismarck had achieved before and after 1871, not only through three wars but also by an extremely shrewd diplomacy, namely the acceptance of the German Reich as a full member of the "Great Five," became questionable. Three of the five—Great Britain, France, and Russia—bonded together against the other two, Germany and the already substantially weakened Austria-Hungary. Eventually the Great War was unleashed through the fight between Austria, supported by Germany, and Serbia, supported by Russia, over the Turkish heritage in the Balkans. The German defeat of 1918 and the ensuing peace treaties cut short any dreams of German world power as the fleet and the colonies were handed over to the victors.

With the greater distance afforded by time, it is, however, clear that the "dictated peace of Versailles" was by no means a crushing peace. More important, it did not substantially touch the position of the German Reich as a world trading power and a European political power. The isolation of Germany among the Great Powers, the "encirclement" so often bemoaned by the German public was not solely the fault of Bismarck's successors, especially Wilhelm II, nor was the resentment on the part of the older competing powers against the rising newcomer. It must be traced back to Bismarck himself and his foreign policy system. The Reich's founder ordered his creation not to enter into any long-term alliance with the other four but instead to form tactical alliances with this or that member of the club according to changing situations. There was only one exception, the ever tighter alliance with Vienna. This bond was lauded in true Wagnerian style as *Nibelungentreue* although one could hear and see every year in Bayreuth that such loyalty would lead to destruction.

It did not end so badly for the German Empire. Given this precedent, the leaders of the Weimar Republic, even under the impact of the defeat, did not make any fundamental changes in the field of foreign policy. The Republic also followed Bismarck's maxim of securing the Reich through shifting alliances. In the terminology of the later epoch of the Cold War between West and East, this was a policy of nonalignment. In theory, there was nothing wrong with such a policy, but it left a precariously positioned Germany unprotected against attacks by other powers. World War I had proven that Britain's principle of "splendid isolation"—thought to be the reason for its success—was not applicable to a nation-state in the heart of Europe that had only recently joined the club. On the other hand, Germany was much too big to retreat into a neutral and remote position, following the example of Switzerland or Sweden.

Thus, it appeared necessary to form at least one reliable long-term alliance among the other Great Powers. For this purpose, Communist Russia, despite Rapallo, was not an option due to its weaknesses and its world revolutionary ambitions. The Americans were not eligible because they had departed from Europe soon after the war. Great Britain continued to adhere to its chosen role as the independent arbiter in continental fights. Only France remained. Together with Paris, Berlin would have been able to create a stable European order. The Treaty of Locarno, concluded in 1925, could have been the basis for such a policy. Indeed, Gustav Stresemann, the long-successful foreign minister of the Reich and architect of Locarno, came close to this insight. Unfortunately, he died shortly before his French partner and friend, Aristide Briand, in 1930 suggested the creation of a European Union. And Briand failed in the midst of the deepening economic crisis. When Hitler was appointed Reich Chancellor, an isolationist state fell to him, true to the legacy of Bismarck.

In order to put his plan for world power into action as quickly as possible, Hitler needed only to withdraw from the weak League of Nations and to "throw off the chains of Versailles," as he demagogically put it. Without any regard for close or distant neighbors, he set about achieving his goal, eventually by war. "A strong man is most powerful when he is alone," said Friedrich Schiller's Wilhelm Tell. This was meant to be the lighthearted talk of a politically inexperienced man soon proven wrong by the union of Switzerland's founding fathers on Rütli Meadow. With Hitler it became a state maxim, producing disastrous results. Again, there were forerunners. In 1895, in a lecture at Freiburg University, Max Weber uttered the following famous sentence:

> We must understand that the unification of Germany will be no more than a youthful exploit which the nation committed in old age and which it should have refrained from due to the great expense, if this unification would have marked the end and not the beginning of a German policy towards world power (*Weltmachtpolitik*).[4]

Sixty years later, the nation stood shattered, helpless, and bewildered before the ruins of its existence as a result of *Weltmachtpolitik*, which had bet everything on its own power and had been proud of defying, as the phrase went, "a world of enemies."

Did the German nation know that it was marching into catastrophe? Are the critics correct who compare it to that romantic yearning for death that Richard Wagner brought to the opera stage? Is the irrational excessiveness that led to two world wars part of the national character of Germany? Would the Germans have to do as Karl Jaspers, among others, advised after the catastrophe, namely to take leave of their national history and dismiss the dream of having a nation-state like others in Western Europe?

These questions are not outdated by the fact that the German nation-state was surprisingly restored—reduced in size and constituted as a democratic republic based on a forty-year-old constitution and the political experience of the old Federal Republic. Yet, it is again a Great Power. If the theories about an unchanged German national character are true, if the Germans still long for the loneliness that the strong have to endure, if they again desire to dominate their neighbors, and if they are still possessed by that yearning for death, then the diagnosis and prognosis for united Germany is grim and these questions are all the more important.

To base thoughts and actions in the international field on the assumption of unchangeable national characters is a precarious practice. In Europe, as in other places, there is a superfluity of examples of how the behavior of a people can change in the course of history. Sweden and the Netherlands, for example, in the seventeenth century pursued a course of *Weltpolitik* in the concert of European powers; today they comfortably and contentedly exist as small, though economically productive nations. In contrast, the United States, founded on ideals of isolation, is the only remaining World Power and is the dominant member of the Atlantic Treaty.

It is no different with the Germans. Two hundred years ago, Goethe and Schiller doubted that Germany was a nation at all and wondered whether the Germans had the gift to build their own state. At the same time, Friedrich Hölderlin scorned them because they were "rich in thought and weak in deed." This was no more true after Bismarck, two or three generations later. The historical reputation of the Germans of yesterday—that they are especially efficient and disciplined managers and soldiers—grew out of the surprising victories of the Prussian Army during the founding of the Reich and the equally unexpected rise of the Reich during the Wilhelmine era to the status of a first-class industrial state.

The self-perception of a nation and its image in the world's eyes change in accord with historical events. Yet, self-perception and image are rarely identical. In the German tradition, loyalty is seen as a national characteristic, but to the rest of the world the seesaw-politics of Bismarck's Reich made the opposite impression. To Germany's neighbors, the Germans, as a political entity, seemed unreliable, unpredictable, even mysterious. Even today, the German chancellor and foreign minister must constantly assert the predictability and reliability of the Federal Republic.

What, then, can be said of the Germans if national characters are shaped by historical events? The failure of Germany's two attempts at world domination and the total collapse of the totalitarian rule are central experiences with deep and lasting effects on Germany and the Germans. World War I was fought almost entirely outside the German borders; it was experienced at home as a mental burden with material sacrifices and not in its immediate gruesomeness. When Hindenburg and Ludendorff gave up the battle against the superior strength of the Allies in the autumn of 1918, there was not yet one Allied soldier on German soil. Thus, at the end of the war only a small minority of Germans rejected the war outright, while a large majority felt the defeat to be unjust and believed the German Army had remained "undefeated in the field." The Weimar Republic was never able to rid itself of *Dolchstoßlegende*, which proved to be a powerful political myth. Hitler, the front soldier, was increasingly thought to be the one who would wipe away the humiliation done to the beloved fatherland. This confusion, in concert with the Great Depression, paved Hitler's path to power.

In 1945 and afterwards, the situation was fundamentally different. To Hitler's threat of world domination, the Allies responded with the demand for unconditional surrender not only of Hitler's regime but of the whole country and people. Hitler did not surrender and preferred, in keeping with the "Twilight of the Gods," to take his people with him to destruction. Even before occupation, the "air war" had brought death, terror, and destruction directly to the experience of most Germans. When the war finally ended, almost all of the Reich territory, including the capital, Berlin, had been bombed into ruins and conquered. Contrary to the situation of 1918 and after, the continuity of the government was completely disrupted for four long years, during which time the Allied Control Council exerted power on the national level. In view of this total collapse, a new *Dolchstoßlegende* could not be created. More importantly, the overwhelming majority of Germans had come to hate war and to detest the whole military business, which had characterized the Second and Third Reichs. In contrast to 1914 when young men went to war singing, supported by the whole people, Hitler's war had never been popular, not even during its first three victorious years.

To the surprise of many foreign observers, the Germans were resistant when their wartime enemies demanded at the beginning of the Cold War that German soldiers be incorporated into their respective alliances. Those who started to build a new democracy on the ruins of the hegemonial dictatorship followed a threefold

"Never again!": No more dictatorship, no more war, no more imperial power. From this three goals ensued: democracy, peace, Europe. Many of the older generation who had lived through World War I found this change difficult to accept. It was a new beginning endeavored by a politically active minority. Over the years it became a basic consensus among Germans and was reorganized under a name with no historical associations—the Federal Republic of Germany.

When the founding fathers of the Federal Republic chose this name for the second German democracy, they were fully aware of the symbolic weight of their decision. It was a symbol of the deep change not only in attitudes and habits but also in aims, ways, and means of the new Germany. While they adhered to the right of the German people to a nation-state, even to the point of decreeing continuity of the state from the Reich to the Federal Republic, they wanted to open a new chapter of German history. Their leaders— Konrad Adenauer, Kurt Schumacher, and Theodor Heuss, among others—had in mind not only the catastrophe of 1945 but also the failure of the Weimar democracy.

The creators and supporters of the first German Republic certainly had not intended its failure, and there were many contributing factors, among them primarily the world economic crisis. Yet, the massive polemics that Hitler and his followers directed against the Weimar democracy must not cover up the extent to which the isolationist foreign policy and the authoritarian domestic policy of the Republic contributed to its downfall. Karl Dietrich Bracher illustrated this with great clarity, particularly in regard to the domestic scene, in his classic work published in 1955 about the disintegration of the Weimar Republic.[5]

In his 1951 keynote speech before the *Deutscher Historikertag*, Ludwig Dehio articulated his thoughts on the balance of power and hegemony in Europe.[6] Dehio noted that in Germany after the defeat of 1918, both elements of hegemonial demonism—blindness and the sensation of power—retained their strength. As a result, and also because those were times of need and of a continuing disintegration of traditional social structures, resentment and dreams of revenge found fertile ground. Dehio wanted to explain why Germany and the Germans, although defeated in World War I, were once more, after only fifteen years, reaching for hegemony over Europe and for status as a World Power. Yet, his is not a complete explanation. Perhaps the answer lies in a combination of the internal and external aspects: On the one hand, the decision to centralize and expand political power rather than, as Montesquieu had advised, to tame and limit it through division and control; and, on the other hand, the will to use this concentrated power to gain control of Europe, instead of joining the European family of nations as Stresemann had tried.

Neither the rulers nor the ruled in the Hohenzollern Reich had ever abandoned the common history, traditions, and ideas of Europe in their will to power and in their emphasis on a special character and mission of the Germans. The idea of defeating and destroying the archenemy France had not occurred even to the pan-German extremists. Ludendorff's military dictatorship was not intended to last beyond the war, and free elections were only postponed as long as the war lasted.

With Hitler in power, however, the dictatorship was declared the highest form of state, the final goal of history, and it prepared to conquer and extinguish its opponents politically and militarily. The Holocaust was neither an aberration nor an act of defense during war times. Rather, it was a result of the totalitarian character of this new type of dictatorship, a dictatorship that, as a reign of terror, surpassed Stalin's sinister gulag regime. As time passed, it came to depend less on the approval of its subjects and more on the horror and aura of invincibility. The latter moved the opportunists to comply, while the former produced the necessary obedience. During his first years in power, Hitler became popular first because he seemed to have saved Germany from economic crisis and mass unemployment, and then because he gave validity to national aspirations. Thus, he drove a whole civilized people to madness with tales of German superiority and invincibility. Such approval was not, however, the deciding factor for Hitler: he began his war in 1939 against the dominant mood of the people.

Today, almost fifty years later, we can conclude that the incredible excessiveness of this second attempt at world domination and its complete failure have achieved what was not gained in and after 1918: the awakening of the Germans from their dangerous dreams. The heroism that had been instilled in the Germans since 1914 was abandoned, and they entrusted themselves to the protection of the victors. The mistakes made by the Allies in 1918 were not to be repeated, and the door through which the Germans could again join the family of nations was opened.[7]

The Russians were the first to try to win the confidence of the defeated by allowing the reconstruction of political institutions, by stopping the dismantling of industry in their occupation zone, and by playing the card of national unity. The American campaign began in the autumn of 1946. American popularity increased as the communists established their power monopoly in the Soviet part of Germany. In 1948, when President Truman decided to counteract Stalin's blockade of Berlin by establishing the airlift to the city, the Americans had won the game. The British and the French supported the airlift to Berlin after having decided, together with the US government, to establish not only a new German currency but also a new German state in the Western occupation zones.

It has often been said that this development, which in 1949 led to the simultaneous creation of the Federal Republic and of the German Democratic Republic (GDR), was a result of the conflict between West and East. This conflict, having begun in 1946 with a communist armed uprising in Greece and the Truman doctrine guaranteeing American protection for the noncommunist side, reached its first peak in 1948 when the communist minority took power in Prague and Stalin started his bid for Berlin. From then on, the Cold War was waged along the line demarcating the zones of influence between West and East. Germany, itself divided, was the biggest prize, but to win Germany, the cooperation and confidence of the Germans first had to be won. While the division of Germany lasted and became ever deeper, it also became clear that the West had won the struggle for the German soul. The proof was given when those in the East revolted against the Soviets on June 17, 1953, and when those in the West, a few months later, voted for Konrad Adenauer and for his policy of a firm and lasting alliance with the West. These events proved that there was much more than sheer opportunism behind the newly adopted allegiance to the West.

Of course, there was opportunism. Across Western Europe uncertainty ruled public opinion during the Cold War years. The Soviet Union was perceived as a huge economic and military power with unlimited development potential, driven by an ideology that had already taken possession of half of Europe. Even Hitler had failed in his attempt to stop communism, and his defeat invited Russia into the heart of Europe. Would the West be able to put Eisenhower's "Roll Back" policy into practice, and would it be willing and able to defend what was left of free Europe? Many believed communism to be the stronger force, and therefore either supported the communists, at least in private, or strove for neutrality. When Stalin, one year prior to his death, in his famous note of March 10, 1952, offered German national unity at the price of German neutrality, he hoped to strengthen these tendencies and maybe bring them into power.

He failed, primarily because of the resolve of the leaders of the three Western Powers as well as of the Federal Republic not to submit to communist pressure and to resist the idea of a neutral Germany. The resolve of the German leaders, based as it was on the support of the majority of Germans, can be traced back to the first years after the end of the war, and even to the policy planning of the German resistance against Hitler. The groups of the German resistance, conservatives, socialists, and liberals alike, agreed that Germany should be a constitutional democracy based on the values and beliefs first formulated by political philosophers and put into practice during the eighteenth century in Western Europe and the United States. Under the heavy pressure of the Nazi regime, they had experienced what it meant to concentrate power, to abolish human rights, to persecute and murder innocent people, and to violently strive for world power. Hence, their policy papers concentrated on three aspects: the protection of human dignity and human rights; the limitation and control of power and its democratic legitimation; and the creation of a united Europe.

These ideas survived Hitler and became the basis for the political programs of the German democratic parties formed after 1945. The first party leaders are characteristic examples: the Christian Democrat Konrad Adenauer, formerly Mayor of Cologne, and later President of the Parliamentary Assembly that elaborated the new Constitution, had, before 1933, worked hard for friendship between Germany and France; the Social Democrat Kurt Schumacher, having suffered for many years in a Nazi concentration camp, led his party in a fierce struggle against the communists; Theodor Heuss, the leader of the liberals and later the first President of the new Republic, in his public speeches set the tone in favor of human rights and the dignity of the individual.

They all were well aware of how enormous and fundamental was the change that they worked for. It can safely be said that the second German democracy was constituted as a result of the total defeat of 1945. But it is wrong to conclude that this democracy was imported into Germany by the occupying Powers. It is true that the three Western Allies first decided to establish a new central state and to convene the Parliamentary Assembly. They also interfered with the deliberations and decisions of the Assembly and eventually gave their agreement to the result. But this result, the Basic Law, passed by the Assembly in Bonn on May 23, 1949, while incorporating important parts of the first German Constitution passed in 1849 by the Paulskirche Parliament in Frankfurt and of the Weimar Constitution of 1919, was the product of men and women who followed their instincts.

The Basic Law of 1949, though incorporating older democratic traditions, truly marked a new beginning. In this regard, three main elements deserve special attention: the unconditional recognition of individual basic rights; the division and control of power; and the inclusion into a peaceful European and world order.

The first element, the catalog of basic rights, was intentionally placed at the beginning of the Basic Law. Its nineteen articles incorporate the results of two hundred years of European and American constitutional development. On the basis of American experience, these rights were declared unconditionally binding and subject to interpretation by the judiciary, in the last instance by the newly created Federal Constitutional Court. The persecution and forced emigration by the Nazis led to ARTICLE 16, guaranteeing political asylum to any persecuted foreigner who enters German soil.[8]

The second element is more American than any other, namely the limitation of power through division. The German system differentiates itself in some aspects from the American model: the president is a representational figure, not the center of power, and is elected not by the people but by the deputies; government is responsible to parliament; there are more than two parties because of the proportionate electoral system; and the *Länder* (states) are directly involved in federal legislation through their membership in the second house, the *Bundesrat*. The system has worked satisfactorily for more than forty years, in part because it provides for strong, but not unlimited leadership by the Federal Chancellor.

The third element sets the basic rules for a foreign policy of cooperation and integration instead of nationalistic isolation. The preamble of the Basic Law describes the will of the German people to serve world peace as an equal member of a free Europe. This is consecrated in ARTICLE 24, until recently the only one of its kind in the world, which expressly allows for the transmission of important parts of national sovereignty to supranational institutions, such as the European Community (EC), and to international systems of collective security, such as NATO and the United Nations, by decision of a parliamentary majority.

Of course, paper, even the sturdy paper on which constitutional texts are printed, will eventually fall apart. Yet, after forty years the Basic Law stands as a solid framework for both domestic and foreign policy and has gained the support of an overwhelming majority of German citizens. Economic progress, political stability, and intellectual freedom have become trademarks of the Republic. In the international field, it managed to gain confidence, to join NATO and the EC on equal terms, and to be accepted as a member of the United Nations as well as of the Western "core group." Even before unification, discussions had started concerning the Federal Republic's acceptance as a permanent member of the UN Security Council.

Will the success story be continued after German unification? Four years after the fall of the Berlin Wall, many problems posed by unification remain unsolved. The constitutional system provided for in the Basic Law has stood the test of change: from consequences of the Maastricht Treaty over the role of the armed forces outside the NATO area to the inclusion of the protection of the environment into the catalog of basic policy aims. The basic directions defined in 1949 are not affected. Neither the division of power among parliament, government, the courts, and the federal structure nor the catalog of basic rights of the individual are challenged.

The political party system of the West was transferred to the East and has won the electoral support of the great majority despite the ongoing critical discussion of their general performance. There is no danger to the system from the extreme Left or Right. However, combating the recent wave of right-wing violence against foreigners and Jews is one of the priorities of the day. Much will depend on how quickly the heavy economic problems can be solved. Unemployment, now reaching the four million mark, poses a serious threat to political stability. Seen in a historical perspective, however, it does not compare to the desperation of the early 1930s.

Less certain is how the German self-perception will develop under present and future conditions. On one hand, unification opens the way for a satisfied national feeling. The deep wounds inflicted by the two catastrophes and by the division of Germany can now gradually heal. There has been no outburst of nationalism and prospects are that the nation will continue to prefer a "good neighborhood" over power and glory.

On the other hand, the internal division between West and East still exists in the minds of the people and may become deeper as the first joys over unification give way to an increasingly bitter fight for pieces of the economic cake. So far there are no signs that this will lead to basic changes of the constitutional and political structure of united Germany, but future leaders might be tempted to strengthen the sense of national unity by a nationalist approach to foreign policy.

Much depends on how European integration will develop. If the aims set in the Maastricht Treaty can be reached, the EC, changed into the European Union, will bind its member countries together into a strong network of common policies and institutions. But if the Union fails and the transfer of national sovereignty to the European level is suddenly reversed, those forces in Germany who long for "real national independence" would gain strength. The more the present tendency of renationalization gains strength across Europe, the more the temptation will grow in Germany to blow the national horn resoundingly.

Under such circumstances, the decision to move the political center of united Germany from Bonn to Berlin might have ominous significance. Those opposing it did so with the argument that the transfer of government and parliament to Berlin would strengthen the centralizing tendencies in domestic politics and weaken bonds to the West. Of course, the transfer will take time, but there is no reason to revive the ghosts of the past. Still, this is a point for watchfulness and for a decidedly European policy not only in Germany but in all countries involved.

The happenings of Germany have never been the affairs of the Germans alone but rather questions central to Europe and hence to the world. Germany's two attempts during this century to unite the nation by authoritarian and totalitarian means and thus to become a World Power have made this more evident than ever before. Since then the German contribution to peace and freedom in Europe and the world has been indispensable. Though this better world may be called a utopian dream and certainly will be built only partially during this and the next generation, it is a worthwhile aim justified by the course of history. The German experiences of the first half of this century have proven to be more than past history and more than just a German affair.

ENDNOTES

[1] Francis Fukuyama, formerly a member of the US State Department, proclaimed the "end of history" in several publications following the breakdown of communism in 1989.

[2] Thomas Mann, *Der Tod in Venedig* (*Death in Venice*), first published in 1913.

[3] Fritz Fischer, professor of history at Hamburg University, started a heated debate over Germany's foregin policy before and during World War I with his book, *Griff nach der Weltmacht* (Düsseldorf: Droste-Verlag, 1961).

[4] Quoted from Max Weber, *Gesammelte politische Schriften* (München: Drei-Masken-Verlag, 1921), 29.

[5] Karl Dietrich Bracher, *Die Auflösung der Weimarer Republik* (Stuttgart/Düsseldorf: Ring-Verlag, 1955).

[6] Published in Ludwig Dehio, *Deutschland und die Weltpolitik im 20. Jahrhundert* (München: R. Oldenbourg Verlag, 1955). Dehio was an influential professor of history at Marburg University.

[7] For the following considerations, I am indebted, among others, to Christoph Klessmann's account in Christoph Klessmann, *Die doppelte Staatsgründung. Deutsche Geschichte 1945–1955* (Göttingen: Vandenhoeck & Ruprecht Verlag, 1991), and also to Hans Peter Schwarz, whose masterpiece, *Vom Reich zur Bundesrepublik* (Neuwied: Luchterhand Verlag, 1966), still is worth reading, especially with regard to US policy towards Germany between 1945 and 1949.

[8] Due to mass abuse in recent years, restrictions were placed on ARTICLE 16 some months ago.

If by the class structure of a society we understand the relationship of its members to the exercise of power, there are above all four groups which demand our attention: (1) those who, by virtue of their position in a given country, are able to lay down the law for others in both the literal and the metaphorical sense (*the ruling groups*); (2) those who assist the ruling groups in their legislative task by executing and adjudicating law as well as by advising and generally helping those in power (*the service class*); (3) those who are subject to the power of the rulers as well as their servants, even if their citizenship rights enable them occasionally to make their voice heard (*the ruled or subjected groups*); (4) and finally, those who stand outside this whole structure of leaders and led, the "free-floating intellectuals," "those who"—in Bertrand Russell's words— "withdraw" and who therefore "do not fit readily into the social structure, and in one way or another...seek a refuge where they can enjoy a more or less solitary freedom" (*the intellectuals*).

If there is any formula to describe the change in the interrelationships among these groups with which I am above all concerned in this essay, it would be the enormous expansion of the service class at the expense of all others and—even more significantly perhaps—the infusion of the values characteristic of this class into the behavior of all others, including even the ruling groups.

Ralf Dahrendorf

From "Recent Changes in the Class Structure
of European Societies"
Dædalus 93 (1) (Winter 1964)

Richard Schröder

The Role of the Protestant Church in German Unification

I N THE YEARS SINCE 1989, the Protestant Church in East Germany has undergone—one might say suffered—a peculiar transformation in the eyes of the public. Celebrated at first as "the mother of the Revolution," it is now accused of having been a "pillar of the system." Those in the German Democratic Republic (GDR) who actively professed the Protestant faith find the situation absurd: During the GDR era, Protestants were suspected of collaborating with the "class enemy"; today they are suspected of having collaborated with the communists. How could this have come about?

Let us look first to the East. The GDR was not only cut off from the West by the Wall; it was also a nation without a genuine public sphere. People were cut off from one other in what was called the "cubbyhole society." They knew little about each other and dared to speak openly only with trusted friends. Immediately after the Wall opened, many teachers invited pastors to come into the schools and talk to their students about religion and the Church. Many of these teachers were surprised that the Protestant Church had suddenly become a significant institution in East German society and they found themselves at a loss to explain it.

Interest in and curiosity about the revival of Protestantism faded quickly however. Since the collapse of the GDR, the churches in the East have experienced no significant increase in membership. The *Jugendweihe*, the ceremony introduced by the communists as a secular substitute for confirmation, is still celebrated—although

Richard Schröder is Professor of Theology at Humboldt-Universität zu Berlin.

without its former component of Marxist ideology—and the number of young people participating rose again this year. There were many in the West, too, who found it difficult to accept the Church as a key agent in bringing down a dictatorial regime. Many West Germans, influenced by the student protest movement of the late 1960s, had based their ideas about religion on the writings of Marx and Freud. At the other end of the Western political spectrum, the confrontational ideology of the Cold War lives on; many reproach the churches in the GDR for not having been clear and outspoken enough in their stand against communism.

Such Western criticism of the path followed by the Protestant Church in the GDR is coupled with the criticism voiced by East German opponents of the old regime, who found a refuge within the Church at one time, but now believe that the Church tried to domesticate and contain them.[1]

A PROTESTANT CHURCH IN A COMMUNIST COUNTRY

To understand the development of the Protestant Church in the GDR, knowledge of a few historical facts is essential. The GDR was the only country in which the communists encountered a large and well-established Protestant Church. They had difficulties in grasping its particular nature, for the communists were familiar only with the Russian Orthodox Church—a church characterized by an almost exclusive concentration on a resplendent service, or rites, which is intended to reflect something of the glories of heaven here on earth; a very traditional theology and hierarchy within the church; and close ties to the nation and its rulers. In contrast, in the Protestant Church, the primary focus of the service is the sermon. Protestant churches function more as gathering places than as places to conduct religious rites.

Committed Protestants see their religion as a creed to be practiced in everyday life as much as in church, and the various circles or groups that meet for parish activities are an integral part of the Church community. The Protestant Church in Germany is actively involved in charities, hospitals, nursing homes, and community health centers. Protestant clergymen are "ordained" to a particular ministerial function in their congregation, but they do not receive a sacrament or join a different "order" of the priesthood. At every level of the Protestant Church, governing bodies consist of ministers and lay people alike; the structure is democratic. In addition, Protestant theology in Germany is traditionally linked to the universities, and thus is closely involved with secular intellectual life.

Protestant history certainly contains its share of ties between altar and throne, but in Germany, which long remained divided into dozens of small principalities and was slow to achieve nationhood, the Protestant Church has acquired a strong federalist character: the churches in the various states have a greater weight than does the national church association. Furthermore, a long time has passed since the official link between secular rule and the Protestant Church was severed in 1918.

When the Soviets occupied East Germany in 1945, they tolerated and even supported church activities. They did so partly because the German Confessional Church (*die Bekennende Kirche*) had actively opposed fascism and had been persecuted by the Nazis. During the Third Reich, many communists encountered Christians in concentration camps, including the later State Secretary for Church Affairs Hans Seigewasser. Church educational activities and youth groups were not permitted, however, and the Party soon took a harsher stance toward the Church. Antichurch policy reached a peak in 1953, when the Communist Party initiated massive repressive actions against religious youth groups, the *Junge Gemeinde* (Youth Congregation), and university student groups. Ministers were arrested, and openly Christian students were expelled from school. In 1958, a second wave of intimidation followed with more arrests of clergymen and show trials. Thereafter, the Church and state coexisted without further dramatic confrontations.

The state repeatedly attempted to limit church activities to "rites" or services. All church work with young people was forbidden to ensure that the Church would eventually die out. The German Protestant Church succeeded to a considerable degree in withstanding these efforts and continued to work with young people and university students. The "Protestant Academies" sponsored conferences on a variety of topics and provided a forum for dissident writers. The three seminaries and high schools maintained by the Church were never recognized or accredited by the government, and thereby were spared from having to inculcate the communist ideology. In addition, annual church congresses (large-scale meetings for Protestants actively involved in church affairs) were reluctantly permitted by the state and gained in significance as the number of active Christians in the GDR dropped.

The Protestant Church managed to retain such a relatively high degree of independence largely because the churches paid the ministers themselves. In other socialist countries, the state paid clergymen's salaries and thus acquired the most important means of control.

CHURCH-STATE RELATIONS IN THE GDR

The constitution of the GDR, adopted in 1949 and remaining in effect until 1968, granted the Church rights similar to those it had under the Weimar Constitution, including collection of church taxes by the government and the right to give religious instruction in public schools. The Socialist Unity Party (SED) did not abide by the provisions of the constitution, however. Religious instruction was banned in public schools beginning in the mid-1950s, and the Church was forced to establish a separate system for teaching Christian principles. At the same time, the state ceased to assist the Church in collecting church taxes from citizens. In response, the Church created its own means of collecting taxes. No constitutional rights could be obtained by legal appeals in the GDR, and so the state was free to follow a policy of harassing the churches at every turn—the simplest matters became subject to endless negotiations at all levels.

The ambiguous legal position of the Church created an enormous number of issues that needed to be clarified with the authorities, but the Church had no bargaining power to bring to the negotiations. It could appeal neither to the courts nor to the public, as both options were blocked by the SED. Collection of signatures for church-related matters was against the law. And if a pastor had suggested an election boycott to his congregation, he would have been liable to arrest and a prison sentence.

The privileges of the churches could be revoked at any time, and infractions of the law that the state routinely ignored could suddenly be enforced. The illegal or semilegal actions on which the authorities turned a blind eye included meetings with Western congregations in Berlin or Hungary, importation of books on theological subjects, and distribution of mimeographed pamphlets, but also events sponsored by the Church that did not fall under the headings of religious services or "Sunday school." For a long time the government insisted that events such as seminars or retreats could be held only with special permission; the Church refused to recognize the legitimacy of this restriction, however, and preferred to pay the fines until the regulations were changed.

Marxist doctrine held that religion would die out on its own. The question of how much the Party could or should do to hasten its end was debatable, and the SED altered its policy on the matter several times. In the spring of 1953, a campaign against the Church was begun, with arrests, actions against youth groups, and seizure of church-owned property by the state. Yet, this campaign was halted even before the uprising on June 17, 1953. The SED continued a rigorous propaganda campaign against the Church well into the 1960s. After the summit talks between the heads of the Protestant Church and the state in 1978, relations improved somewhat, but tensions began to increase again in the mid-1980s.

That the goal of the SED remained unchanged was openly acknowledged. A doctoral dissertation written by a party official in 1983 contained the statement, "The Church is the sole institution in socialist society which neither corresponds to the *spirit* of socialism nor springs from it, and which is superfluous for both socialism and its development." [2] As statements of the Party's position go, this was quite moderate: It left out the usual comments about the Church being "a breeding ground of reaction" and the door through which "hostile enemy forces" would enter socialist society to attack it.

The GDR referred to itself as a "dictatorship of the proletariat" but was in fact a dictatorship of the Politburo. The GDR citizens had three alternatives: passive acceptance; active siding with the government; or trying to exert a positive influence. Those who chose the third possibility, however, could hardly step up and announce, "You have taken us hostage and we despise you for it." Rather, they had to say something like, "I do understand your position, but. . . ." It became difficult to determine when one had gone too far in trying to understand the SED and its motives.

Those who protested loudly and uncompromisingly against conditions in the GDR and those who went to prison or were expelled to the West deserve respect. However, it is wrong to suggest that everyone had an obligation to do the same. The Church could not have emigrated, nor should it have. In order to continue playing an effective role, it had to ensure its own survival. Self-preservation is not a despicable aim. One can go too far in pursing it, of course, but that line is not crossed until ideals are abandoned or betrayed.

A further aspect of the lack of a public sphere or public dialogue was the fact that Party members and state officials were forbidden to discuss matters related to the Church and even to have any contacts with the Church. The Party feared "ideological diversion." The first discussions between theologians and Marxists occurred as part of the observance of the Müntzer and Luther anniversary years (1973 and 1983). The first (and last) Christian-Marxist dialogue in which the Protestant Church participated took place in 1989.

State and party policy toward the Church thus consisted of a refusal to engage in discussions, although individual representatives of the Church were often summoned for informal talks. The members of a synod might be called in, for instance, shortly before the synod began. In order to present its concerns, the Church repeatedly sought discussions with the state. Church representatives were required to outwardly preserve the confidentiality of their talks but to report fully to colleagues within the Church. In the climate of official prohibition, such informal contacts were welcomed as favorable opportunities, but their importance was overestimated. It is now widely known that the state's policy toward the Church was a centrally planned and managed strategy of "divide and conquer."

THREE GENERATIONS OF EXPERIENCE

The experience of the first generation was marked by Nazi anti-church activities, Stalinism, arrests, the antichurch campaign, and the uprising of June 17, 1953. It also experienced the introduction of the *Jugendweihe*. This generation saw the GDR as a provisional arrangement that would end with reunification, and since the regime was unpredictable, this generation decided the best strategy for survival was to hibernate until the thaw came.

The second generation experienced the building of the Wall. The GDR no longer seemed provisional or transitory; the Soviet Empire, known as the "international socialist camp," appeared stable. The survival strategy of this generation was to adapt to existing conditions, as fundamental political change could not be expected. The aim was to improve the relationship between the state and the Church, and to avoid any major confrontations. The new foreign policies in the West, the ongoing Conference for Security and Co-operation in Europe, and Gorbachev's *perestroika* initiative all nourished hopes of improved relations. The motto, "the Church under socialism" grew out of this context. The Church never intended it as a declaration of general approval for the policies of the SED, let alone of the Party's ideology. It did, however, signal a willingness to seek out and emphasize the common ground shared by Christians and Marxists.

The third generation, having grown up after the Wall was built, was too young to regard present circumstances as an improvement over the Stalinist climate of the 1950s; they chafed under all the restrictions and the denial of freedoms. They saw the misery in the Third World and the destruction of the environment. Students at the Protestant seminaries often knew nothing about the events of 1953. They insisted on demonstrating against the prohibition of a church newsletter. When the State Security Service (*Stasi*) arrived and tried to single out individuals for arrest, all fifty demonstrators jumped onto the waiting trucks. This is the generation of the "opposition groups."

The opposition groups affiliated with the Church were motivated by questions of human survival: environmental pollution, the disparities between North and South, and threats to peace. Denial of human rights rarely stood at the top of the list. Their criticisms of social ills were usually formulated as appeals to improve socialism, not to overthrow it, and they were usually combined with criticisms of capitalism that were in line with Marxist views. The political goals of these groups had a strong orientation toward direct and broad-based democracy; their grasp of the importance of institutions, of *representative* democracy, and the formal constitutional state, however, was clearly underdeveloped. The groups were endearingly chaotic: freedom to travel took top priority among their political demands. The attention they received from the Western media made them better known in the GDR, but it also led to overestimation of their importance, both by others and by the groups themselves.

Although the opposition groups were affiliated with the Church, non-Christians who were interested in the same issues also joined. Some were former communists who had left the Party; often they had no interest in the Christian faith and merely wished to avail themselves of the opportunity for "public" protest. In not a few cases such newcomers held anarchist or extreme left-wing views. To be granted shelter within the Church, these groups had to be assigned to congregations. This was not an easy task when the majority of a congregation did not sympathize with their political views or feared that the new members would bring increased harassment from the authorities.

The conflict between the church congregations and the opposition groups reflects to some degree the incongruous experiences of the second and third generations in the GDR. For some Christians, an acceptance of socialism (combined with a striving to improve it) had something to do with atonement, but it was an atonement without any sense of proportion. They charged that the Church had failed to improve the lot of working people, and they accused the Church of having previously taken the side of the exploiters and oppressors.

THE ROLE OF THE PROTESTANT CHURCH DURING THE BREAKDOWN OF THE SYSTEM

In 1989, the Protestant Church in the East had neither a program for reshaping the GDR nor one for German unification. It did, however, much to the annoyance of the SED, maintain its particular sense of community with the churches in the Federal Republic (ARTICLE 4.4 of the constitution of the Protestant churches in the GDR). The Church, though actively engaged in the struggle to turn the GDR into a constitutional democracy, hoped for détente in Europe and in domestic political reforms. The collapse of the GDR was not primarily the work of opposition groups, but the result of a fortunate set of circumstances.

First, the SED refused to accept Gorbachev's new course. When the Party leadership went so far as to ban *Sputnik*, a Soviet periodical published in the GDR, it aroused widespread opposition within the ranks of the Party. The Politburo contained too many aging leaders who were both unwilling to admit younger members and incapable of major shifts in policy.

Second, West German television, which could be received throughout the GDR without interference after 1972, kept East Germans quite well informed about West German politics and society. When the German-German negotiations achieved a slight relaxation in travel restrictions, and more people were able to experience life outside the country, dissatisfaction with conditions inside the GDR grew.

Third, when Hungary opened its border with Austria to East German citizens in the summer of 1989, the wave of emigration that ensued took the government by surprise.

The role of the Church in this breakdown of political authority can be outlined as follows. First, because the state was prevented by world opinion from attacking the Church too harshly, the Church was able to shelter opposition groups. However, not every group was granted such protection. As Bishop Leich once said, "The church is there for every*one*, but not for every*thing.*" Nonetheless, it gave opposition groups a certain voice and access to the public, especially in services where litanies and prayers of intercession were said. The Monday demonstrations in Leipzig, the only mass protests of those days, grew out of the Leipzig "Pray for Peace" services.

Second, the two large churches organized and moderated the "roundtable" around which the old Party leaders and the opposition groups carried on their debates over who would wield power in the future. The debates finally compelled the SED to give up the *Stasi.* Parallel to this development, "roundtables" were meeting all over the country, in almost every town, usually moderated by Protestant pastors. The new political movements forming in the autumn of 1989 usually introduced their platforms in churches, in lieu of the unavailable marketplace. It is largely due to the roundtable debates that the SED did not succeed in recommending itself to the population, under a new name, as the medicine to cure its self-inflicted ailments.

Third, both in the formation of the new political movements and in the first freely elected *Volkskammer,* the experiences of practical democracy acquired in church synods proved very important. A great many of the people who have now become active in politics came from the Protestant Church.

The Protestant Church has been accused of cronyism in its relations with the SED. In the whole spectrum of discussions that took place between representatives of the Church and state authorities, there were cases in which acceptable limits were exceeded. The communists expected the Protestant Church to guarantee fair conditions for the departure of the former rulers. Some members of the SED even expressed the hope that the Church would "rescue socialism." But it must be remembered that the Church is not a political party.

DIFFICULTIES WITHIN THE CHURCH AFTER UNIFICATION

The unification of Germany, a union of two most unequal partners, has brought momentous change to the East. Because the SED preempted all the high-level positions in the government, the legal system, higher education, and the economy, the East Germans find themselves dependent on West German experts as they set about rebuilding their society. As a result, many people in the East feel that they have been "colonized." Many had overly optimistic expectations in the autumn of 1989 about what a change of government could accomplish, and West German politicians made elaborate promises that they were unable to keep. All this has given rise to a high degree of discontent, mingled with the disorientation resulting from the collapse of an entire social order and its ideological foundations.

The Protestant Church itself had difficulty adjusting to reunification. In some areas, the Church was convinced that it was superior to its counterpart in the West. It was no longer an established church, and it did not owe its role in society to any "privileges" awarded by the state. [3] It believed itself to be more clearly identified with the goals of the Ecumenical Convocation, with justice, peace, and preservation of the creation. The Protestant Church in Germany is criticized for cooperating too closely with the state, as evidenced by religion classes in public schools, pastoral activities within the military services, and support from taxes collected by the government. Sometimes it is also reproached for too uncritical an acceptance of "market economics" and "capitalism." These points must all be further discussed and clarified. Many East Germans are unable to recognize the difference between an ideologically oriented state that served as the instrument of one party, and the ideologically neutral state of the German constitution, which merely provides a legal framework for living within the society. To many Easterners the state is suspect in and of itself.

The churches, like the rest of East Germany, are preoccupied with adapting to the new circumstances. Congregations are as small as they were before the transition. The joy felt at regaining freedom is overshadowed by the difficulties presented by the new situation. The hope has not been fulfilled that the Church could provide a new intellectual and spiritual orientation to fill the void left by the collapse of a dominant ideology. The churches are clearly struggling to make the shift from their earlier mind-set to participation in the public sphere of a pluralistic society, where in order to be heard one must be willing to speak up.

There is no cause for resignation. The fact that the Church has not emerged from this process as a shining hero may simply mean it will keep its reserve. Everything will go more slowly and be more difficult than we thought in the heady days of late 1989. But fortunately, there is no turning back.

Translated by
Deborah Lucas Schneider

ENDNOTES

[1] The material for these debates is gleaned from the archives of the *Stasi* and the Socialist Unity Party (SED).

[2] G. Lewerenz, "Kirche im Sozialismus" ("Church under Socialism"), a philosophical dissertation, the Pädagogischen Hochschule in Güstrow, 1983, p. 31.

[3] In West Germany, citizens who register their religious affiliation (most do) have "church taxes" withheld from their income. The government collects this money and distributes it to the church organizations in each state, which use it to pay the clergy's salaries and maintain church property. To this extent, the Roman Catholic and Protestant Churches in Germany can be called "established."

The losers of World War I are back; such is the gloomy outlook of geopolitical analysts and retired generals. But it misses the obvious. The link between German reunification and the breakup of Yugoslavia (or Czechoslovakia) is not a new *Drang nach Osten* but simply its precedent: the primacy of self-determination of nations over the postwar status quo. How could Germany deny to Slovenia, Croatia, or the Baltic states the implementation of the right to self-determination which it had just used for its own reunification? No less importantly, Germany did nothing to encourage the secession of Slovenia and Croatia until the war broke out at the end of June 1991. The fact that, unlike other West European countries, Germany's constitution prevents it from intervening militarily outside its borders did not prevent the Serbian defense minister from claiming, shortly after sending troops to quash Slovenia's and Croatia's bid for independence, that "Germany has attacked us for the third time this century."

The result might well be a greater imbalance between the smaller and weaker Central European nation-states and their increasingly powerful German neighbor. The new nation-states' "sovereignty" could bring some of them into a state of economic or even political dependency on Germany and Austria. But that, surely, would be the consequence—not the cause—of their bid for independence.

Jacques Rupnik

From "Europe's New Frontiers: Remapping Europe"
Dædalus 123 (3) (Summer 1994)

Jochen Thies

Observations on the Political Class in Germany

I

ERMANY HAS PAID A HIGH PRICE for Hitler's war and its consequences—so high, in fact, that Germans tend to repress it. Three consequences stand out: first, the disappearance of the Jewish population through the Holocaust; second, the exodus of those who managed to leave in time, including a number of distinguished writers, artists, and scientists—every autumn, when the Nobel Prizes are announced, this becomes painfully apparent; and third, large population losses, which have had grave demographic consequences for the development of German society. It is impossible to recreate prewar German society, a loss for all, not least for the city of Berlin.

Of course, it was not only German society that was devastated by the Third Reich and World War II. The Nazi Reich inflicted incomparably greater damage on the countries of Eastern and Central Europe; Russia, Poland, Yugoslavia, and the Czech Republic show the scars of those terrible years. By some criteria, the Germans of the Federal Republic suffered least. They experienced totalitarian rule for only twelve years; the citizens of the German Democratic Republic (GDR), like those of many states in Central and Eastern Europe, were obliged to endure totalitarian regimes for fifty years. Who knows whether the Soviet dictatorship would have survived for seventy years had Stalin not emerged as the hero of his federal republic, the man who had defeated Hitler. The destruction of an older middle-class society and the virtual extinction of a traditional political class is the condition that obtains in Germany and in all the countries to the East that Germany invaded. A great deal of time

Jochen Thies is Foreign Editor of Die WELT, Berlin.

281

must elapse before Germany and these other states are able to enjoy political advantages that accrue to those who live in Western Europe. This is not to deny the crisis of political legitimation that exists everywhere in Europe today, even in the West, but it is to emphasize that the situation in Germany, and in the countries to the East, may be particularly acute.

A political class exists in France and Great Britain today that has no parallel in Germany. The successes and celebrity of a group of prominent German chancellors—Adenauer, Brandt, Schmidt, and Kohl—ought not to confuse the situation; it ought not to conceal what lies beneath. The political class in Germany today is only a pale reflection of the one that exists in the older European democracies. All developments toward normality, which would see Germany assume its proper share of responsibility within the international community, are today threatened by the absence of a political class rooted in German society. Nazism achieved at least one of Hitler's goals: the destruction of the traditional elites.

What distinguishes the German political class today from those in Western Europe is the striking taboo against the principle of elitism. In the Federal Republic, political leaders take their values and their orientations from a newly-prosperous middle class. In France, by comparison, every function in society, in government, has its specially trained elite. That situation also obtains in Great Britain, where the public schools and the "old boy" network, symbolized by Oxford and Cambridge but not exclusive to them, continue to dominate, not least in politics. In Britain and France, the members of the political class know each other. They live in capitals with highly centralized national governments; they are not scattered throughout the country as the German professional elites are. In Germany, politics is concentrated in Bonn; banking and business in Frankfurt; the arts in Munich; the media in Hamburg. Because of this fragmentation, representatives of the political class encounter each other relatively late in life, often when they are aged forty or older, if at all. In a crisis, they lack the familiarity of each other's habits and reactions; they are constantly surprised by both.

Another difference with Great Britain and France, not to be underestimated, is that Germany lacks any experience of colonial rule worth mentioning. Germany has a tendency towards provinciality, a tendency that has become more apparent since unification.

Whereas her neighbors in the West remained linked to their former colonial empires in many ways, and are therefore able to understand societies massively different from their own, Germany lacks the advantage of such a perspective. While Germans travel abroad a great deal these days—holidays are both long and frequent—such experiences provide few permanent impressions.

This provincialism was not nearly so apparent in the first generation of leading Federal Republic politicians after the war; the biographies of men like Willy Brandt, Helmut Schmidt, and Franz Josef Strauss suggest this. For all their differences, they had some knowledge of the world outside Germany, some sense of its complexities. Brandt turned to politics during the period of his long exile in Scandinavia. Without Hitler, he might well have ended his days as a prominent journalist. Schmidt and Strauss, in the absence of their experiences in the war, might have chosen careers as civil servants in their localities. By comparison, Adenauer, and a number of others in his Christian Democratic entourage, were much more thoroughly German, substantially more provincial. These qualities went unnoticed at the time principally because Germany, unlike its neighbors, France and Great Britain, lacked the status of a fully sovereign nation. Germany's foreign policy, required to fit into a mold determined by others and by the exigencies of the Cold War, which perpetuated the division of the country, was very delimited in its objectives. Until 1989, German political and foreign policy provincialism went largely undetected.

The situation is very different today. The Gulf War and the civil war in the former Yugoslavia have given an early warning of how unprepared Germany is to confront complex foreign policy issues. While few would argue that Helmut Kohl, Hans-Dietrich Genscher, and Klaus Kinkel are knowledgeable in matters of foreign policy, they have been shaped by experiences quite different from those of the generation of Brandt, Schmidt, and Strauss. Their subordinates are even less prepared to deal with this new era of troubles. Too young to have seen active service during World War II, too little informed on the world outside the Community, they take pride in the Federal Republic's economic prowess, but they have no traditions to guide them in the turbulent world that now engulfs Germany.

To make the situation even more serious, there are signs that the Federal Republic is itself becoming more German. Noticeable in the media, which has moved away from a model once provided by the BBC, it is even more striking in the German educational system. Now that the influence of the Western occupying powers is rapidly fading, the ideal of "character building" as an integral part of education is gradually losing ground. Because the idea of elites has become taboo, schools and universities do little to select and sift out the gifted. German institutions of higher education have degenerated into gigantic waiting rooms, where large parts of the population between the ages of twenty and thirty are parked for five to seven years, waiting for society to find a place for them. Germany, in all these respects, reveals a political and social culture significantly different from that of the Anglo-Saxon world, but also from France.

Concurrently, the phase of internationalism created by the Western Allied presence in Germany during the last fifty years is drawing to an end. It is now evident that the Germans' growing independence from the once admired American model began as early as the Vietnam War. A curious reversal of political attitudes has occurred since then. In the 1950s and 1960s, conservatives in Germany often kept their distance from the United States; the Left, until the Vietnam War, was more enthusiastic, embracing much that was American; today, the opposite is true. While American influence remains very strong among young people, particularly in popular culture, the more elite influences that tended to come from France and Great Britain have virtually disappeared.

The impression that Germany is becoming increasingly German is strengthened by the addition of East German populations, who arrive with their own parochialisms. Prohibited from traveling freely for decades, lacking the linguistic, scientific, and political skills of the more advanced countries of the West, they bring no memory or experience of modernity. When the Honecker regime collapsed, East Germany was a "headless" society; during the dramatic weeks of upheaval, no charismatic leader emerged, none comparable to Lech Walesa or Václav Havel. This helps explain the unsatisfactory course of today's political debate over who is to succeed Richard von Weizsäcker as federal president. Chancellor Kohl has few candidates to choose from, given that he wishes for the new president to come from the East.

The pool of potential leaders on which the former GDR can draw is small: a few writers, scientists, and artists; a handful of business-men with international professional contacts; a small group of pastors and others closely associated with the Protestant Church. The new East German elite is very small, substantially different from the political class in the West, and it will not be easy for the two to reach a consensus. Unification has bred distrust; many in the GDR resent the fact that the constitution of the old Federal Republic was imposed on them. In 1949, the newly created West German government was able to retain many of the civil servants of the Third Reich; this has not proved to be possible with the civil servants of the GDR.

It remains to be seen how citizens in the newly incorporated states will vote in the upcoming elections in 1994. Voters from the five new states may well tip the scales in favor of a new governing coalition at the federal level. One thing is clear: citizens in the former GDR, shaped by their experiences of dictatorship and excessive militarization, have little desire to see Germany play a more active role in international affairs. Unlikely to favor military interventions abroad, they retain the mental reservations about the West that have been characteristic of the older generation of East Germans. It is not likely that they will be especially friendly to the Federal Republic's old allies. It is all the more important for the three Western powers in the coming years to bestir themselves in the East, to invent policies, political and cultural, that will fill the void created by the end of communism, with its very different value orientations.

II

Who belongs to the political class today in Germany? According to the classic definition, members of the federal government and the *Bundestag*, and of the governments of the *Länder*; heads of state-operated agencies and public corporations; top-ranking civil servants in the various ministries; members of political advisory groups; leaders of political parties; and heads of major interest groups. If this definition is expanded to require that these men and women have some international experience, if we ask how many follow world events closely, maintain contacts abroad, are listened to or consulted by their counterparts in neighboring countries and around the world, their number shrinks dramatically.

Opportunities to observe those who fulfill the last condition are offered in a handful of top-level international conferences held in Germany every year—the Military Science Conference in Munich, the Forum for Germany in Berlin, the German-British Königswinter Conference. A close look at the lists of participants indicates that they fall into eight subgroups: top-ranking civil servants and generals; officials of international organizations; university professors; journalists; directors of independent research institutes; members of foreign policy and defense policy think tanks; top business executives; members of the *Bundestag* and their advisers. In the opinion of those involved, such attempts to define the political class in Germany will be thought too narrow. They may insist that there is also a political class at the state level, perhaps in every large German city. Certain doctors, lawyers, and heads of medium-sized corporations, as well as mayors, top city administrators, and editors of local newspapers, may seem appropriate members of the political class.

In this context, journalists deserve special mention. Until the mid-1980s, they considered themselves the true political class of the country. That putative monopoly condition was lost through recent dramatic changes in the media, particularly the rapid and large expansion in the number of television channels. The press lost its dominance as a prime source of information. The politicians had themselves contributed to this special position of the press; for a long time it was they who sought close contact with the media, and not so much the media who had pursued them. The country's relatively short life as a democracy contributed to the power of the media; after the war the press in Germany was shaped and set on its course by the occupying powers.

Another group that even today sees itself as playing a key important role in defining policy is the top corporate business elite of Germany. This group functions quite differently from the rest of the political class, and in fact has few connections with it. There are reasons for this: the significantly higher salaries that exist in the corporate world; the esprit de corps that prevails there, even at the bottom rungs of the career ladder. In certain respects, the German corporate business elite has taken the place of the traditional aristocracy, which still plays a small role within business, but not in society as a whole.

If we add all individuals at the national, regional, and local levels, it is possible to speak of a German political class of some fifty thousand, roughly equivalent to the group included in the German edition of *Who's Who.* A hereditary elite has been replaced by another kind of elite; they occupy key positions, carry out specific functions, are rarely in contact with each other. They come from very different worlds; one must never forget that some twelve million Germans were expelled from the territories in the East, settling in the Federal Republic; also, that there have been very large-scale migrations from East to West within Germany itself. Today, foreigners are seeking to migrate to Germany in large numbers; they are likely to affect the composition of the political elite in the next generation, but the real question is how the East Germans will be absorbed, what their role will be.

As Germany provides no special education or training for an elite, the political parties have stepped in to fill the gap. The consequences of this intrusion are conspicuous in the case of the Foreign Office. That ministry, headed for eighteen years by the liberal Hans-Dietrich Genscher, is today very much the creation of his tenure; he had a decisive influence on the careers of many. While the classic German diplomat, typified by someone like Berndt von Staden, the former ambassador to Washington, has largely disappeared, his place has been taken by a new type of career diplomat, molded to fulfill Genscher's public-relations needs. Those who worked for Genscher at the beginning of his time in office, whether as personal aides or ministry spokesmen, are today likely to be serving as ambassador or under secretary. The rapid promotion of a small group, with access to the former Foreign Secretary, has created a considerable imbalance in promotions throughout the Foreign Office. Genscher's successor is faced with a difficult situation, exacerbated by the fact that today's problems call for a reconceptualization of Genscher's more rhetorical sallies. Reports persist that many top officials feel a greater loyalty to Genscher than to Kinkel. This has apparently led to considerable tension as Germany seeks to develop a new security policy with regard to Eastern Europe.

The situation in the foreign service is very different from that which prevails in the defense establishment. The promotion of General Staff officers is proceeding according to established patterns. The army played a key role in the opening phase of German reunification, successfully effecting the merger of the East and West German military forces. This feat, largely accomplished in 1991–1992, has reduced the total German military force by almost half, a situation little noticed by the general public. The *Bundeswehr*, charged with the sensitive and difficult task of overseeing and coordinating the withdrawal of the former Soviet Union's troops from Eastern Germany, appears to be accomplishing its purposes rather well. For all these reasons, it is not surprising that the strongest pan-German consciousness is to be found in the *Bundeswehr*.

It is not commonly known that some 40 percent of the top-ranking civil servants (under and assistant secretaries) in the federal ministries were born either in Prussia or in North Rhine-Westphalia, a state with strong Prussian influences. A large number in this group were born in Berlin. Indeed, Berliners and East Germans more generally are also strongly represented in the top echelons of German journalism. Similar constellations exist among the leaders of industry, suggesting that it may not be too farfetched to believe that personal background factors played some role in the reunification process.

Two of the more positive developments in Germany during the last twenty years are the diminished separation between the Catholic and Protestant segments of the population and the increased tendency for many in the political class to be university-educated. Whereas the dominant orientation of the political elite in Germany prior to 1945 was Protestant, there are today no significant distinctions between Protestants and Catholics in this regard. The period of Helmut Kohl's chancellorship will be remembered for the opening of the Berlin Wall; it will also be recalled as the time of the final breakthrough of Catholics to top positions in government and society.

A further development of the last years may prove significant if the trend holds: children of the German elite in all fields are increasingly attending colleges and universities abroad, in English-speaking countries. Only twenty years ago, the young rarely studied abroad. In the 1980s a greater number of students attended universities outside Germany, primarily in Europe, often in France. One can only speculate about the reasons for the new transatlantic orientation; while it represents in part a flight from the overcrowded and anonymous conditions of German universities, it may reflect also the conscious career planning of a younger generation, having certain assumptions about the kind of world it will be obliged to live in.

The younger members of the two largest political parties are conspicuously different in the way they approach this problem. While the up-and-coming generation of Christian Democrats, particularly those connected with the Konrad Adenauer Foundation, have an Anglo-American orientation, the younger Social Democrats tend to have a domestic orientation, or look toward Eastern Europe. Two consequences follow: if the trend persists, it will give the Christian Democratic Union (CDU) a strategic advantage in the future; it may presage a new division in Germany's political class, particularly if the East German segment of the Social Democratic Party (SPD) is widened. At the present time, it is impossible to exclude the possibility that Germany may one day face a fundamental decision with regard to its political orientation: East or West? Until 1989, it appeared as if this question had been settled once and for all by the parliamentary elections of 1949, an outcome confirmed by the elections in 1953. Today, the issue is again being raised. It may be a factor in the almost instinctive refusal of many members of the political class in Bonn and the Rhine Valley to accept the projected move of the capital from Bonn to Berlin.

If the largest portion of Germany's political class works as civil servants, employed by the government at the federal, state, or local levels, it is also true that their salaries are roughly half of what they would be in comparable positions in private industry. Many of today's decisionmakers belong to a generation that did not become prosperous until they were well into middle age. Having witnessed the displacement of millions of people at the end of World War II, their most profound hope is for stability, including stability in their personal lives. Many own homes to which they have strong emotional attachments. Growing up in an atmosphere dominated by tales of World War I and the grievous inflation crisis that followed, having lived through the upheavals of World War II, they crave only stability. Such longing is common in the generation born around 1930, to which the Chancellor himself belongs.

III

If Germany is to achieve true unity, if it is to exert a calming influence on its neighbors both in Eastern and Western Europe, it must develop a homogeneous political class that recognizes that today's problems are not those of 1953 or 1968. Such a development would be helped by the capital being moved from Bonn to Berlin.

Berlin's recent failure to win the invitation to host the Olympic Games in the year 2000 has more significance than is generally acknowledged. Sidney was always the clear favorite in the Olympic stakes, but the circumstances surrounding Berlin's defeat ought to give Germans pause. Three reasons for the loss may be discerned: first, the bid was not supported by all groups in the country, in part because of the continuing battle with Bonn over moving the capital; second, members of the International Olympic Committee were frightened by the militancy of a small group of anti-Olympic protesters; finally, Germany's image has suffered greatly abroad in recent years, not least because of the serious foreign policy mistakes made since the Gulf War. And the wave of xenophobia that has swept over the country since the summer of 1992—the firebombings and the attacks on refugee centers—has not gone unnoticed. Germany's prestige has been seriously affected.

Moving the capital to Berlin expeditiously and enthusiastically would represent a conscious decision to confront recent German history, with citizens of the Federal Republic coming together with the citizens of the former GDR. East Germans have never really dealt with the Nazi era; their Communist leaders taught them that they had been on the "right side" of the conflict in the years 1933–1945, that they had nothing to excuse themselves for. West Germans created their own myths. Thus, in addition to their current problems, both are now obliged to face up to their different pasts, to come to terms with the present, and to conceptualize the future.

Berlin would be an ideal site for such candid and open discussion. The city itself is virtually an outdoor museum, filled with monuments to the disastrous failures of German nationalism. This chapter of history must now be brought to a close if Europe is to proceed with unification. Even if Europe were to achieve political union soon—an increasingly dubious prospect—the nation-states will continue to exist. Identification with Berlin is necessary for Germany; the city symbolizes the heights and depths of German history. It was never the cradle of Nazism—in free elections, the National Socialists never won more than 30 percent of the vote in Berlin; in no other city were so many Jewish citizens hidden during the Third

Reich. Hitler instinctively disliked Berlin, much preferring to stay in Southern Germany, returning only after he assumed power in 1933, and again when the Allied armies were nearing the German borders. The Allied airlift confirmed the city's image as a national symbol of resistance; this remained the situation until the 1970s, when an attitude of acceptance of the country's partition set in; it led to a "status quo" mentality, not only in Bonn but in the entire country.

Seen from the vantage point of history, cost has never played a decisive role in establishing or moving a capital city, nor should it do so now, despite the fact that rebuilding the new *Länder* and Eastern Europe is requiring the transfer of immense sums of money. The politicians and bureaucrats in Bonn who oppose moving the government on financial grounds are suspected of having concealed their true motives. Instead of ordering a halt to all construction work in 1989, when the Berlin Wall came down, Bonn continued on its building spree, investing even more heavily in the Rhine capital. Since then, more than a billion marks have been spent on renovating, expanding, and constructing major government buildings. If plans for the initial phase in Berlin were reduced even slightly, it would be possible to transfer a great part of the government within four years.

Almost all capital cities within the European Community are located in the Western part of the continent. With Berlin, the Community would acquire something like a bridgehead to Eastern Europe; the old links to Prague and Vienna would regain their rightful importance. The Community might wish to use Berlin as its headquarters for the enormous efforts that will have to be made to bring the standard of living in the East up to that in the West. Germans and Poles would be given the opportunity for a full reconciliation, rather like the one that occurred between Germany and France in the 1960s.

The move to Berlin and the healing of the profound rifts that have developed since unification will not be accomplished unless the process is set in motion by the present generation of German leaders, who have some recollections of a united Germany from their childhood, who have some vision of a united Europe in the future. The *Bundestag*, in 1998, two elections hence, will include many younger members, who will be less able to grasp the historical significance of the vote on Berlin, which is well understood abroad.

Berlin is today, admittedly, a conflict-ridden city, with a deeply divided population. Still, it has begun to attract a courageous and interesting youth, who have some sense of the need to go beyond the conventional attitudes of the old Federal Republic. Compared to other cities in the Rhineland and Southern Germany, Berlin is poor. During the transitional phase, the arrival of federal civil servants from Bonn would give the city the much larger middle class it lacks at the moment. This group, twenty to thirty thousand strong, would help set in motion a dynamic development that could lead to considerable population growth.

One positive by-product of all this would be the growth of a truly national press, on a scale that Germany does not today possess. The fear exists that in a capital the size of Berlin, mass demonstrations would be mounted to intimidate a democratically-elected government; the counterbalancing gain, however, is that politics would be taken less seriously in Berlin than in Bonn. The "power triangle" of politicians, diplomats, and journalists would be broken; the splendid isolation of a highly privileged mini-elite on the Rhine would be ended. The new political class would be required to compete with other worlds—of culture, banking, and business—a situation from which all would stand to profit.

Even more decisive, however, would be the politicians' direct exposure to the problems facing Berlin and the five new *Länder*. In 1948–1949, the German leaders who favored Bonn as the West German capital managed to complete the necessary preparations within a matter of months; had Helmut Kohl followed their example and agreed in 1990 to shift some of the government departments to Berlin immediately, a great many misunderstandings with the East Germans might have been resolved.

A case in point is the failure to absorb into the West German civil service able bureaucrats who served during the Honecker regime. Why was it possible, for example, for the *Bundeswehr* to accept a number of East German army officers substantially greater than what the Foreign Office was able to do with its much smaller complement from the former GDR? With their knowledge of Russian, their experience in the states of the former Soviet Union, Germany could certainly make excellent use of them. The argument that this group could not be considered for ideological reasons does not hold when one recalls that while Bonn rejected East German diplomats, the Foreign Office held classes for Polish, Hungarian, and other East European diplomats, intending to retrain them for work in a democratic society. Other Bonn ministries were much more accommodating.

In Berlin, the groups and factions that comprise the political class will find it necessary to shed some of their mutual suspicions, to overcome some of the self-hatred that still characterizes so many of them. Unification has created new rifts; the question of who believed in reunification, and at what point, is being asked in too self-righteous a tone by many. It serves no purpose to pin the "realist" label on some, and to deny it to others.

German unification has destroyed the "postmaterialistic" dreams of many veterans of 1968. The group known as Willy Brandt's "political grandchildren" has been particularly hard hit. Concentrating their efforts on ecology, imagining that they enjoyed a monopoly of wisdom on issues of international peace, their rhetoric has been called into question. At least for the interim, the SPD will need an intermediate generation of political pragmatists, who have been losing ground in the party since the era of Helmut Schmidt.

The East Germans are in an even more difficult situation. Having grown accustomed to the limited possibilities of existence under communism, they must now come to terms with the burdens of the past. Having accepted no responsibility for the events of 1933–1945, they must do so now. Without any emotional support from the West, they must clear away the rubble created in their own minds by an authoritarian communist regime. Natural demographic processes had begun to resolve certain of Germany's problems—including that of an aging population and the gradual disappearance from professional life of the wartime generation—when reunification brought new ones. Once again, Germany is a country of men and women with twisted and shattered lives, whose biographies show that their ambitions have been skewed, interrupted, or thwarted for decades. For the next generation and a half, the German political class will be largely occupied with healing the internal rifts of the nation. Simultaneously, Germany is compelled to regain a certain normal balance as a nation-state but also as a responsible member of the international community. The enormity of the task is not likely to be seen in proper perspective from Bonn.

The political class of Germany must learn the virtues of competition; it must learn that the shift from the public sector to the private, and back again, is a desirable thing that is happening in many places in Europe today, that it ought to happen also in Germany. The federal president, Richard von Weizsäcker, in a recently published interview, criticized the utopia of status-quo thinking in German society and indicated how important it was that innovative thinking replace the lackluster rumination that has been so characteristic of Germany these last years since unification.

A functioning political class will develop in Germany when widely accepted notions of state authority are overcome. The present tendency toward a monopoly on power by the major political parties cannot long continue. In offering programs and scholarships for the gifted young—a phenomenon replicated nowhere else in Europe—the major German parties, through their party foundations, are beginning to recognize that the country's future depends on the creation of a more venturesome and less parochial political class. Their calculations may be upset by recent developments, which show that the established parties are suffering dramatic memberships losses; new protest parties on both the Right and the Left are appearing. This trend has alarmed those who hoped to be able to form the political class of the future; they were unprepared for such dramatic change. If it is confirmed by the elections of 1994, this will certainly not help to provide the changes in attitude that are so desperately called for. Germany is required to rethink its foreign and military policies, not to speak of the domestic conventions that have reigned supreme to this date. Such a reconfiguration of policy may be more easily achieved from Berlin than from Bonn.

Translated by
Deborah Lucas Schneider

Joachim Gauck

The German Way of Dealing with a *Stasi* Past

I N THE AUTUMN OF 1989, FOLLOWING A PERIOD of crippling depression, after years of remaining silent, a great number of men and women began to protest against a fossilized dictatorship no longer able to persuade its citizens that it was doing its job— taking care of the people's welfare. The lavish celebrations laid on by the evil old men at the top for the fortieth anniversary of the German Democratic Republic (GDR) was, in the beginning, accompanied only by small-scale protest from splinter opposition groups. However, the hard line taken by the state authorities against these protesters resulted in a sudden wave of solidarity, particularly evident within the churches. Civil movements were formed, and the Social Democratic Party (SPD) was refounded in an East German vicarage. The protest, initially heard at church services and other Protestant gatherings, soon emerged from the churches and spilled out onto the streets.

The courageous protesters of Leipzig were symbolic of the rebirth of citizenship. It was a heady period for all who for decades had been forced to keep their heads down. The weekly demonstrations, in large and small towns, and the catalog of demands for human and personal rights and for radical political change became more and more determined. These protests culminated eventually in growing demands for German reunification; not because the Easterners had suddenly become nationalists, but because in this manner they were most clearly able to express their desire to turn away from socialism.

Joachim Gauck is Federal Commissioner for Documents of the State Security Service of the former GDR.

The street protests in my home town of Rostock were fairly typical: they were regularly held in front of the local State Security Service (*Stasi*) offices. There we were able to do away with long discussions about ideology. By simply pointing at the edifice, so to speak, we were able to present the real character of the "socialist" system for popular judgment. The decision was clear—the *Stasi* and tank socialism were on the way out. The *Stasi*, the prime instrument of oppression, was to be the first victim. "Put the *Stasi* men to work in the factories" was the rallying cry of the protesting masses. After that, the demonstrations were directed against the Party's branch offices. The protesters outside the *Stasi* buildings were especially determined, word having gone around that enormous numbers of documents were being destroyed. The revolutionaries knew how important it was to save this data, the old regime's hold over its former subjects; it was expected that political use of these materials would one day be made.

In early December 1989, a decision was made to occupy the *Stasi* regional centers. Unfortunately, the main office in Berlin-Lichtenberg was not reached until January 15, 1990, which gave the *Stasi* officers six weeks longer there than elsewhere to destroy vital material. Thousands of sacks full of shredded or damaged dossiers testified to the zeal of those fearful of the typewritten evidence of their activities. All over the GDR civil committees were formed to supervise the winding-up of the secret police, to guard documents, and, where possible, to collate the files they found. Many of these groups produced pamphlets on *Stasi* activities, edited *Stasi* materials, and from time to time informed the press that someone seemingly destined for high political office had worked closely with the MfS (the official short form for the *Stasi*).

Following the first free elections in the postcommunist GDR (in March 1990), the parliament, the *Volkskammer*, decided at a very early stage that all MPs should be vetted to see whether they figured in *Stasi* records as *Inoffizielle Mitarbeiter* (IM, undercover collaborators). A special parliamentary committee was set up for this purpose. Later, another committee was formed, and the author of this article (at that time an MP representing the civil movement called "Bündnis 90") was elected to be its chairman. This body's task was to supervise the breakup of the MfS, which took place on the orders of the Minister of the Interior. The committee also influenced legislation; it presented a draft bill that became law in August 1990 that fixed the methods for dealing with the *Stasi* legacy. This law took up many of the themes of the 1990 civil protests; its main thrust was to allow former *Stasi* documents to be used for "political, judicial, and historical reckoning with the past." Each citizen was to be allowed to examine his or her own file to discover if and how the *Stasi* had acted. The East German parliament's intention was to return the former rulers' instrument of knowledge to those it had ruled and oppressed. "Political reckoning with the past" (*politische Aufarbeitung*) meant, among other things, the right to vet MPs and all elected bodies, as well as public employees, to see if they had previously worked for the MfS, either as *Inoffizielle Mitarbeiter* or even as *Hauptamtliche* (full-time collaborators). Where the vetting process revealed such collaboration, the MP or public servant was to be dismissed from his post.

Why did the East Germans decide to embark upon this process in 1989? It was not a quest for vengeance; there was no majority in the *Volkskammer* for such vindictive action. On the contrary, the MPs recognized the following problem: In East Germany, from 1933 onwards (i.e., the start of the Nazi dictatorship), the entire public administration, government, and parliament had been largely comprised of people who, to a greater or lesser extent, had collaborated with the antidemocratic rulers. They included judges, lawyers, police, teachers, university professors, and other representatives of the federal and regional legislature and executive offices. If, after more than fifty-five years of Nazi and Communist dictatorship, citizens were to trust elected officials under the new democratic system, it was important that those officials be trustworthy. The intention was not to remove former Communists (members of the Socialist Unity Party, SED) from all posts, but rather to respond to the East German people's minimal demand that persons who had conspired with the regime, unbeknownst to their fellow citizens, should be deemed unsuitable for public positions of trust.

Following the establishment of a democratic state in East Germany, only a few full-time state employees attempted to reenter public service; those without such a handicap applied in large numbers for posts, including major political jobs. The screening process was never designed to deprive individuals of employment; former high officials were allowed to work in business and the professions, as doctors or artists, for example, but not in the service of the democratic state. The *Stasi* files were to be used for "judicial reckoning with the past" in order to facilitate prosecution where crimes had been committed, but also to vindicate those who had been wrongly accused. Finally, there was a historical justification for this legislation. With the aid of the files, historians would be able to portray the actual processes of domination and organization, demonstrating the interplay between the ruling party and its instruments of surveillance and oppression.

The bill passed by the *Volkskammer* in August 1990, which contained these three essential features, was welcomed by the overwhelming majority of the public, regardless of political affiliation. For many MPs the decision to make a clean breast of their country's dark past was linked to a desire to do so in an open, self-critical way, very different from the situation following the end of World War II. This time, collaboration, failure, and guilt would not be suppressed; they would be acknowledged, faced up to.

The sheer speed of the German reunification meant that this bill's life was short-lived. While the Unification Treaty contained clauses restricting freedoms in this regard (for example, taking away a citizen's right to view his file), use of the files was allowed in principle and the Act declared that, following reunification, the new pan-German parliament would adopt a bill restoring most of the features of the *Volkskammer* law. The German *Bundestag* complied with this declaration in 1991 in the "Act concerning the Documents of the State Security Service of the Former German Democratic Republic" ("*Stasiunterlagengesetz*"), which came into effect at the end of that year. Since 1992, a surprisingly large number of individuals and institutions have made use of their legal options.

The Federal Commissioner for Documents of the State Security Service of the former GDR (my official title) and the body that bears the same name began work on German Unity Day. The Commission is specifically enjoined to work towards the above-named objectives, but also to facilitate the press's constitutionally-regulated access to the *Stasi* files (excluding only those relating to victims). It has more than three thousand staff members, divided between the main office in Berlin and fourteen branches in the five East German federal states. The need for such a high level of manpower is dictated by the enormity of the archives (almost 120 miles of shelves) and the number of applications for access to the files. More than 1.85 million requests for access have been made, over 650,000 by private citizens wishing to see their own files.

The Commission's main activities consist of providing data for the public service and preserving and arranging the archive. In 1989–1990, the data was in total disarray; the archivists' main task was to create a reliable archive, reconstructing dossiers that were completely or partially destroyed. Since the electronic data bases had been wiped out on the orders of the Modrow transitional government, the archive section has the urgent task of sorting, reconstructing, and completing the card-indexes, the principal means for linking names to files. Another principal objective, likely to gain significance in the coming years, is provided by the education and research department, where requests from historians and press research applications are processed. This department's task is to inform the public about *Stasi* structure and methods of operation by publishing books aimed both at laymen and experts, by holding seminars on the *Stasi,* and by organizing exhibitions held in Berlin and in the new federal states.

* * *

There has been for some time now a feeling of unease about this digging up of the past. It is less marked in East German public opinion, and rather more conspicuous in certain media dominated by the "old West." This unease is clearly caused by many factors. Some individuals are simply averse to the media treatment of the issue. For a long time, the public was bombarded with reports about the *Stasi.* In many cases, particularly where political, cultural, religious, or sports personalities were reported to have been IM, there was, especially in the tabloid press, overgeneralized and sensationalist treatment. This, along with oversaturation, caused public frustration and confusion. It is important for readers in the West to realize that the East German secret service had many different methods for recruiting and guiding IM.

As a rule, the IM undertook to collaborate with the MfS by means of a written or oral statement. But, in the case of a small group of intellectuals and churchmen, the *Stasi*'s rules allowed for a more circumspect recruiting method. "Confidential talks" were arranged, which, after a time, were held in secret ("adhering to the rules of conspiracy," as the MfS termed it) by agreement between the two parties. This agreement was typical for the initiation of an IM dossier of this special type. Persons recruited in this way often did not know the term "IM," received no money or presents, apart from birthday gifts, did not intend to betray anyone, and continue today to reject vehemently the charge of collaboration uncovered by the examination of the files. They consider themselves untainted by their past, choosing to forget that they fully accepted long-term contact with a *Stasi* officer, kept the relationship secret, acquiesced in a role rejected by others in comparable positions in the East. They also fail to see that the *Stasi*, very naturally, pursued its own interests in processing the data gleaned from the IM, that such information was used, regardless of the supplier's motives, to support the regime's hold over its subjects.

While such collaboration must be distinguished in the public mind from real treachery and espionage, in many cases sensationalist witch-hunting reports (never based on the work of the Federal Government Commission) precluded such a distinction being made. It contributed to the frustration expressed by many. Apart from the special problem of media coverage, there are, of course, other political objections to the German method of dealing openly with the past. Let us consider, for example, the interests of those removed from public posts, who understandably protest such action. In the universities, to cite a single instance, some of the IM would prefer that the public regard the special treatment they received as a result of their collaboration with the MfS as quite irrelevant. They often do not grasp the fact that they are quite correctly being compared with their East German colleagues who did not allow themselves to be drawn into working with the *Stasi*. Many seek support at home and abroad, claiming that West German attempts to dominate the East following on reunification cost them their jobs. This sort of argument needs to be approached with extreme caution. While West German "neocolonialism" does take place from time to time, the investigation of public servants for *Stasi* collaboration is a result of pressure from the East German democracy movement, legalized by two German parliaments, and cannot be explained as a Machiavellian scheme by the old Federal Republic.

It is important to note that such protests are often taken up or favorably reported by West German politicians, journalists, and scholars, who, in earlier contacts with the East and in their appraisal of Eastern politics, demonstrated a high level of support for the GDR, often refusing to perceive what was really going on. In this way, from time to time, alliances are created between former *Ossis* and *Wessis* whose common interest lies in their fear of being compelled to acknowledge past mistakes, or sometimes to admit past guilt.

The attempt to deal with the *Stasi* past reflects the wish, at least partially, to bridge the gap that existed in the former GDR between "us" and "them," the people and the elite. The majority of the oppressed and spied-upon population had a legitimate interest in publicizing the *Stasi* files. They hoped that the new knowledge would have consequences. The minority, the collaborators, were to be disadvantaged, a justifiable result, given the advantages they had enjoyed in the past.

In united Germany, the (Western) majority is not sufficiently aware of this discrepancy; it is very apparent to all in the East. The new German contradictions (the East-West postunification tensions, but also to a great degree the political party discrepancies) have drowned out the old ones. We find it difficult to comprehend fully the history of individuals who have had different experiences of suffering and alienation. Many East Germans today have great difficulties in explaining their very different pasts to West German countrymen. The gap is too wide, the burdens borne over long decades are too unequal. And if it turns out that their Eastern neighbors were indeed oppressed and discriminated against, many Westerners draw back, wishing to protect themselves from the suffering of others. They cannot begin to grasp the magnitude of what was experienced under a totalitarian system; they try to equate the injustice and shortage in Communist countries with what they themselves experienced under democracy.

It is perhaps normal that not everyone is able to understand the emancipatory approach we politicians in the East use in order to rake over the ashes of the recent past. Some accuse those who refuse to forget of being vengeful. They fail to see that there is a need to remember the times and those who restricted our right to freedom and personal expression, not least because these inalienable rights need to be defended now and in the future. The present-day dissension need not be seen as precluding reconciliation and inner stability. We will be in a position to forgive and forget only if we are given enough time and the right to heal our wounds, to calm our anger, and, yes, to curb our hatred. Reconciliation with such a past can only be achieved not simply through grief, but also through discussion and dialogue.

If this fact was not evident to all Germans after the fall of Nazism, we ought to welcome the changed situation that now makes it possible. However, any foreign reader who thinks that our way of coming to terms with the past is too strict and too organized must realize a simple truth: only in such a distinctively German way can a dictatorship set up on the German model be destroyed.

Translated by
Martin Fry

Michael Mertes, Steven Muller, and Heinrich August Winkler

Coda

THE PRINCIPAL CONTRIBUTIONS IN THIS VOLUME were written in 1993. At that time Germany was facing the deepest recession of the postwar period. Violence against foreigners became headline news throughout the world as reports came in with alarming frequency from the Eastern *Länder,* followed by news of attacks in the Western *Länder,* too. This led to fears, both in Germany and abroad, of a return of German nationalism and a resurgence of far-right parties. Had reunification set free ghosts of the past that were thought to have been banished when Germany was still divided? Was the "Berlin Republic"—still governed from the Rhine—becoming more like the Weimar Republic than the Bonn democracy? Was there not much evidence to support the suggestion voiced by skeptics that the nation-state and democracy were simply incompatible in Germany?

None of the authors in this volume yielded to the temptation of responding to the anxious questions so in vogue in 1993 with quick and easy answers—whether confirming or denying the dangers. Nevertheless, the problems that appeared so pressing at the time are naturally reflected in their essays. In the two years that have since passed, much has changed in and around Germany and this cannot have failed to influence the authors' perceptions. Were they to write their essays today, some would certainly shift their emphasis on certain points.

On the whole, however, this collection of essays has demonstrated a remarkable durability, which is first and foremost Stephen Graubard's achievement. With his Socratic approach, with his characteristic mixture of kindness and rigor, he has seen to it that the contributions meet the high standards of quality by which *Dædalus* has earned its world-wide renown.

In the spring of 1995 the authors had the opportunity—albeit with severely limited time—to revise their contributions in the light of current developments. We can therefore genuinely call this book a new edition, especially since Timothy Garton Ash's essay, "Germany's Choice," has now been added to the collection. The editors are very grateful to *Foreign Affairs* and above all to the author for permission to reprint this essay. As a result, the book contains a chapter dealing specifically with foreign policy, an essential part of any really comprehensive account of "Germany in transition."

Germany has since emerged from the depths of recession, even if the structural weaknesses in her economy have not yet been overcome. The democratic system has proved to be remarkably stable, as a glance at the outcome of the federal election of October 16, 1994 shows. Support for the extreme right-wing parties (again not represented in the newly elected *Bundestag*) declined when the democratic parties finally managed to reach a compromise on the hotly disputed issue of reforming the asylum laws. That compromise defused the problem and it has since rapidly disappeared from the headlines. New right-of-center anti-establishment groups, for which a great future was still being prophesied as recently as late 1993, have—at least at the national level—disappeared from view, while the traditional parties—to which *Bündnis* 90/The Greens can now also be accounted—together hold 92 percent of the votes.

The "party of non-voters" was also less successful than had been feared: on October 16, 1994 some four-fifths of the electorate cast their vote, roughly the turnout that has been customary for decades. Many observers today are more concerned with a party that discovered "democratic socialism" only at the end of 1989, which still finds support among many voters in the new *Länder*. Thanks to four direct mandates, three of them won in East Berlin constituencies, it is again represented in the new *Bundestag*: we are referring, of course, to the Party of Democratic Socialism (PDS), which emerged from the East German Communist Party.

The PDS's success at the polls casts a cold light on the state of internal unification. The former Communists are in no sense a classical worker's party. Although the PDS can count unemployed workers among its voters, its most important base lies among the members of the former GDR state intelligentsia, including many who have lost their jobs in the civil service, the Party, or mass organizations, who now find themselves in early retirement and—despite their objectively comfortable material situation—are suffering from a feeling of relative deprivation.

If the PDS has on average a reservoir of around 20 percent of the voters in the new *Länder* (representing just under 5 percent of the national average), that indicates the extent to which the East German Communist Party was successful in integrating the population of the GDR into its system. The Party never had a majority behind it, but it was able to depend on the loyalty of a relatively broad layer of the upwardly mobile who would probably not have been able to enjoy an academic education without the SED's "cultural revolution."

Half a decade after reunification, Germany is still divided into two political subcultures. The fact that the proportion of votes going to the PDS was many times higher in the new *Länder* and that the turnout there was 8 percent lower indicates, with particular clarity, that the relationship to parliamentary democracy in East Germany is different from that in West Germany. In the new *Länder* there is no militant anti-parliamentary movement (the PDS is not that either) but there is a great deal of indifference toward the essential elements of a Western democracy. In February 1995 a poll conducted by the Allensbach Institute for Opinion Research found that 80 percent of East Germans could see no connection between the separation of powers and the protection of human rights. When asked about the most important human rights, respondents in the new *Länder* ranked the right to work far above freedom of speech, which was not the case in the old *Länder*.

What journalists frequently refer to as "GDR nostalgia" or ironically "Ostalgia" does not entail a genuine yearning for the political conditions that prevailed in the GDR before 1989. Rather, there is a widespread longing for the sense of being cared for from the cradle to the grave, which Erich Honecker's state bestowed on its people with a certain degree of success. This is closely connected with a distinct need for harmony, such as that found to a similar degree in the old Federal Republic during the 1950s.

Many East Germans tend to regard the consensus model of the round table as the expression of ideal democracy rather than the clash of opinions openly debated in the manner characteristic of parliamentary democracy. Finally, much like the situation in the

1950s, one also finds a refusal to accept the painful insight that a major part of one's lifetime, or perhaps even the whole of one's previous biography, was wasted on a dictatorial regime. Whether those years were given willingly or not, they can never be brought back. As a result, many try to seek some superficial comfort in the idea that not everything past had been all that bad and that some things had actually been better.

Assimilating the patterns of political behavior in East and West Germany—and in East and West Berlin—may take more time than approximating the state of economic conditions in both parts of the country and of the capital. The PDS, therefore, will remain for some time an important political factor. At present, up to one-fifth of the East German electorate tends to regard the PDS as an efficient representative of East German interests (or, at least, of the interests of a particular group of East Germans).

As a consequence of the strong position of the PDS, the formation of parliamentary majority governments has been very difficult in some East German *Länder* and in Berlin. Absolute majorities of one party exist only in Saxony, governed by the CDU, and in Social Democratic Brandenburg. In Mecklenburg-Western Pomerania and Thuringia, "Grand" (or "Black-Red") Coalitions of the CDU and the SPD were established in the fall of 1994 after long and tiresome negotiations. A completely different development has taken place in Saxony-Anhalt: Since July 1994, a "Red-Green" minority government, led by the Social Democrat Reinhard Höppner, is being tolerated (i.e., tacitly supported) by the PDS.

The "Magdeburg model" violated a West German taboo, namely an unwritten law that states that democratic parties shall not cooperate with parties that have a dubious democratic reputation. After the national convention of the SPD, held in Mannheim in November 1995, this law was no longer respected—at least as far as the PDS was concerned. Oskar Lafontaine, the newly elected chairman of the SPD, has come out in favor of treating the PDS as a normal democratic party. After the political turn of the SPD, changes in government in Mecklenburg-Western Pomerania, and perhaps even in Thuringia, can no longer be excluded. There are, however, some uncertainties. It is not clear whether the PDS can afford to move beyond mere tacit support and enter a coalition government without risking its unity. The Social Democrats face an analogous problem: It is unknown whether an arrangement with the PDS, either a toleration pact or a coalition, will split the SPD in the *Länder* concerned. A split would most likely mean that there is no parliamentary majority as an alternative to a Grand Coalition.

The Mannheim party convention of the SPD has, virtually overnight, dramatically changed the strategic configuration of the German party system. The most severe polarization in the history of the Federal Republic can be predicted for the next *Bundestag* election in 1998. A left-wing alliance, consisting of the SPD, *Bündnis* 90/The Greens, and the PDS, will confront the right-of-center government forces—the CDU, the CSU, and the FDP. It is questionable whether a majority for the "left-wing camp" really exists. Experience suggests that elections in Germany are won in the center, not at the fringes of the political spectrum.

The FDP, which has in the recent past failed to gain the necessary 5 percent of the votes in most elections to *Land* parliaments, puts its hope for 1998 on the prospect that it might benefit from the vacuum at the political center that a more left-wing SPD would leave behind. If the Free Democrats' new hope turns out to be in vain, the CDU and the CSU would have to openly fight for an absolute majority in order to prevent a left-wing coalition. In the aftermath of the Mannheim convention, other options, such as a Grand Coalition on the national level or the "Black-Green" (CDU, CSU, and *Bündnis* 90/The Greens) alliance that has stirred for some time the imagination of politicians, journalists, and the public, have become merely theoretical models. The order of battle for 1998 seems clear—much clearer, at least, than the outcome of the election.

The title "In Search of Germany" is completely appropriate considering all the above observations. This is particularly true of united Germany's foreign and security policy. In the summer of 1994 the Federal Constitutional Court set a precedent by deciding that the deployment of German armed forces outside NATO's operations in the context of multinational peacekeeping and peacemaking operations does not contravene the Basic Law. That ruling by Germany's highest court has passed the whole issue back to the politicians who had tried earlier to escape it by submitting it to the court. Only now, on secure legal foundations, can the necessary political consensus emerge in Germany as to the duties of the

German armed forces beyond those of defending the country and the Western Alliance.

There is already unanimity on the necessity of performing such duties only in a multilateral framework. There is also no dispute over the fact that in military matters Germany should continue to exercise restraint with regard to the understandable fears of her neighbors. However, Germany will now have to realize that her partners and friends will increasingly suspect that German references to history are often a convenient excuse for noninvolvement. This was the response in early 1991 during the Gulf War, and it has been even more evident since 1992 in the context of the war in the former Yugoslavia.

A Germany trying to claim a special pacifist role for herself would endanger the cohesion of the Atlantic Alliance just at a time when the latter is seeking a new definition of its role. It would also call into question the substantive progress made towards foreign, security, and defense policy integration in the framework of the European Union (EU). Germany would also compromise those partners and friends who are advocating a permanent seat for the Federal Republic on the Security Council. Most foreign policy experts in the Social Democratic group in the *Bundestag* agree with the coalition on this issue. However, the ideas of the new SPD chairman, Oskar Lafontaine, point elsewhere. At the party convention in Mannheim, he was able to assemble a majority vote for a resolution against deploying any German combat forces (i.e., peacemaking as opposed to mere peacekeeping forces) outside the NATO area. As a result, a power struggle is developing within the SPD between the party organization and the party's parliamentary group, the outcome of which, at present, is still unclear. All this is happening at a time when the chairman of the parliamentary group of *Bündnis* 90/The Greens, Joschka Fischer, is asking his party to abandon its traditional all-out pacifist stance.

The right answer to the partly contradictory expectations facing Germany lies neither in neo-Wilhelmenian pleas for more national "self-confidence" nor in idealistic dreams of merely "civilian" power. In the first instance, it is purely a matter of soberly (i.e., without ambition) defining one's own interests—interests that on vital matters coincide with those of one's immediate neighbors. Here, then, is the answer to the question of reasonable alternatives to the existing integration of the Federal Republic in the Euro-Atlantic community: there just are not any.

Should anyone in united Germany have seriously contemplated a return to an old-style policy of oscillating between East and West, then the war in Chechnya must have finally dispelled any such illusions and demonstrated that Russia would be a very problematic coalition partner. In any case, the Federal Republic would in no way be capable alone of carrying the burden of Western support for the necessary reforms in the states of the former Soviet Union, so that even in this respect Germany needs a multilateral framework.

Germany has a vital interest in stable democracies and market economies in the neighboring countries of East Central Europe—and thus, of course, also in countries further to the east, above all the Ukraine and Russia. In 1989, the dominoes of Soviet imperialism began to fall, tumbling from west to east. These dominoes must be prevented from tipping back again one day, this time in the other direction. In the context of the German debate on the future role of the North Atlantic Alliance, the historically rooted fear of a security vacuum between West Central Europe and Russia has encouraged particularly candid and numerous voices in favor of NATO expansion.

Voices to the contrary can no longer be dismissed these days. Out of the ranks of the SPD come warnings about a confrontation with Russia as a consequence of admitting former Warsaw Pact member states to the Atlantic Alliance. Of course, those who support an eastward enlargement of NATO also want to prevent such counterproductive effects; this is why the problem is always being discussed in the broader context of a Europe-wide security system that includes Russia. For the time being, the question of how opinion will develop within the SPD remains open. However, it can be argued that under Lafontaine those who view an eastward enlargement of NATO with skepticism will win influence. There is, however, a broad consensus that Germany should be more committed than others to the early accession of East Central European countries to the EU. European integration has, from its beginnings in the 1950s, proved to be a force for peace and a program of economic growth of the highest order.

As one of the leading export nations—the per capita export performance of the German economy (6,500 dollars) is four times higher than in the United States (1,500 dollars) and almost three times higher than in Japan (2,500 dollars)—Germany has a vital interest in dismantling trade barriers. Here, too, there is a high degree of common interest with Germany's neighbors in the East. As producers of textiles, steel, or food, they need improved access to the EU internal market so that, through their own efforts, they will be in a position to produce the means they require for economic construction (without which some of them will never be able to qualify for EU membership).

On the other hand, Germany does not have the slightest interest in returning to those times when other European states tried to limit her demographic, economic, and thus (potentially) politico-military predominance by forming coalitions against her. In the Federal Republic only very few would deny that attempts to domesticate political rivalries between states by using the classical instrument of the balance of power would be a far too risky game. This game can only be prevented if Germany repeatedly and firmly demonstrates a willingness to share national sovereignty with her EU partners on the basis of reciprocity. Moreover, the continuing presence of the United States in Europe helps subdue nation-state rivalries on the Old Continent—quite apart from the fact that, as a non-nuclear state, the Federal Republic is far more reliant on the US guarantee of nuclear protection than is France or Great Britain.

An important reason for Germany's pro-integration policy can be found in the way her political culture continues to be shaped by that markedly European and Western mind-set that arose in the old Federal Republic. From this point of view Germany's institutional integration in a supranational European framework constitutes the partial realization of a cosmopolitan vision—and thereby a value in itself.

Nevertheless, the supranational definition of European integration is facing a challenge from two sides: on the one hand, there appears to be a feeling spreading throughout united Germany (i.e., not only in the eastern part) that the question of one's own national identity has to be answered before one can (again) turn to the issue of "European identity." On the other hand, it has become clear in recent years—not least throughout the arduous process of ratifying the Maastricht Treaty—that Germany's partners in the EU are concerned less with modifying, within a supranational perspective, their own self-perceptions as nation-states. There certainly is no sign of a willingness to relinquish the nation-state in favor of a "European identity," and in this respect the case of the former Yugoslavia is surely a bad omen. The old-style national self-interest may be strongest in the case of Great Britain, where the idea of what Churchill once called a "United States of Europe" meets with particularly forceful opposition. But it is even true, in a milder form, of France, which has in the past been and remains Germany's most important partner in elaborating common strategies to deepen European integration.

There is much to suggest that German policymakers will need to learn to move forward by taking small steps rather than leaps. In any case, most of their energy will for now be focused on realizing the most ambitious goal of the Maastricht Treaty by 1999: the economic and monetary union to be formed by those EU member states who qualify for such a "union within the Union." The new pragmatism is likely to make itself felt no later than the 1996 EU intergovernmental conference scheduled to examine the progress of the Maastricht Treaty and to discuss how the EU can be expanded eastward without losing internal cohesion. Yet realism does not have to mean dropping a European vision, which in the view of the editors is still one of the best things to have come out of the "Bonn Republic."

Translated by
Grahame Lucas

Index